ROTH FAMILY FOUNDATION

Music in America Imprint

Michael P. Roth

and Sukey Garcetti

have endowed this

imprint to honor the

memory of their parents,

Julia and Harry Roth,

whose deep love of music

they wish to share

with others.

The publisher gratefully acknowledges the generous support of the Music in America Endowment Fund of the University of California Press Foundation, which was established by a major gift from Sukey and Gil Garcetti, Michael P. Roth, and the Roth Family Foundation.

Ronnie Gilbert

The publisher gratefully acknowledges the generous contribution to this book provided by the following:

The Constance and William Withey Endowment Fund for History and Music of the UC Press Foundation

The Gustave Reese Endowment of the American Musicological Society, funded in part by the National Endowment for the Humanities and the Andrew W. Mellon Foundation

Ronnie Gilbert

A Radical Life in Song

With a foreword by Holly Near

UNIVERSITY OF CALIFORNIA PRESS

University of California Press, one of the most distinguished university presses in the United States, enriches
lives around the world by advancing scholarship in the
humanities, social sciences, and natural sciences. Its
activities are supported by the UC Press Foundation and
by philanthropic contributions from individuals and
institutions. For more information, visit www.ucpress.edu.

University of California Press
Oakland, California

© 2015 by Ronnie Gilbert

Library of Congress Cataloging-in-Publication Data

Gilbert, Ronnie, author.
    Ronnie Gilbert : a radical life in song / with a
foreword by Holly Near.
        pages   cm
    Includes bibliographical references and index.
        ISBN 978-0-520-25308-7 (cloth : alk. paper) —
    ISBN 978-0-520-96244-6 (ebook)
    1. Gilbert, Ronnie.   2. Folk singers—United States—
Biography.   I. Near, Holly, writer of foreword.
II. Title.
ML420.G438A3   2015
782.42162'130092—dc23
[B]
                                            2015016336

Manufactured in the United States of America

24 23 22 21 20 19 18 17 16 15
10 9 8 7 6 5 4 3 2 1

The paper used in this publication meets the minimum
requirements of ANSI/NISO Z39.48-1992 (R 2002)
(*Permanence of Paper*).

For Donna

CONTENTS

List of Illustrations ix

Foreword by Holly Near xiii

Acknowledgments xvii

1. Songs Are Dangerous

1

2. Family

3

3. Making My Own Way

41

4. The Weavers

55

5. Moving On

120

6. Theater

133

7. Heading West
157

8. British Columbia
178

9. The Winter Project
196

10. The Weavers' Last Concert
210

11. Women's Music
223

12. Women in Black
252

13. Learning to Be Old
260

Postscript 265
Index 267

ILLUSTRATIONS

Following page 54

1. Three-year-old Ruth Alice "Ronnie" Gilbert, Queens, New York City, 1929

2. Ronnie with her mother, Sarah, and sister, Irene, New York City, 1930

3. Ronnie and friends Greta Brodie and Jackie (Gibson) Alper singing rounds at a hootenanny with Pete Seeger, New York City, c. 1947

4. Pete Seeger, Fred Hellerman, Ronnie, and Lee Hays at the Village Vanguard, Greenwich Village, New York City, 1950

5. Ronnie dressed for stardom, 1950

6. Wedding portrait, Ronnie and Marty Weg, 1950

7. Ronnie and baby Lisa at home in North Hollywood, California, 1954

8. The Weavers' reunion concert at Carnegie Hall, with the three post-Seeger tenors, Bernie Krause, Erik Darling, and Frank Hamilton, 1963

9. Ronnie in a scene from Open Theatre's production of *America Hurrah,* by Jean-Claude van Itallie, at the Pocket Theatre in New York City, 1966

10. Joe Chaikin, founder of the Open Theatre, 1978

11. Director Jim Brown filming the documentary *The Weavers: Wasn't That a Time!,* New York City, 1980

12. Ronnie and Will Patton in the Winter Project's production of *Tourists and Refugees,* New York City, 1980

13. Ronnie and Holly Near at the Sisterfire music festival, Takoma Park, Maryland, 1982

14. Ronnie and Holly Near about to go onstage at the Sisterfire music festival, Takoma Park, Maryland, 1982

15. Ronnie as Saint Joan in *Top Girls,* by Caryl Churchill, directed by Larry Lillo at the Grand Theatre, London, Ontario, Canada, 1988

16. Life partners Larry Lillo and John Moffat, 1992

17. Ronnie and her partner, Donna Korones, 1987

18. Ronnie and Lisa kayaking in Sausalito, California, 1993

19. Ronnie with her mother, Sarah, and lifelong friends Jackie Alper and Dottie Gottleib, Cambridge, Massachusetts, 1994

20. Ronnie, Lisa, Donna Korones, and Donna's daughters, Harlene and Alicia Katzman, Hawaii, 1998

21. Ronnie and Donna with their new grandbaby, Sara Zoë, Berkeley, California, 2001

22. Ronnie and Zoë at the zoo, Oakland, California, 2003

23. Ronnie with Faith Petric at a Women in Black silent demonstration for peace in the Middle East, San Francisco, California, 2003

24. Lisa and Zoë, Mendocino, California, 2004

25. Ronnie and Donna, Mill Valley, California, 2012

FOREWORD

A small child on a Northern California cattle ranch begins her journey to understand the world through the songs on those magical vinyl circles that her parents bought through mail-order catalogs. The child listens with great care and curiosity. One such recording is called *The Weavers at Carnegie Hall*. Maybe the girl is six or seven or eight. The songs are forever invited into her brain and her heart. "Kisses Sweeter than Wine," "Darling Corey," "Rock Island Line," "Shalom Chaverim," "I Know Where I'm Going," and more. There are four voices. The little girl stares at the picture on the cover of the record, figuring out which voice came out of which singer. One is obvious, the female voice. The photo suggests that the singer throws her head back when she sings. The little girl tries it out, throwing her head back and singing along. The singer's voice sounds like she looks. It is a powerful, joyful voice. It is a tender voice. It is the voice of Ronnie Gilbert.

The child? That is me. A few decades later, I was singing with Ronnie Gilbert—not along with a record but in real life on a real stage with a real audience.

In 1972, I had started a record label in order to sing lyrics that the mainstream was not interested in: songs that opposed racism and the war against Indo-China, and songs that let me begin to investigate my newly discovered feminism. I dedicated my second recording to Ronnie Gilbert. I confess, I didn't know where she was or if she was even alive. Understand, this was before the Internet.

Apparently, Ronnie's daughter brought the recording to Ronnie's attention. And that was the beginning of a long and creative relationship. It would be boring and unrealistic to say our collaboration was without challenges. We are two strong-minded women! But on stage, that power was thrilling. Audiences came in multiple-generation configurations. They came to hear "I Know Where I'm Going," about a woman dreaming of marrying her "handsome winsome Johnny," smashed right up next to "Imagine My Surprise," about a woman contemplating lesbianism and the "rugged women" gone before her. We sang "Si me quieres escribir," which remembers the Abraham Lincoln Brigade of the late 1930s, who fought against Franco in the Spanish Civil War. And we sang "Biko," in remembrance of a South African leader who stood up against apartheid and was tortured and killed.

I remember walking to Lincoln Center in New York City and seeing "SOLD OUT" written across the ad for our two-night engagement at Avery Fischer Hall.

Ronnie will tell you the rest as she puts together the many and varied pieces of her life. A memoir isn't a well-researched biography by a historian. It is a remembering fat with feelings. This memoir is a gloriously personal invitation to us to see how *she* saw it. Any of us who remember it differently can write our own damn books!

I'm thrilled that Ronnie took the time and made the effort to put her stories onto the page. During the process, I saw her room strewn with loose pages, news clippings, PR photos, records and CDs, Post-its, and red-pen-marked drafts. I did not envy her task. How does one write about eight decades in a book light enough for people to read on a park bench or an airplane? But then again, we don't have to write about it all. We can write about the parts we remember, the parts that interest us. And Ronnie was interested in so much! Anyone who thinks Ronnie was "just a folk singer" (as if that weren't enough) can come take a ride with Ms. G. as she remembers the first time she heard Paul Robeson sing, her travels with the Weavers, becoming a mom, the devastating disruptions of McCarthyism, touring Israel, her solo career, experimenting with drugs, becoming an actor, living in Paris during a workers' uprising, meeting Vanessa Redgrave, becoming a therapist, coexisting with bears in Canada, and discovering feminist and lesbian culture.

Thank you, Ronnie, for picking and choosing and committing to this part of your story. The rest we will remember in our hearts, in the way we love you, in the way we throw our heads back and sing!

Holly Near
December 21, 2014

ACKNOWLEDGMENTS

Abundant thanks to Annie Stine for urging me to continue writing this memoir, which had its inception in Wendy Lichtman's writing class; to Deborah Ann Light, Clare Coss, and the Grandmother Winifred Foundation for supporting and helping me through the first phase of the project; to Lynda Winslow for uncountable hours spent organizing my files into working order; to Kate Dougherty for reworking my scribbles into readable paragraphs and challenging my compulsive revisionitis; to Annette Jarvie for proofreading, to Lisa Weg for editing and rearranging the manuscript and helping me to finish it already; to Donna Korones for her support and companionship on this decades-long journey; and to the many friends, acquaintances, and soulmates who encouraged, inspired, and supported me along the way.

ONE

Songs Are Dangerous

Songs are dangerous. So said HUAC (the House Un-American Activities Committee) in the 1950s, and its anti-communist investigators did their best to prevent us from being un-American in public. Nevertheless, the Weavers endured, and on November 28, 1980, at New York's Carnegie Hall, four aging Weavers waited to walk onstage for our first reunion concert in nineteen years, and presumably our last. Actually, only three of us would walk. Lee Hays, "the 'senior member' of the Weavers," as he liked to call himself, would roll on in a wheelchair. A double amputee with a bad heart, he was losing his long battle with diabetes. As we waited for the signal to go on, I wondered how the audience would handle the shock of seeing big Lee so cut down. And how would he, grinding his teeth, face and hair already wet with sweat, handle his key role as emcee?

Movie cameras rolled and the noise of wild welcome cheering and applause flared as we entered, but it gradually subsided as we crossed Carnegie's huge stage, wheeling Lee, a blanket covering his stumps, to his microphone behind a small table.

The air was electric with anticipation. Then, in the silence, a familiar baritone voice, gravelly with disuse and age, announced: "Good evening, I'm Lee Hays ... more or less." A nanosecond of quiet, and then an explosion of cheers and laughs rocked the staid old auditorium. The tension evaporated. Onstage, backstage, and in the audience, we all settled down to enjoy the concert. The years had altered us: Pete with turkey neck and his hair almost gone, Fred with a full goatee and post-middle-age paunch, and me with my plus size 3X figure. But we were survivors, and we were there anyway. If I hadn't known that Lee would be annoyed and embarrassed, I would have said in public what I know we were all thinking: that Lee's appearance that night was the most valiant and generous act of his career. To which he might have replied, as he had to a showbiz promoter twenty-five years earlier: "Act? That was no act; that was the real thing!"

TWO

Family

I was born Ruth Alice Gilbert in September 1926 to Charles and Sarah Gilbert of Brooklyn, New York. I was a chubby, bookish child at a time when every mother imagined her darling to be the next Shirley Temple, and tap dancing lessons were practically obligatory. I loved the dancing, but it was the singing that I excelled at, and it soon became my path.

I trace my part as a "political" singer to a tradition my mother learned as a child laborer in pre–World War I Poland. Before she immigrated to America as a teenager to work in the dress factories of New York, the tradition of meetings and discussion groups, demonstrations, plays, poetry, and singing had already crossed the ocean and met its American counterpart in the songs, parodies, and street theater of the Wobblies and the American trade union movement. It was into that fine international stew that I was born.

PAUL ROBESON, 1936

One morning, my mother, Sarah, an activist International
Ladies' Garment Workers' Union dressmaker, shook me awake.
 "Get dressed, get dressed, we're going downtown to a rally."
 "Oh no! Why do I have to go? It's Saturday. I want to go to the
movies."
 "No, Ruthie, you're coming with me today; it's something
special."
 The outdoor event was on Thirty-Eighth Street near Seventh
Avenue, in the Manhattan garment district. I stood in the street,
miserable, brooding over my mother's unfairness, jostling with
grim-faced strangers for my space, and gritting my teeth at the
incomprehensible speeches delivered from the back of a truck to
applause and boos from the audience. I was just about to start
complaining again when my mother grabbed my arm and pointed
up toward the platform: "Look, Ruthie, look! There's Paul! Now!
Now you're going to hear some real singing." It was as if someone
had sprayed the crowd with a can of happiness. The somber faces
disappeared. People shouted, cheered, laughed. A woman near us
took off her gloves to sharpen her applause. I looked up to see a
black man standing at the microphone smiling, taller and broader
than everyone else on the platform. Finally, he leaned down to
speak. Everyone hushed. "Comrades," he began with a voice so
deep I felt a rumble in my chest. He said something about "my
people and your people," and I looked at my mother for an explanation. She was fumbling for a handkerchief, her eyes full of tears.
 Paul Robeson—actor, singing star, lawyer, football hero—in
the garment district amid the short, pale, adoring, mostly Jewish
garment workers! He cupped his hand behind his right ear and
sang a song familiar from grade school music:

When Israel was in Egypt land, let my people go ...
Oppressed so hard they could not stand, let my people go ...

The words wrenched at me as if I'd never heard them before, carried by the thrilling sound of his voice settling around us like a velvet carpet. Now I was full of questions: What's a pharaoh? Who were the firstborn? Why did Moses threaten to kill them? My mother and I talked all the way home on the rattling BMT subway. It was the first of our lifelong gabfests about politics, power, and songs.

MY PARENTS

"Silly, how can you grow up to be a cowboy? You're a girl," chided Mama. Satisfied at last with the latest hem on my old green party dress, she pulled out the remaining pins, bit off the thread, and steadied the rickety kitchen chair for me to jump down. "Women don't do such things," she threw in for good measure, and pulled the dress off over my head, muffling my retort. "They do too, Mommy, I saw in the movies!"

I remind Daddy to give me a dime to "go see the cowboys tomorrow."

"No! No movies," he said. "Do not ask me again!" He threw down his napkin and walked out of the kitchen.

"Why is Daddy mad at me? I was only reminding him tomorrow is Saturday."

"Don't pester," Mama said. "There's no money for foolish things. Daddy had no work again this week."

"A cyclical downturn of the market," Daddy's newspaper had said. "The worst depression in a decade." This particular cycle had wheeled us into a sandpit from which there seemed to be no getting out.

"If this country had socialism like in Russia …" Mama had said several times.

"Do they have movies in Russia, Mommy—cowboys?"

"Silly, it's not about cowboys."

Because of the Depression, we were a family always on the move, looking for cheaper rent. I rarely spent a whole semester in the same school. In a move to Queens, we stayed still long enough for adventures with my neighbors the Flynn twins, Mary and John. One Saturday, Mrs. Flynn invited me to have lunch with them. She served us sandwiches with a thick layer of peanut butter and a thin line of red jam. I took a bite and started to chew, but then I began to choke and tear up as the wad adhered to my palate and would not move. Mary stared. John laughed. Mrs. Flynn brought me a glass of milk and pounded on my back. Finally, the bolus dislodged, and I gulped it down, very embarrassed. The lesson "don't talk with food in your mouth" had impressed itself upon me forever. I had been trying to say, "This is good. I've never had peanut butter before." My family's sandwiches were always cream cheese and jelly.

After lunch, we watched Mr. Flynn cleaning something over newspapers at the dining room table—a gun, black and shiny with oil. He offered it to me. It was cold and heavy, nothing like the boys' fake guns. A flutter started at the pit of my stomach and reached all the way up to my throat, like the time I had held a dead bird in my hand. I handed it back quickly. Mr. Flynn chuckled and gave me a rag to wipe my hands. At home, I told my mother about the sandwich and Mary and John's policeman father. "Policeman? He's no policeman. He's a gangster!" It didn't seem safe to question, so I didn't. Who was Mr. Flynn? A nice person in a blue uniform who you went to if you got lost? Who'd help you find your mom? Or a bad guy like in the movies? I thought I'd ask the twins, but I never did.

Mary and John took me to church. I loved the theatrics. I imitated my friends' genuflections and self-crossings and knelt alongside them before the altar. There, the priest, in his pretty white and gold brocades, pushed a smudge of something black onto my forehead with his thumb and put a tasteless cookie on my tongue. I went home in a mood made dreamy by candles and incense. "Wash that off," my mother said, with a cluck of impatience at the ashes on the bridge of my nose. But when I told her that I wanted to go to the convent with Mary and be a nun, she said in a voice sharp with scorn: "Jewish girls don't marry Jesus!" What did getting married have to do with nuns? They had such allure, floating in pairs or threes along the street in their long black gowns; you never saw their feet move. Even gruff men said "Sister" with a kind of tenderness, as if nuns were delicate or royal—certainly special. I imagined Mary and I gliding together along Eighty-Second Street, members of that mysterious club.

But the Flynn-twin adventures ended when we again moved to a different neighborhood. Our new home was a long, third-floor apartment in a wedge-shaped building, perfect for roller-skating around, except when the barber came out of his shop screaming at us about the noise. One night, I awoke from sleep to shadowy voices from deep in the apartment—Mama, and Aunt Pauline maybe. I held my breath to hear better. "... not a man you can depend on." Mama's voice sounded like she was crying. The moon a huge platter outside the window. Branches and leaves, traced on the windowpane, hardly moved. The rail at the foot of my bed was shiny with moonlight. I lay as still as the moon and started to sob, although I didn't know why.

My mother came, sat on my bed, held me close, and told me I had had a bad dream. I knew I hadn't. I pointed to the window and whispered into her bosom, "There's somebody bad there!" "No, no, darling, there's nothing there," she said, "just the moon. See? Look how beautiful the moon is." Held safe in her arms, half-remembered scenes flashed through my mind: Choking— Daddy and I in the green waves, bouncing up and down. "My god, Charlie, why didn't you hold onto her?" Daddy teaching me to skate—metal wheels—*chee, chee, chee, chee*—my hand in his warm hand until the top of the street, the pavement below so smooth. Mama, sponging blood from my knee. "Why did you let go of her hand!" Daddy, biting his lip. I didn't tell her it was me, that I had let go.

After that, we moved to Judge Street, which had leafy trees and no barbershop. Our apartment had one bedroom for my sister, Irene, and me, and a pullout couch in the living room for Mama and Daddy. The kitchen was a sort of closet called a "kitchenette." Mama joined a club called the Party. They met at different people's houses. One night, it was our turn to host. I was doing my homework on the living room table, when the Party people came, three men and a woman. One man was black, and he wasn't our janitor. They talked quietly so as not to disturb me, but I heard names and places—Mussolini, Italy and Spain—like on the radio. I finished my homework, put my books together, and was saying goodnight when I heard a key in the door—it was Daddy home from work. Daddy worked hard, and many nights he came home late and tired. He said hello. Everyone said, "Hello, Mr. Gilbert." I kissed him and Mama goodnight and went to bed. Pretty soon, Daddy came in and tried to lie down on Irene's bed. "She sleeps like a wild one, all over the bed," Mama always said. Not me. I sleep very still. Sure enough,

Daddy couldn't make Irene move over. He came to my bed. I pretended to be asleep. He knew I was pretending. "Ruthie, move over." He got in, turned his back to me, and fell asleep. He smelled like cigarettes. He was snoring a little. I fell asleep hearing the Party people still talking.

On Sunday mornings, Mama served us breakfast from the kitchenette stove. Daddy sat across from me at the little pull-down table, having his favorite breakfast—orange juice, bacon and eggs, Silvercup bread, and coffee. I would drink my juice and watch him eat. He would take up his knife and fork and cut into his eggs: a horizontal cut above the yolk, then a cut to the right of the yolk, then a horizontal cut below the yolk, and then a cut to the left of the yolk. Now the yolk was sitting in a small, white square and was free. Next, he cut the two whites apart, lay down his knife and fork, picked a piece of bread from the bread dish, tore it in half, and put one of the halves back. I would tell myself not to watch the next part, but I couldn't keep my eyes from following his hands. Daddy would pick up his fork in his left hand and, using the bread as a pusher, fold the free egg white in half on the fork and lift it slowly. His mouth would open very wide. Slowly, slowly, everything went in, even the white slime, which had begun to drip. He would close his mouth and chew, the fist holding the fork resting on the table. The round place on his jaw would rise and fall, rise and fall. I would go back to my orange juice, but the squishing sound behind his lips would pull my attention back.

And now he would eat the yolk. Daddy would slide the tines of his fork under the yolk and lift it from the plate. I would keep telling myself, "Don't watch this," but I would watch. Again, the mouth would slowly open wide as the hand slowly moved upward. But this time, halfway up, the slime would begin to drip, and there was no bread to catch it. I would hold my breath, wondering if the yolk would make it, and then I would see yellow oozing between the tines. I would tear my eyes away and dive into my orange juice. But there was still another egg on Daddy's plate ...

THE FOLKS, GREENPOINT, BROOKLYN

My father's father had been a blacksmith's helper in the Ukraine. In the early thirties, in Brooklyn, New York, he was the only one in my family who had a job. He hammered out metal staves for illicit wooden beer barrels. My atheist mother teased my Orthodox Jewish grandfather, "Don't forget to thank God for Prohibition." I was happy because we were spending the day with Gramma and Grampa. Grampa sometimes gave me a dime to see the children's matinee at the Meserole. But it was Saturday, the Sabbath.

"Jews don't spend money on *Shabos!*" he said.

"But the cowboys only ride horses, Grampa."

"Jews don't ride horses."

"*Vos redst du, Mottel?*" Gramma scolded. "Give the child a dime, for God's sake!"

I was eight years old, and my sister, Irene, was six. She was little—she got in free. "Be sure you hold Sister's hand!" Mama warned as we ran down the stairs. I promised I would, praying that Irene wouldn't have to go pee-pee when there was a good part. Mama read my mind!

"Make sure you both wash your hands when you go to the toilet!"

"We will, we will!"

"Come right home and don't talk to anyone on the street, and don't run, you'll fall!"

And we were out the door and up Manhattan Avenue to the Meserole Theater to watch Ken Maynard, Tom Mix, or Bob Steele flash across the screen on their fabulous horses and win against the bad guys. Then there were Busby Berkeley's movies and music! Rows and rows of silver ladies singing: "In my song of love, the moon above makes the music ..." On the way home, we passed the tobacco store's rolled-up awning hanging lopsided like a wink over thick white letters on the glass. Next door hung a sign—"Haberdashery/Gone Out Of Biznis!" An empty display case stood crooked in the middle of the floor. Suddenly, an unpleasant smell wafted into the street and jolted me. I held my breath as we hurried past the Polish butcher shop: two dead pigs' heads in the window, fury in their terrible smiles and no-eyes. Then I saw a movie poster in the window of the shoe repair shop: a lady lay on a table, her yellow hair trailing on the floor. A drooling giant ape-man held a spike over her. Two jars filled the display window of the store next door—one held a red liquid, the other green. What did "apothecary" mean? What was in those huge jars? Could they hold a person? A child?

Crossing the street, I took Irene's hand. The corner building was boarded up, and there was a man with crutches in the door-way. I couldn't keep from staring as we passed. One trouser leg was folded and pinned up. He was trying to get both crutches under one arm while holding onto a small bottle. He grinned at us and waved the bottle. Holding tight to Irene's hand, I looked straight ahead and pulled us past. We went a couple of steps and just behind us, crash! I peered over my shoulder. The bottle was smashed on the sidewalk, and the man was staring at me. My stomach turned. Should I have helped him? I was full of curios-ity about cripples. Mama told me that the war had taken away their legs. What did the war do with those legs? I also wanted to know about the beggar man, or half-man really, who I often saw on a rolling board: How was he attached—with glue? Nails? Did he sleep on the board at night? How did he go to the bathroom?

Once, Gramma took me to her Orthodox synagogue. We climbed stairs up to a narrow space with wooden benches, where women greeted Gramma in Yiddish. One smiled at me. Shy, I looked away. Suddenly, this stranger was sitting right next to me, pinching my cheek between her knuckles. When I yelled, everyone laughed. Not wanting to be called a crybaby, I concentrated hard on the floor down below, where men with large scarves stood about the big, dark hall, muttering, bowing, and swaying. A rumbling sound spread through the hall.

"Gramma?"

She put her finger to her lips.

"But Gramma, who are they? What are they doing?"

"Look, there's Daddy, and there's Grampa," she whispered. "You can't see them?"

From where we sat in the balcony, the men below in caps (beanies that I was told to call "yarmulkes") looked pretty much alike. (Not long afterward I got the glasses I needed.)

"How come some of them have their shawls over their heads?"

"*Nisht* shawl," Gramma corrected, "tallis."

"But why are they bowing up and down?"

"Davening," she whispered, "they're davening. Now, *shah*, be a good girl."

It was another mysterious Jewish ritual, like when Grampa would wind his arm with leather thongs when he prayed at home. Nothing was explained.

I later wondered if it was sad for my grandmother that her granddaughter grew up without comprehending the rituals connecting observant Jews to past and future. My grandparents died when I was seventeen, and this trace of my religious identity was buried with them.

GROWN-UP PROBLEMS

I was about ten years old—Mama, Daddy, and I were standing inside the entrance to the playground with a tall man in a dark suit. He was a detective. "Is this the man who touched you?" the detective asked. I looked at the playground man standing stiff in front of us in his green uniform, then glanced over at the swings, where there was another man in the same uniform. How could I tell? "Is this the one?" the detective insisted, like in school, when the teacher asks you a question that's in your homework and you don't know the answer. Only in school, I always knew the answer. Now though, I couldn't breathe, couldn't talk, was not sure. The man in front of us began to cry. "I'm sorry, I'm so sorry, I swear I didn't mean anything!" He clasped his hands in front of him. "I prayed to God all night to forgive me." Tears poured down his cheeks. I was so shocked; a grownup sobbing out loud in front of everybody, the people watching, the children coming over from the swings.

Suddenly, Mama leaned toward him.

"You bastard! You beast!" she screamed. "Is this what they teach you in your church?"

"Sarah ..." my father pleaded, and touched her arm. She shook off his hand. He looked around, studied the ground, and bit his lip.

"I prayed, I prayed ..." sobbed the man, tears and snot all over his face. I was wishing he'd unclasp his hands and find his handkerchief.

"Yes, tell your priest, you pig!" Mama hissed, and spat on the ground right in front of him. I looked at the detective, but his face didn't say anything.

"You can go home now," he said, dismissing us like a teacher. Then I could breathe; I was so glad it was over.

The day before, we'd had visitors who had two children. Our apartment on Judge Street was small, and the grownups wanted to talk, so they sent us out to play in the park. We fooled around on the swings for a while, waiting for a basketball to be freed up. You could get the ball at the shed from an attendant in a park uniform that was green, like the Girl Scouts'. Finally, we got a ball and took turns shooting baskets. Some other kids that were waiting played with us. They were all older than me, and everybody laughed at the way I threw the ball, underhand. It was fun, though. But after a while, it began to drizzle, and kids left the game until there was just me, trying to throw the way the others did. When I felt a little drip run down my nose I realized my hair was pretty wet. I looked around, and there was no one else in the playground. It was time to quit. The attendant was standing at the open door of his shed, watching me, holding his clipboard over his head. I brought the ball to him, and he motioned for me to put it inside. Everything was stashed in shelves, but the shelves were full. He came in behind me.

"Put it there," he said, pointing to the floor under a shelf, "and sit down until the rain stops." "I have to go home," I said.

"Sure, sure," he said, "but it's raining too hard now." He shut the door. A single bare light bulb was burning. The door had a hook and eye. He latched it and handed me a towel to dry my hair. It didn't look clean, but I blotted my hair.

"Sit down. Here." He smiled and moved something off the bench. His voice was scratchy. His hair was black and gray like my Grampa's. The space was small. I pressed back against the wall to avoid his behind, which was almost in my face. I felt the material of his pants rubbing my bare knees and moved over a little. He finished arranging and tried to sit down and almost sat on me. Now I was pressed against the wall, behind a little shelf jutting out in front of my face. The two of us filled up the whole bench.

"Nice girl," he said, smiling and patting my knee. "You like to play ball?"

"Yes," I whispered.

"Yes," he repeated. "I seen you here before. You like to throw the ball in the basket, huh?" I nodded my head. "Don't be afraid. You're a nice girl. I like you, that's all." He patted my knee again. Then he put his hand under where my shorts ended and took hold of my thigh, and he gave the inside a big squeeze. I was paralyzed with embarrassment. I tried to pull my legs together and pushed hard at the wall, trying to move away. "No, no, don't be scared. I won't hurt you. I like a good little girl, a pretty girl." His voice was mushy. My face was burning hot. I felt like I was choking.

His hand shifted a little. I thought he was letting me go, but he held on to my thigh. Now I felt his finger scratching against my panties, stroking through my panties. Then his hand was still. He let go of my thigh and patted my knee again. "Listen, girlie," he said, "you wait here, OK? I'm gonna go get my car, I'm gonna take you home. You wait right here, alright?" He was standing up, his back to me, doing something with his pants in front. I could see only a little bit of his face. He opened the latch and opened the door. Light came in around the dark shape of his body. "You sit right here, yes, like a good girl?" I nodded. He was gone. I got up and ran out of the shed and ran and ran. "Never!" Mama had said—I could hear her voice—"never, never get into a car with a stranger!" Running felt good. I didn't feel scared; no, I was smart—I fooled him, I didn't wait for the car. I felt excited, happy. I got home to our apartment building, ran upstairs, and told Mama how I fooled the man, how I ran away from his car! She called the police.

A long time later, maybe a week or two, Mama and I sat on a wooden bench with slats in a long hallway in a strange building. I was trying to run my finger along the edge of every slat, and I had three more to go, but a man with a badge on his blue shirt came out from a door and nodded to us. Mama took my hand, "Don't be scared. Just tell the truth." Fooey, that story again. On the other side of the door was a big room with mostly grownups and some children, all sitting in rows of seats behind a railing, like the front rows of the movies. The man with the badge took me to a table on the other side of the railing and told me to sit down. I waited. Three old men in black robes stared at me and didn't say anything. They were judges; I knew from the movies. I was beginning to feel scared and looked around for my mother. She was sitting just on the other side of the railing.

Finally, the judge on the right went "*grmm, grmm,*" and said, "Ruth, do you know what will happen if you tell a lie? What happens to you when you lie?" Hah! I knew the answer to that one. "My mother will be mad," I said. "I'll get punished." He leaned back and looked away. Uh-oh, I could see from his face that something was wrong. He looked at the other judges. The one at the other end stared hard at me. They whispered something to each other. Then the baldish judge in the middle leaned forward and looked straight toward me. He said quietly: "Did he touch your privates? Did he touch your private parts?" I didn't know what to say. What were "private parts"? He touched my panties. You're not allowed to let anyone see your panties. You always have to close your legs, pull down your dress. Was that it? I looked toward my mother and was not sure what she was thinking. "Did he touch your private parts, little girl?" the judge asked once more, now very stern. I thought she nodded. "Yes," I said.

Later, after we left the courtroom, Mama cleared up some of my confusion: "The first judge wanted you to say that God, not your mother, would punish you for telling a lie. The other two were satisfied you told the truth, and the man is being sent to jail. The women in black who were crying and shaking their fists at us on the way out were some of his relatives, an Italian family. They wear black whenever relatives die."

When I got back to school, my teacher asked what had happened. I answered with the short phrase Mama had taught me to say: "I was molested in the playground." Mrs. M. gasped and closed her eyes. When she opened them she stared at me so hard over her spectacles that I wondered if I had given another wrong answer, and I had to look down to the floor.

More problems arrived a year later, when I was eleven. Mama said she needed to talk to me about something important. We were alone in the apartment, sitting together at the living room table. She started to talk, saying something about problems grown-up people sometimes have. I was proud to be talked to about something grown-up and tried to listen carefully, but then she mentioned something about Daddy, and my own thoughts about him made me lose the thread of her voice. I was thinking how mad I was at Daddy; he would say that we could go for a walk but then he would fall asleep on the couch. You couldn't play the radio when he was on the couch sleeping; you couldn't even talk out loud. Suddenly, something she said interrupted my bad thoughts. I wasn't sure I had heard right. Sad and soft, her head tilted over like a bird's, her nose getting red, like she was going to cry.

"What do you think, Ruthie, should I?"

"Should you what?"

"Should we leave Daddy?"

I imagined our house with the couch empty, the radio playing, and Mama laughing. I let out my breath. "Maybe we should." Did this mean we would? When? She didn't say. I didn't ask. I just wanted to forget about that conversation.

SPRINGFIELD, MISSOURI

The back of a family photo read, "Sussmans, Springfield, Missouri," showing three girls in hats and white gloves, the demure daughters of my mother's half-brother Ben and his wife, Eva. Another photo showed the adults in front of their home, which had a front porch built of stone. "Would you like to spend a few weeks there?" Mama asked. Go "out West" to Springfield, Missouri? Meet my cousins, Florence, Ruth and Sarabelle, who was my age, whose movie star blondness cast glamour over the notion of family? Oh yes!

I didn't know that Springfield was the first of a series of steps on a journey that would lead to California, where my mother would eventually move—without my father. My memories of Springfield began with the smell of jasmine and the feel of cool stone on the porch, lawns melting into each other like a green river, evenings bewitched by fireflies, and the sensation of being an outsider, totally alien. As it turned out, my beautiful cousin Sarabelle and I had almost nothing in common to shape a relationship. Shy, bookish, and buxom, I felt clumsy next to her brisk, athletic little self. I couldn't ride a bike—I had never owned one—whereas her bike was as much a part of her daily life as her arm or leg. I clung to the safety of the house, baking cookies and listening to Aunt Eva's table-model Philco, to which I owe my later professional comfort with hymns and fiddle tunes. A fondness for "serious" vocal music was a prize I carried home from the middle sister, Ruth, a college freshman and voice student. I yearned after the passionate sounds she made from her G. Schirmer *Book of Art Songs* and would sit at the piano picking out the melodies and imitating her pronunciation of the French lyrics. I have never forgotten the songs she sang—"Habanera" from Carmen, "Mon cœur s'ouvre à ta voix" from Samson and Delilah, and others. Ruth's singing teacher should have collected a double fee that summer for inspiring my pear-shaped tones, which reviewers have occasionally mistaken over the years for a "trained classical voice."

Uncle Ben Sussman was king of his castle, obeyed and catered to by his family. It confused me that the lively, assertive women, each a distinct personality in the daytime, would hush and blend in together in Uncle Ben's presence. A small man with a prominent nose and taciturn manner, my uncle owned a shoe store downtown. Some of his business was in secondhand shoes. On Saturday mornings, farm families from the surrounding Ozark Mountains turned Springfield's downtown streets gray, the color of poor rural America's wagons, buckboards, and whatever was left of their worn autos in 1937. Sarabelle and I walked downtown late one afternoon to meet Uncle Ben and be taken to dinner. A buckboard was stopped in front of the store, the horse dozing. A woman sat high up, reins loose in her lap, a boy about my age next to her. Both were barefoot. Two small children were playing with something at the back end of the wagon. The boy and I stared at each other for a second or two and then quickly looked away. Inside, Uncle Ben was fitting a small girl with shoes. Her hair, so pale yellow it was almost white, matched the hair of the children outside. A man in faded coveralls stood by watching, turning a battered hat round and round by the greasy brim. The child sat gripping the chair arms, her expression like her father's, mouth slack, eyes shifting from Uncle Ben's face to a rack of old shoes of mixed sizes. Her legs startled me. They were white from bare toes to calf, where grime began, ascending to her knees—and perhaps beyond. "These should be fine," said Uncle Ben, choosing a small pair of pink Mary Janes from the rack. He bent, slipped one of them on, and squeezed at the toe. "There you are," he said decisively to the father, who nodded quickly. Uncle removed the shoe, stood up, wrapped the pair in newspaper, accepted some coins from the man, handed the package over, and turned to other things as they left the store. Through the glass front door, I watched the man lift the girl up onto the bench next to the woman and hand up the package. The view to the back of the wagon was blocked; I couldn't see the boy or the other children. Uncle Ben tidied up, rang up the cash register, and locked up the shop, and we went out the back door to meet the rest of the family for the weekly treat.

We went to a restaurant—an elegant cafeteria, where a waiter in uniform carried trays from the steam table to the dining table. A musician played an electric organ on a raised platform during the dinner hour. I was glad Uncle chose a table near the organ. I was fascinated by the elusive connection between the music and the movement of the organist's feet on the wooden pedals. On our way home, Uncle Ben stopped at the store to retrieve something. When we got there, the buckboard was still parked out front; the woman appeared not to have moved. The boy was seated next to her again, and the girl who had "new" shoes was curled up next to him on the seat. She sat up as we parked and stared at my uncle as he let himself into the store. He did not greet her. I wondered if I should say hi, but I didn't. Heading home, I asked Uncle Ben if he knew them.

"Well, they buy shoes from me," he replied.

I wondered why they were sitting there all that time.

"Saturday night. That's what they do. Come in, buy something they need, wait for the father while he drinks at the bar."

I thought about the mother without shoes, wondering if that had something to do with her not getting down off the wagon, wondering why she didn't just drive away and come back, wondering if the little girl's new shoes would be comfortable or pinch her feet, and if she would have to wear them anyway. I kept the wondering to myself.

My visit with the Sussmans ended with their yearly automobile trip to St. Louis to buy shoes wholesale for the shop, a trip of several hours, winding through the Ozark Mountains. I begged to be allowed to stay at home. I dreaded carsickness. I was so susceptible that just smelling the interior of an automobile while walking past a car with its door open would bring on an attack of nausea. But no, I could not be left behind—I had to go. It was a sparkling day when we set off, but the beauty of the gently rolling hills was wasted on me, and likely also on my relatives, when it became all too obvious I hadn't exaggerated the problem. They were solicitous, but I felt doubly miserable for spoiling their good time. On the drive back to Springfield, though, Ruth began singing, encouraging me to sing along. Grateful for her good cheer, I did. It was nothing fancy, just the old chestnuts: "You Are My Sunshine," "Down by the Old Mill Stream," "Wait 'till the Sun Shines, Nellie," and so on. Ruth and I took turns with the simple harmonies, everyone joining in. By the time we reached Springfield, we had orbited the repertoire of public school music classes several times, and I had not been sick even once! Doth music soothe the timid stomach as well as the savage breast? In any case, I was done with car phobia and have rarely been troubled by carsickness since.

BRIGHTON BEACH, BROOKLYN

I came home from Springfield to Brighton Beach, where my mother and Irene and I were to live. My father stayed in Manhattan. Brighton Beach was a neighborhood so different from Jackson Heights that it might have been another country. Even in 1937, it was 90 percent Jewish. For my mother, Brighton Beach might have been a reminder of the Warsaw neighborhood of her youth, where Yiddish had been her first language. For me, it was culture shock. Why was there so much noise? The overhead train clattered by, and people's voices were so loud! Why did everyone laugh so boisterously and gesture with their hands, which I had been taught not to do? And Yiddish—the language my parents fought with—was everywhere. At first, Brighton Beach sounded like a place full of angry people. Strong odors assaulted my nose on the street: fish here, knishes there, poultry a few doors down. I missed calm, leafy Jackson Heights. I missed tying knots with my Girl Scout troop every week in the big echoing emptiness of the Catholic Church basement. At recess on the first day of school, I asked a girl in the schoolyard, "Do you think Mrs. K. will be nice? She seems strict." Uh-oh, what did I say? Her face scrunched up with distaste. "Gee, you twalk fohnny," she said. I guess, coming from Queens, I did "twalk fohnny." I was exotic in Brooklyn! It would take more than memorizing a new address to locate myself in this milieu.

Every other Saturday, the doorbell would ring. "Answer the door, Ruthie, it's your father." I knew that. It was my week to go out with him. Closing the book over my finger to hold my place, I thought, "It will be a while. He won't come in. He will stand there shifting from foot to foot, biting at his upper lip until Mama calls out, 'Come inside, Charlie.' She will take her time saying it." I tried to finish the page of my book. Daddy joined Mama at the dining table, sat down, and cleared his throat. They talked softly, but I could hear.

"Again nothing, Charlie?"

"Trouble at the shop, Sarah..."

They began to speak louder and then switched to Yiddish. I put down my book, walked slowly to the door, opened it, and looked at them with a grin. They stopped talking, although I could see their eyes were still yelling. Slowly, Daddy stood up and joined me at the door. Mama said, "Have a good time. Do you have a handkerchief, Ruthie?" I waved at her with my hanky and closed the door.

The train ride from Brighton Beach to Manhattan's Times Square was long—sometimes elevated, sometimes underground. We didn't talk much; I could hardly hear anything at all over the rattling of the train. Daddy would yell a question about Irene. I would yell back—yes or no or I don't know. He always asked about Irene when I was alone with him. I always wondered if he asked her about me.

I yelled, "Are we going to the movies?" He yelled back, "Yes, sure." Daddy liked musicals. Boy, so did I. He loved Jeanette MacDonald and Nelson Eddy; I loved Deanna Durban and the new star, Judy Garland. Deanna Durban was so beautiful, and you could see right down her throat when she sang.

I was a quick study with melodies and lyrics, and Daddy liked that I could sing most of the songs by the time we came out of the theater. Usually, we went to the Automat for lunch. I chose what I wanted from a big wall of glass cases, each with a serving of food inside. When I was little, Daddy used to lift me up to put the coin in, turn the knob, lift the door, and take out my food. And I still liked the Automat. They had my most favorite—cherry pie. When we finished lunch, Daddy would say, "Let's go for a little walk." And I would think "Uh-oh—that means he wants to look at model hats." Daddy made ladies' hats in his factory, copied from hats in stores. As we walked, he might see a hat with a net hanging down around the edge, a feather in the band, or flowers on it, or even just a plain hat, and he'd walk around the window looking at the back and the side. Maybe the shop would have a stylish hat. Or maybe not. And maybe it would get too late for the movies. You just never could tell.

"Daddy," I'd say, "do you like that hat?"

"Yes, maybe."

"Why?"

"It's stylish."

I nodded, even though I didn't really know what that meant. He didn't like to be asked too many questions when he was thinking. He would move slowly along the glass front, and when I thought he had looked at all the hats in the window, I would remind him softly, "Are we going to the movies now?" He'd squeeze my hand and whisper, "Wait, wait just a minute," like it was a secret.

In Brighton Beach, my mother became a member of the International Workers Order (IWO), a Communist-affiliated insurance and fraternal organization. The Brighton Community Center, a sprawling building of many rooms and a large proscenium stage, was the local IWO's hub of cultural and educational activity. Perhaps reflecting on my fascination with marrying Jesus, Mama signed me up for a children's class to learn Yiddish. I don't remember being consulted about it, just going to the class. Chaver ("comrade") Leib—kind, patient, and rotund— was the teacher. With his help, I rapidly learned to read and write the Yiddish alphabet. I even won a spelling contest, and my prize was a place in a group trip to historical Philadelphia. Like the Liberty Bell, though, my triumph had a small flaw. I did not understand a single word I had spelled. Undeterred, Chaver Leib gave me a line to speak in his Yiddish-language children's play. I have never forgotten it. It translates as: "It has been a long time that I have not seen Jacob." Fluent Yiddish speakers with whom I have laughed about my one line assure me that the grammar is impeccable and my pronunciation outstanding. However, apart from that line, I learned no more Yiddish that semester. Once again I was an alien. My classmates, all younger than I, had grown up in a Yiddish-speaking community. They were in the class to improve their grasp of the language; I had no grasp to begin with.

My next taste of IWO culture was a bit more my eleven-year-old style: the Brighton Beach Drum and Bugle Corps. We practiced all winter in order to march in the May Day Parade. I thrilled to the marching drill, perfected the roll and the single paradiddle on a drum pad, and emerged proudly on May Day as drum sergeant. Mama was pleased, although she had initially asked, "Why not the bugle?" Irene got the bugle. I remember the parade that year clearly—the yellow silken banner that hung across the avenue with the message "Remember the Haymarket Martyrs" in red and the excruciating pain from the sharp rim of the field drum bouncing against my left thigh for blocks. I enjoyed the lessons though, at least as much as I had enjoyed tying knots. However, the volunteer instructor quit after May Day and was never replaced. So much for my career as a percussionist.

CAMP WO-CHI-CA (WORKERS CHILDREN'S CAMP), 1937

Then came summer and a new IWO activity—sleepaway camp. Thanks to my mother's resourcefulness and various philanthropies, I'd experienced a range of children's summer camps by the time I was eleven, from two weeks on a horrible beetle-infested New Jersey beach to a full summer at an elegant girls' camp in the piney woods of Maine. At the camp in Maine I learned to ride horseback, an indescribable thrill for me because of my cowboy fixation, even though there was nothing western about Camp Wazayata. The saddles were the size of postage stamps, meant for serious English-style riding. Seniors practiced jumps. I was content to post and canter and climb back up when I fell off—a frequent occurrence, due to my short legs and round bottom—which earned me a pat on the head from Major Church, the riding master.

The IWO's Camp Wo-Chi-Ca in New Jersey was a completely different world. As the bus pulled into the Schooleys Mountains campsite after the long, hot ride from New York City, we passengers were greeted by a chorus of campers and staff passionately singing:

> You are the best, I love you best,
> Wo-Chi-Ca mine, oh camp so fine,
> There's not another camp like mine.

I hadn't been there two days before I agreed they were right—there wasn't any other camp like this one. The Wo-Chi-Ca repertoire came from the *Wobbly Little Red Songbook* and the *Songs of the Abraham Lincoln Brigade*. I was introduced to my secular Jewish identity by the old Yiddish folk song "Tumbalalaika," and the newer "Djankoya."

We sung a lot at camp. Once, we even had a special visitor. "Extra rehearsal! Paul Robeson is coming to camp! We're going to perform the 'Ballad for Americans' for him at the evening program." Music counselor Millie reminded us: "Don't forget to listen to each other on 'so-o-o-me' and to hit 'birthday' together." We sang in unison:

> In seventy-six the sky was red
> Thunder rumbling overhead
> Bad King George couldn't sleep in his bed
> And on that stormy morn—
> Ol' Uncle Sam was born.
> SO-O-O-ME BIRTHDAY!

Suddenly, the door of the dark barn slammed open to blinding sunlight, and Robeson himself was there, his huge silhouette filling the doorframe, singing the next verse:

> Ol' Sam put on a three-cornered hat
> And in a Richmond church he sat
> And Patrick Henry told him that
> While America drew breath
> It was "Liberty or death!"

At least a quarter of the campers were black (we said Negro back then), which was unusual in those days, even at other leftist camps. Many of the staff came from the African American cultural world: singers Paul Robeson and Kenneth Spencer; the dancer Pearl Primus; the actor Canada Lee; artists Ernest Critchlow, Charles White, Jacob Lawrence, Gwendolyn Knight, and Rockwell Kent; the writer Howard Fast; and the poet Gwendolyn Bennett. Political figures such as Mother Bloor, Albert Kahn, and Dr. Edward Barsky came and talked about their experiences and struggles to change the world. The world needed changing, we kids learned, and we could be involved in changing it.

We eleven-year-olds were going through some big changes ourselves. That summer, the girls in Marie Curie Bunk decided en masse to change our names to boys' names. Cheating, I borrowed mine from a girl, Ronnie. Maybe some essence of the tall, blonde, popular senior would dust its magic over short, awkward, roly-poly me. Was it the incipient little dykette in me? Hard to know. I also had a deep crush on a male counselor. In any case, I was growing up. My menses began that fall. And oddly, although the glamour dust blew away without having done much good, the name Ronnie stuck.

These were the years when my sister and I developed a fierce struggle for Mother's attention and approval. Mother gave us little of this and would not allow us to do anything for her that might have lightened her load. Why didn't she have me do the shopping or fix a simple dinner for us now and then? I was surely capable of it. But her tempo was prestissimo. She couldn't stop to make lists, and I was "too slow" or "too sloppy." Both of our parents had primitive beliefs about behavior modification. Verbal abuse and slaps, good old European traditions, were their methods. Perhaps the anger Mother spit out helped her discharge some of the stress that ultimately brought her an ulcer. Irene and I reacted in different ways—I with guilt and passive aggression, Irene with efflorescent fury.

In the meantime, I was gathering my new life around me. A friend of my mother's had heard that a children's radio program was recruiting young singers for a choir. She thought of my strong voice and sent in my name. A postcard arrived announcing the time and place of the audition. My mother knew nothing about it, and neither did I, but at her friend's urging she agreed to take me there. It was a long ride on the subway train. The scene as we emerged from the station into Manhattan is imprinted on my memory: 1440 Broadway, the building that housed the radio station WOR, loomed before me like a huge iceberg, and I hung back on the subway stairs, frozen, unable to make my legs climb.

"What's wrong?" asked my mother. I didn't know. I just stood there, waiting for her to tell me. "What do you want to do?" she kept asking, starting to sound very annoyed. I began to cry. I was stuck, my mother was stuck, and my sister was looking on, puzzled. Finally, Mother had had enough. "Well, make up your mind," she snapped, "Do you or don't you?" Did I or didn't I what? I only knew that I didn't want to go back down the stairs and bear her disapproval all the way home, so I forced myself forward. Inside the building, I stood next to a piano keyboard, facing a man with untidy red hair and a large mole next to his nose, his eyes crinkled in a smile. I sang the scales and tunes he played on the piano. "That's nice, very nice, Miss Gilbert. Thank you. I'll see you Sunday," said Dr. Dolph Martin, the choir director.

I sang in the alto section of his Rainbow House Children's Radio Choir for three years. Every Sunday morning, Jonah Javna (another Jewish child from Brighton Beach) and I helped the choir open the show, proselytizing for the Christian triune God:

> Praise God, from whom all blessings flow;
> Praise Him, all creatures here below;
> Praise Him above, ye heav'nly host;
> Praise Father, Son, and Holy Ghost.

Then we sang one or two of Dr. Martin's choral arrangements—which ranged from Fauré to French folk songs, Bach chorales, old parlor songs, barbershop harmony, and Christmas carols. But our Jewishness managed to survive the doxology, for Jonah eventually became a rabbi. My Jewishness wasn't religious anyway. Years later, Pete Seeger offered this reworking of the words for the Common Doxology, also known as the hymn tune "Old Hundredth."

> Old Hundredth, please don't think us wrong
> For adding verses to your song.
> Sing peace between the old and young,
> 'Tween every faith and every tongue.
>
> Between the white, black, red, and brown,
> Between the wilderness and town,
> Sing peace between the near and far,
> 'Tween Allah and the six-pointed star.

BEATTIE

It was in Brighton Beach that I found a true best friend: cheerful, witty, and buoyant Beatrice Levinsky. Thoroughly Jewish Beattie (she hated "Beatrice") was the perfect tonic for my overserious, self-conscious, Waspish, socially-shy self. She was curious and amused at my life experience in *goyishe* Queens. I admired her poise, her happy rootedness in the culture of Brighton Beach, and her stories about helping with her mother's kosher catering business—preparing buffets and waiting tables to earn an allowance. She admired my "interest in politics," as she termed my concern with the lost Spanish Civil War, my worship of the volunteer American soldiers who fought for the Loyalist cause, and my worry about the Spanish refugee children. "How do you know about those things?" she asked. "Oh, I read the *Daily Worker*," I bragged, although what I spouted was mostly parroted back from adult discussions. But I was in fact wrapped emotionally in the red, yellow, and purple flag of the Spanish Republicans—my first activist cause. I would go out into the street with my *pushka* (charity box) to collect coins. Mother acquired some sheet music with lyrics as passionate as my cousin Ruth's ardent art songs. I spent hours at the piano working out the rhythm for "¡No pasarán!" (they shall not pass). This had been the motto of the Loyalist defenders of the city of Madrid against Franco's Nazi-enhanced fascist forces.

> Spain darkens under a cloud where sun should light the land.
> Spain thunders out clear and loud to stop the fascist hand.
> ...
> Spain bleeds for a world that would be free—
> O Republic! *No pasarán!*

Lounging on her bed or mine, Beattie and I always had something to talk about. We were growing up with the rise of the big bands, and we jitterbugged and lindy-hopped ourselves silly at Beattie's cousin Eleanor's house, dancing to Glen Miller, Harry James, and the Dorseys and singing along with Helen Forrest, Connie Haines, and Frank Sinatra hits: "Begin the Beguine," "You Made Me Love You," and "All or Nothing at All." "Your voice is better than Helen Forrest's, Ronnie. You should be singing with a big band," insisted Beattie, my first avid fan, her encouragement feeding my dreams of going on the road with Tommy Dorsey.

Across the Atlantic, however, drums beat less appealing rhythms. Unopposed in Spain by the major world powers (the United States, for instance, had declared itself neutral in the conflict), Hitler's troops continued to goose-step across Europe—taking Poland first, then Czechoslovakia, Austria, and Hungary. Nations headed by proto-fascist governments were declaring themselves "neutral" while falling in line behind the Nazis, who were filling concentration camps with political dissenters, social nonconformists, and thousands of Jews.

I was almost fourteen in August of 1939 when little groups of older campers and staff at Camp Wo-Chi-Ca gathered in tearful discussion about the staggering news from Europe. Had the Soviet Union really signed a nonaggression pact with Nazi Germany? Surely it wasn't true! Hitler, the slaughterer of Jews and co-destroyer of Spain, and our respected Comrade Josef Stalin? At a general meeting on the subject, camp director Dick Crosscup's quiet, reasoned analysis was meant to reassure. He told us that, unopposed by the United States, Britain, and France, Hitler was overrunning Europe. Hostile forces would surround the Soviet Union. The pact gave Stalin time to build up the Soviet Union's military so it could protect the country against an inevitable attack by Hitler. But his explanation did little for my thirteen-year-old sensibility. How could I get past the vision of Stalin shaking Hitler's hand? And why would Hitler let Stalin build up a defense against him? I decided that when I went home from camp I would ask my mother what she thought. Meanwhile, though, I wouldn't think about it. I had more important business that summer: Bill Pevsner's thrilling drama group. I was playing Ma Joad in *The Grapes of Wrath*, the solo murder-victim-to-be in *Sorry, Wrong Number,* and one of the readers of the horrific antiwar novel *Johnny Got His Gun.* Whew! With so much to tell Beattie, I could hardly wait to see her again. But as it turned out, Beattie wasn't much concerned by my problems with the Hitler-Stalin pact, and she was only slightly interested in my theatrical adventures at camp. Because that summer, Beattie had discovered boys.

"I can't wait for you to come home!" she wrote. "We are going to have the best time!" With war knocking at the door, many eager, small-town boys from Middle America had enlisted and were posted within a day's pass of Brooklyn's Coney Island and its famed Luna Amusement Park. All summer, khaki and navy blue had been brightening up the mile of boardwalk that connected Coney Island to Brighton Beach. Beattie could hardly contain her excitement to show me the photo of a soldier from Kansas with whom she had eaten hot dogs and ridden the Cyclone at Luna Park. "Kansas, Ronnie! Can you imagine? He lives on a farm!" They'd promised to write to each other. Beattie had been an enthusiastic pen pal since childhood. Now, along with Kansas, her list of new correspondents contained an address in Arkansas and one in Texas. I was a little shocked. "But Beattie, aren't you scared? What if someone gets fresh?" She admitted to one uncomfortable experience. She'd been playing pinball with a sailor boy at a boardwalk game concession. He had a bottle of something—rum, she thought—and he kept wanting to pour some in her Coca-Cola, so she told him she wasn't feeling well and went home. "But most of them aren't like that. Their manners are very nice," she said.

She couldn't wait to go walking together. I was more than a little nervous. But, like Beattie, I got myself up in the costume for teen girls of that time, which was copied from sexy movie stars like Hedy Lamarr: a clinging white jersey blouse, dark—almost black—lipstick, hair piled high, a gardenia in my hair (but ugh, there wasn't much I could do about my eyeglasses). And off we went to try out our teamwork, chattering all the way. Gone, the heart-to-hearts about we two. Now the conversation went: he said, then I said, so then he said, so I said . . . It was rather one-sided, since I had nothing to contribute yet. But it didn't matter, Beattie's enthusiasm for potential new friends—cute boys from faraway places—was infectious, and I just loved being with her. Maybe this hunt for cute boys was really okay. Our first promenade together turned out to be what it had always been: a nice stroll to Coney, an ice cream cone, and back. There had been a few servicemen among the walkers, but there'd been no occasion to stop. I was relieved.

The next day, though, as we were heading back and had gotten halfway home, we crossed paths with three boys in khaki. One called after us. Turning, we saw that he was holding up a box camera. Would we take their pictures? Beattie and I looked at each other. "Sure," we said together. We took snaps of each one separately, then all three of them together. Then Albert, the owner of the camera, asked if they could take pictures with us. Sure, why not, we said. From then on, we switched picture takers, posing together in different combinations and dopey positions on the benches and guardrails until the film ran out and we were screaming with laughter. Coming down from the hysteria, Albert—who seemed to be the leader of the three—suggested they take us for Cokes, but I quickly said no, hoping Beattie would back me up. She did, although she gave me a funny look. Really, nothing had happened to worry about, but I just didn't want to be out with them after dark. Beattie made sure to get Albert's address for her pen pal list before we parted.

The war quickly sped up changes in social mores. I got more adventurous but never more comfortable. I didn't have my most reliable prop—conversation—to lean on, since no one else seemed to be interested in the Spanish Civil War or the labor movement. And my attentiveness to sports had been exhausted by the end of the Wo-Chi-Ca baseball season. Beattie and I continued with our boardwalk strolls as long as the good weather lasted, and later would meet each other at that reliable pool of young servicemen looking for female company in Manhattan—the Astor Hotel. But I was always uncomfortable. I'd sit grinning and silent while Beattie carried the ball, keeping the conversation aloft with an easy mixture of gentle kibitzing and seemingly genuine admiration, the perfect response to the young males' awkward attempts at conversation. Pretty soon we were asking each other: "How far should you let him go, and when? First date? Second? Third date?" I had nothing to offer, glad that, for me, the questions were purely theoretical, and secretly thinking, "I wouldn't let him get anywhere at all." The truth is that I was mostly bored with the subject.

An amateur drama workshop started at the Brighton Community Center to study two plays by Clifford Odets that had shaken up the professional theater world a couple of years back. Of the six or eight people who showed up for the reading, I was the one "experienced" actor (You are the best, Wo-Chi-Ca mine!) and was given the part of Flo in the union-organizing drama *Waiting for Lefty* and the role of Henny Berger in *Awake and Sing!* Not quite fifteen, and as yet innocent of the problems of the heavily sex-smitten, I couldn't really have understood the parts very well. Fortunately, the plays were never produced, but when the group broke up, I discovered Gilbert and Sullivan. Although the productions were not politically heady, unlike Clifford Odets's works, rehearsals for *H.M.S. Pinafore* and *The Mikado* were great fun. I was becoming committed to performance.

Beattie and I truly missed each other and tried to spend time together when we could, but our different interests pulled at us. I became careless about keeping dates, especially those of the "let's meet at the Astor" variety, and we drifted apart.

In fact, something in my inner self was coming apart then too. For the first time in my life, I had trouble with a teacher. Mrs. Greenberg, the Spanish teacher, played Mexican popular songs on a small portable record player and handed out lyric sheets, which I loved and gleefully gobbled. But for some reason, she didn't love me. During an exam, she accused me, in front of the class, of an amazing plot to cheat. My mother was sent for, costing her lost hours of work at the dress factory where she was working. The accusation—which was utterly false—was resolved somehow, and Mrs. Greenberg was even somewhat solicitous of me afterward, although she never apologized. But the event shook me more deeply than I could explain. Maybe it was my family drama, or just pubescent confusion, but something solid inside of me began to crumble. It started with Mrs. Greenberg.

Then there was swim class, part of the physical education program at Abraham Lincoln High School. Girls wore a one-piece gray wool swimsuit, which bagged when dry and clung when wet to every embarrassing bump and pucker of our diverse adolescent bodies. And it itched. Disrobing my precociously developed pudge in public was hard enough, but the swimsuit was an insult I couldn't bear. So I began to cut the class, signing my mother's name to the required parental request slip. Deception did not sit easy with me. I walked around in a cloud of guilt, sure I'd be discovered. I should have been, since I used the excuse of menstruation at least twice a month. Having made the leap into "criminality," I understood how easily one could avoid other stressful situations and engage in pleasurable substitutes for school, like the movies. By my junior year, I was behind in my classes and talked about quitting school and getting a job, to the horror of my mother. I couldn't imagine another way out of the mess I'd made. But one presented itself.

My father's greatly admired friend from boyhood, Harvey Lee, was the owner and director of a private preparatory high school, Boro Hall Academy. He offered me a tuition-free scholarship in exchange for several hours work each week in the school office. I supposed this was at my father's request, and it seemed to me a gift from heaven. I could start fresh in school and learn some office skills. Oddly, my mother was vigorously opposed, but she wouldn't give a reason. I couldn't imagine why and thought her completely unreasonable. She finally relented after I loudly and tearfully begged for the tenth time.

I spent my junior year at Boro Hall. My office duties were simple. I was to assist the school principal by opening and sorting mail, keeping track of files, entering tuition payments in a green ledger, making out deposit slips, taking checks to the bank, and answering the telephone smartly. Although I liked saying my crisp lines—"Boro Hall Academy. May I help you?"— I came to hate answering the phone. I always knew it could be Dr. Lee, who would often pop me rapid questions about my studies that I never felt prepared for. I can barely remember classes there, and I recall only one teacher. He was a dandy little fellow who wore a cravat and a black velvet fedora hat, the brim tilted coyly. His breath smelled of the violet tablets he carried in a small tin in his breast pocket. His subject must have been European history. But all I remember of his pedagogy is having to memorize the phrase "kinder, kirche, und küche" (children, church, and kitchen), which he smugly explained was German society's ideal for females.

Boro Hall Academy occupied the upstairs of a two-story commercial building in downtown Brooklyn. A room at the back of a restaurant with a table tennis game served as the "campus" for the older boys' breaks. The majority of the students were male, and part of my job was to herd the boys back up to classes. Most of them put up politely, if reluctantly, with my intrusion. It was a problem only when a student had drunk his lunch and had to be hauled upstairs. The boys were tall and I was short.

In contrast to the school's spartan surroundings, Dr. Lee's private office was furnished in dark wood, patterned carpet, and dark drapes. He was there irregularly, coming in to meet with Mr. Shacket, the principal, on school business, I supposed. Sometimes he was on the phone to his broker. Dr. Lee was a heavy investor in the stock market, much admired and envied by my father. I dreaded his appearances at school. At the end of the day, when school was over and my work was done, he would call me into his office for a private lecture on politics, American history, philosophical thought, and human psychology. I didn't know what he expected of me during these talks, and I wondered if he would quiz me. He never did. But I would try to look alert, nodding now and then when he paused for breath, all the while longing to be released to take the long subway ride home to Brighton Beach.

One afternoon, late in my second semester at Boro Hall Academy, Dr. Lee's lecture was of another order. Suddenly, it was personal.

"You know that your father and I are old friends don't you?" he began.

"Yes, I know that," I replied, surprised.

"Did you know that your mother and I are old friends, too?"

I replied with a nod, thinking, so what?

"You probably didn't know, though, that your mother and I were very close, that we loved each other very much. Did you know that?"

I shook my head no. Indeed, in my father's frequent panegyrics over the years about the successful educator and brilliant Wall Street player, he had never mentioned my mother.

"Oh yes, we were very, very good friends at one time. Much more than good friends, in fact."

All at once, I realized we were in a geography I surely had never studied. What did he mean? Would I be expected to answer questions? My mind tumbled. A love story? My mother a love story heroine? Impossible. And with Dr. Lee? This gross, huge-bellied, big-nosed man? I was in shock. At last, he came to his point. My mother had been "hysterical" to separate from my father, he said. She had married a good man and borne two children; she had been given a fine life. Now, after three years of separation, wasn't it time she came to her senses and brought her family back together? "You are an intelligent young woman," he said. "Shouldn't you give this some serious thought and help bring them back together?"

A half smile frozen on my face, I said nothing, and he indicated with a nod of his head that the interview was over. I got up from my chair and went back to Brighton Beach. At home, I climbed on a chair and reached into the closet shelf where my mother kept a box of old letters and official looking papers and went through them. There was nothing about Harvey Lee, but I found my parents' marriage certificate. They had been legally married three months before I was born. What was I supposed to make of or do with these unwanted family secrets? I struggled through the rest of the year at Boro Hall Academy, vowing to myself not to return the next year. I was grateful to be heading toward a stint as a junior counselor at Camp Wo-Chi-Ca when school let out.

That summer, Mother suffered a ruptured stomach ulcer and barely survived. Major surgery, a long hospital stay, and many weeks of recovery were necessary. The IWO paid our medical bills and gave us our after-school activities, but my mother made our clothes and usually paid for the rent and food out of her wages from the dress factory, supplemented by my father's frequently late child support payments and the bit of money she received from renting a room. But she would not be able to work that fall. Unemployment insurance did not exist yet, and she had no savings. Irene was only thirteen, but I was fifteen, a grown girl. Under our circumstances, it was reasonable for me to look for a real job. It was 1941 and wartime; work was plentiful. I would learn to wait tables, I told her, thinking of my friend Beattie, or else take a job in a war plant. Full of confidence and a craving for adventure, I opened the newspaper to the help wanted section. Column after column leaped out at me. I didn't know how to read them and felt the beginning of fear about the confusing world out there.

While she was in the hospital, Mother had a visit from an old friend, Sara Blackman, from Washington, DC. Sara was in New York visiting her daughter, whose postcard had led me to the Rainbow House Choir. Wartime DC was hungry for clerical personnel, Mrs. Blackman said. Her son Harry headed an accounting office at the Federal Housing Authority. He could probably help me get placed, and Sara had rooms for rent in her big house. "So far away!" My mother wept. But a few days later, I packed her old suitcase and was on my way.

THREE

Making My Own Way

THE PRIORITY RAMBLERS, 1941

Harry informed me that I'd have to take a civil service exam to qualify for a position at the Federal Housing Authority. I bit my nails over the word "exam," but I ended up flying through the questions. My typing, however, clocked in at thirty words per minute, a pace beatable by any healthy snail. It didn't seem to matter—I was certified as a Clerk/Typist Grade 2. My first placement was in a typing pool, where my speed might have improved, but I was quickly moved into Harry's department as a do-everything sort of clerk to three or four superiors, who never required me to type another paragraph.

As an employee of the federal government over the next year, I learned some useful things: how to file, use a comptometer, draft simple graphs, and look serious—Ralph B. thought I smiled too much. He also taught me that there are no slow moments in an agency of the federal government; when you read a magazine or a paperback during a hiatus in the work, you do not rest it on top of the desk, you hide it inside the drawer. I learned on my own which bosses came back mellow after their liquid lunches and which I needed to look out for. That surely cannot be all I learned during the year I was employed by the Budget and Planning Division of the Federal Housing Authority in Washington, DC, but it is what I remember most clearly. That, and the words "WHITE ONLY" or "COLORED" stenciled in all public places—like on benches, over rest rooms, and at drinking fountains. I learned that whites and coloreds sat separately in movie houses (the coloreds had to sit upstairs) and that ordinary restaurants, like lunch counters, were off limits to coloreds. If I and a Negro coworker wanted to eat lunch together, we would go to the Agriculture Department cafeteria, one of the few places we were permitted to sit in the same area, but even there the combination raised eyebrows. I learned that the black woman who ran the mimeograph machine in the basement at a salary and classification as minimal as mine, had a master's degree in English Literature.

Mrs. Blackman's home, which was a short walk from Dupont Circle, was a pleasant place to live. My room was large, airy, and light. That's all I remember about it, because only a few lonely days after I'd settled in, I discovered something at the house that changed my life. Late one evening, I heard singing and followed the sound to the partly open door of a small basement apartment. Two men and a woman with guitars and another woman without an instrument were on the floor on cushions, leaning back against a couch. I half-hid myself behind the door, listening. As they came to the song's conclusion with a couple of quick thrums on the guitars, one of the women saw me and beckoned me in, patting a space next to her on the floor. As I sat, she struck a couple of chords and began another song: "Wish I had a bushel, wish I had a peck." The others joined in: "Wish I had ol' Hitler with a rope around his neck." Then came the chorus: "Round and round Hitler's grave, round and round we go. Gonna lay that poor boy down; he won't get up no more!" I had sung Bach chorales, Gilbert and Sullivan, French folksongs, and the repertoires of choirs and school choruses. I was a quick harmonizer and was soon bellowing the silly chorus with them.

These singers called themselves the Priority Ramblers, a whimsical mating of official government jargon and rural references. They sang the songs of the Carter Family Singers and the Coon Creek Girls, an American country music idiom I hadn't met very often and hadn't been much interested in until that moment of free-throated singing. Their repertoire included smart topical songs—which were not very challenging musically but were great for registering political complaints: "Lincoln set the Negro free, why is he still in slavery? Jim Crow!"—interspersed with Appalachian ballads and country songs. The Ramblers— Bernie and Milly Asbel, Tom Glazer, and Jackie Gibson (the woman with the guitar)—were wartime temps like me, but a few years my senior. They were part of an extended musical community that included Alan Lomax, Jackie's boss at the Office of War Information. Names of absent friends popped up often in their conversations, in particular a Woody something-or-other in the Merchant Marines and a Pete Seeger in the Army. Before the war, these two had been members of a group called the Almanac Singers, which had performed at leftist political rallies and union meetings with a repertoire of folksongs and topical, mainly antiwar, songs written by the group's members. They had traveled the country and had even been on a national radio broadcast, but when the war was declared they had disbanded, leaving a trail of admirers and singers and players like the Priority Ramblers, who followed in their footsteps. Much of Priority's repertoire was borrowed from the Almanac Singers.

Jackie, who was lively, knowledgeable, and, to my eye, the epitome of sophistication, graciously accepted the role of mentor that I tossed at her, and over the weeks we also became a singing duo. She played simple and reliable guitar support for our basic repertoire of sweet Appalachian ballads, such as "I Never Will Marry," "Turtle Dove," and "Who Will Shoe Your Pretty Little Foot," which were enlivened by a teasing song about the Johnson Boys, who "didn't know how to court a maid." Our first engagement together was at The Arena, which was not a venue where prizefights were staged, as I had thought (wondering what the Ramblers had to do with boxing), but a theater, now famous as Washington's Arena Stage. We had great fun, and it was my first public performance as a "folksinger."

Bonnie, a supervisor at the Federal Housing Authority, asked if I would like to hear some blues. "Sure, I'd love to," said I, with nary a clue what blues were about. As far as I could tell, several different kinds of music seemed to be called blues. At dinner, Bonnie played some of her extensive collection of what she called "race records." Thus, Bessie Smith and Ma Rainey first worked their heavy magic on me, nicely balancing Jeanette MacDonald and Deanna Durbin.

After a year, my excuse for earning and adventuring alone in Washington faded with Mother's full recovery from surgery. She came to DC with my sister, determined to get work herself and make a new life there for us. When the Housing Authority came through with a new, spanking clean, two-bedroom apartment in Naylor Gardens, delighting my mother, we moved to Anacostia. But far from the government offices where I worked, central Washington, and my Rambler friends, I was anything but happy. Every day on the long bus trip to work and back, my resentment grew, exacerbated by the vista along the way—the living quarters of the very poor, a view of DC unavailable to those who never ventured beyond the alabaster center. Several streets of cave-like dwellings and tarpaper shacks were like those I had seen in photos of rural Southern poverty—but in the nation's capital? How I missed the Ramblers and their cheer- fully effective songs of conscience. Without the catharsis of singing out protest, I was increasingly depressed by the city. I longed for New York's illusion of integration, at least the seem- ingly common agreement that racial discrimination and the poverty that resulted from it were unfair. Late that summer, I decided to quit my job, go back to high school, get my diploma, and clear out of Washington. Mother was happy for me to go back to school. Pleased with her new city and proud of her office job, which was her first work outside the dress factories, she sim- ply smiled at my promise to leave Washington at graduation.

My last fling with the Ramblers was a blast. The bathtub, scoured and sterilized, held a concoction like fruit punch— several half-gallon cans of grapefruit and pineapple juice plus several pints of sloe gin, the only drinking alcohol available to plebeians in those wartime days of shortages. The singing started early and never stopped. Tom, Milly, Bernie, and Alan, along with some friends who had been Ramblers before I came into the group, were the first to arrive, followed by guests, with and with- out guitars, who filled the entire floor and stood against the walls. To get to the bathroom, one stepped cautiously over and around seated bodies. The more nimble of us (I was an agile seventeen year old) were able to make the journey frequently. As a rest from the sing-alongs, people pulled out their solo favorites. I begged Jackie for songs from Harold Rome's garment worker musical,

Pins and Needles, which was breaking long-run records on Broadway. I loved the way she could drop from the end of an Appalachian ballad right into the sassy, down-and-dirty style of "Picket Line Priscilla." Tom Glazer sang "The Ballad of Anne Boleyn":

> With her head tucked underneath her arm,
> She walks the bloody tower.

I laughed until it hurt. Then he sang his setting to the lovely Housman poem:

> With rue my heart is laden
> For golden friends I had,
> For many a rose-lipped maiden
> And many a light-foot lad.

I sobbed to myself for having to leave my friends (I had taken too many trips to the bathtub, obviously). The huge bed in one of the bedrooms called to me. Pulled by some new party excitement, but unable to turn while the room whirled, I dropped onto the bed, while the music continued in the other room: "If you ain't got the do-re-mi, boys, if you ain't got the do-re-mi, you'd better go back to beautiful Texas."

The next morning, I felt something furry in my fingers—a cat? No, it wasn't a cat. Hair! I leaped out of bed, yelling. An eye opened. A voice drawled, "Good mornin', purty girl." It was Woody Guthrie, who had breezed into town during the night and been given the only unoccupied sleeping space, the excess next to me in the big bed.

· · ·

In September, I entered Anacostia High School as Priority Rambler Ronnie Gilbert, United States Government Clerk/

Typist G2. On the first day of school, I seated myself on the cement abutment at the front steps, lit a Kool, and watched students walking up. Ponytails, bobby socks, and saddle shoes—who could I possibly connect with? Some stared hard at me. A sharp rapping inside a window behind me interrupted my musings. I stubbed out my cigarette and walked into the building, where I met a woman with crimson fury in her face. "How dare you smoke at school?" she shouted. "How dare you sit right in front of my office, brazenly smoking? What right have you to smoke? Do your parents allow you to smoke?" In fewer than fifteen seconds, Mrs. Reardon, the school principal, reidentified me: Ronnie Gilbert, Anacostia High School senior.

As a left-wing New York City Jewish know-it-all, integrating myself was bound to be a challenge. I felt that it was my job to desegregate the disgustingly racist, all-white Anacostia High. When we made masks in art class, I shaped my clay model as my hero, Paul Robeson. A boy snickered over my shoulder, "What are you, a nigger lover?" I whirled on my stool and shoved. Harry, the kid with the twisted spine, who walked with crutches, went down like a stone. We had been friendly at lunch hours. Too shocked to act, I stared as someone helped him up. He was staring at me, his eyes round with surprise, and he was actually smiling. I ran from the classroom in tears to a chorus of hoots from the boys nearby. At seventeen, I was full of politics but not concerned much with humanity, and far less with humility, and I wouldn't apologize, since he had used that nasty epithet.

Later, to compete for a spot on the debating team, I wrote a description of the housing conditions along the bus route to downtown and offered the topic "Should the government in wartime take note of and act upon the condition of people living in poverty in DC?" Mrs. Reardon was one of the advisors. She was firm. "Oh no," she said. "You certainly will not be given an opportunity to give our neighborhood a black eye." The senior project, a minstrel show in blackface, was our final contest. I refused to participate. She threatened to withhold my diploma, but it came in the mail! Free at last, I prepared to run for New York City.

Mother was appalled. Why should she give up a hopeful future in DC? Indeed, I retorted, why should she? We argued fiercely. Why didn't she stay there and let me go? Were the bright edges of DC rubbing away a little for her too? I don't remember what her reasons were, but what seems appalling to me now is my headlong self-absorption. Was that typical of an eighteen year old? In the end, I agreed to a compromise and worked in New Jersey as a Wo-Chi-Ca counselor for the summer of 1944. There, I met Fred Hellerman, a jocular co-counselor, who had taught himself guitar in the Coast Guard and knew the songs of Richard Dyer-Bennet and Burl Ives, which I knew well. All summer, we sang songs like "Jimmy Crack Corn," "Blow the Candles Out," "Greensleeves," and many more. Two years later, we'd be singing together full-time. By that fall, Mother had returned to New York with Irene and done the impossible: in the post-war, space-strapped city, she trawled for an apartment and caught a good one on the Upper West Side of Manhattan.

PEOPLE'S SONGS

In December 1945, Pete Seeger was on his way home from Saipan in the Northern Mariana Islands, where he had produced amateur shows with enlisted men for the Army. Pete and one of his Almanac buddies, Lee Hays, had a plan to reconnect with folks they'd known during their touring days as Almanacs and create a national folk music network that would produce, promote, and distribute songs of labor and the American people. They called it People's Songs. One hundred fifty borrowed dollars secured a used mimeograph machine, typewriter, telephone, a couple of battered desks, and office space in a funky building near Times Square. They mailed their first newsletter, the *People's Songs Bulletin,* to addresses in New York City, Philadelphia, Chicago, Detroit, and Los Angeles. Four pages, written mostly by Lee Hays, encouraged everyone home from the war to join a national community of folks who itched to sing, dance, and play music together.

Around that time, who should come back from DC to run the People's Songs office but my friend Jackie Gibson! She phoned to tell me, "Pete and Lee are putting together a chorus. Wanna sing?" What a question. Jackie and I, our friend Greta Brodie, Fred Hellerman, and enough others to make a joyful noise came together. It was really Lee Hays who was at the center of the excitement. The son of a Methodist minister from rural Arkansas, Lee brought his hymn-singing heritage into the cause of organizing sharecroppers, following the lead of Reverend Claude Williams, known as "the red preacher."

During that Christmas season, I happily entangled myself in the fringes of People's Songs, caroling down Greenwich Village streets with Pete, scratching out a rip-off Currier & Ives cover on a mimeograph stencil for the December bulletin, and singing rounds with Jackie and Greta whenever the chance came along. An example of our oeuvre is preserved on one of Pete's more obscure Moe Asch Folkways recordings.

Jackie, an ace secretary, got hired at the March of Dimes office and tapped us for dime-collecting at hit plays in Broadway theaters, like *A Streetcar Named Desire, Medea, All My Sons,* and *Mr. Roberts.* I was hired by CBS as a typist (I was up to forty-five words per minute at that point!) and, like a good labor activist, joined the office workers union. I agreed to "colonize" my department, which was made up of seven friendly women. Surprisingly, hours and wages were not their issues, but rather a fairer distribution of copy. Scripts and essays were straightforward typing. However, six hours a day of slogging through an unrelieved stack of announcer notes, interoffice memos, and other badly or hastily jotted material was not. This put us totally on the same side, and I collected a tidy pile of "yes I will join" cards. The dreary union agent, however, argued that their demand was frivolous and refused to present it to the union for action. So it went.

Greta, a typographer (a rare female in the craft), did fairly well, and she bought a good used car, putting us on wheels. She and I made a run to Camp Beacon, a leftist resort, to visit Jackie, who was on the entertainment staff that summer. There were several repeat trips to see Jackie, and for me to visit Marty Weg, a good-looking lifeguard at the resort. He was a veteran and a great dancer, and he was about to begin his residency in dental surgery at Mount Sinai Hospital.

That same summer, I was hired by the publicity office of a small chain of New York City theaters that showed Mexican films. My job, which was on a par with my rudimentary command of Spanish, was to translate a few lines of each movie's Spanish ballyhoo into English for the theaters' newspaper ads. A fellow worker in the office was journalist Carlos Mora. A Marxist intellectual, he wrote critical essays for the Spanish-language press. Carlos generously offered hilarious suggestions in very broken English. All the laughter, and our leftist connection, was irresistible. We began to date. The differences between Marty and Carlos kept me fascinated, and I juggled my emotions for many months.

THE WALLACE CAMPAIGN, 1948

Meanwhile, J. Edgar Hoover and the media were busily hyping the Cold War: "Look out everybody, the Russians are coming, the Russians are coming!" The warnings clanged on the air so incessantly that terrified Americans, convinced by the conservatives that Democrats were "soft on communism," gave both the House of Representatives and the Senate to the Republicans in 1946. The coming presidential campaign was the first since President Franklin Delano Roosevelt's death in 1945 and also the first since the end of World War II. It would also be the first for me. I would turn twenty-one in September and therefore be eligible to vote in November.

A third party was in the race—the Progressive Party, whose candidate was Henry Agard Wallace. He had been Roosevelt's Secretary of Agriculture during the New Deal and his vice president during his third term as president. A disciple of Roosevelt, Wallace believed that the United Nations was the place to settle the world's quarrels with the Soviet Union and that capitalism's best weapon against communism was a living wage and decent working conditions for every worker. He told Americans that the twentieth century would be "the century of the common man." It seemed like a no-brainer. Henry Wallace would get my maiden vote in '48. Until then, he could have my voice. The Wallace campaign was a natural choice for Pete Seeger and People's Songs. In 1948, Pete hit the campaign trail with Wallace and his running mate, Idaho senator Glen Taylor. Pete and People's Songs turned the campaign into a musical jamboree, supported by a raft of creative people. The songs were delicious. Edgar "Yip" Harburg, song lyricist of *Wizard of Oz* fame, wrote a parody on an English music hall song:

I've got a ballot, a magic little ballot;
I've got a ballot, and it means my life.
It can bring a living wage, it can pension my old age,
It can make a little home for kids and wife.

Roll it up for WALLACE, roll it up for TAYLOR;
There is magic in that ballot when you vo-o-te.
Happy is the day when the people get their way,
As we go rolling up the vote.

Paul Robeson campaigned as well, and we all sang "John Henry":

Henry's train's a-coming,
Coming round the curve,
Puttin' on the steam and brakes
And strainin' every nerve.
Get on board, little children,
There's room for many a more.

A great favorite was Ray Glaser and Bill Wolff's "The Same Old Merry-Go-Round":

The donkey is tired and thin,
The elephant thinks he'll move in.
They yell and they fuss but they ain't foolin' us
'Cause they're brothers right under the skin.

The battle in the press was between the Democrats and Republicans. But to us devotees of the Roosevelt years and the thousands of liberals, progressives, and a handful of communists who hitchhiked to Philadelphia in July for the 1948 Progressive Party convention and lived in tent towns on the convention hall parking lot, there was only one party, the Progressive Party, and only one candidate, Henry Wallace. Jackie, Greta, and I sang with Pete and the great Paul Robeson. So much joy is not containable—I felt that it would burst through the walls and infect the country with hope and assurance. No one would be able to resist.

Wallace's favorite song was Dick Blakeslee's gentle, hymnlike "Passing Through":

> I saw Adam leave the Garden with an apple in his hand.
> I said, "Now you're out, what are you gonna do?"
> "Plant my crops and pray for rain, maybe raise a little Cain.
> I'm an orphan now and I'm only passing through.
>
> "Passing through, passing through,
> Sometimes happy, sometimes blue,
> Glad that I ran into you.
> Tell the people that you saw me passing through."

In November 1948, the election was over, the results gathered, and the harvest bitter. Jackie, Greta, and I shared brunch and gloom at Lundy's Restaurant. How could it be, after all that work and all those great songs, the rallies so full of joy? "What's wrong with this country?" Greta fumed, tearing her bagel into chunks. "One million five hundred thousand votes? There've got to have been at least ten million people in this country who cheered when Wallace said, 'Peace in the world.' Where the hell were they?" Jackie sighed, stirring sugar into her coffee. "Ugh! When the United Auto Workers pulled out, that was it. But even then, I thought we'd still get at least five or six million votes." I was aghast. "Numbers? You're bemoaning numbers? Wallace was supposed to WIN, wasn't he? Wasn't that what we were working for?" Jackie smiled. Greta shrugged and offered me a Dunhill. Inside of me, anger warred with confusion over the condescension of my friends. Did everyone but me realize that Wallace wasn't going to win? But if they did, why did they put so much effort into the campaign? I lit the cigarette to cover my embarrassment. In my disappointment, I had hardly noticed the big national upset: Harry Truman, every pundit's sure loser, would be staying in the White House as our president for the next four years.

1. Three-year-old Ruth Alice "Ronnie" Gilbert, Queens, New York City, 1929.

2. Ronnie with her mother, Sarah, and sister, Irene, New York City, 1930.

3. Ronnie and friends Greta Brodie (left) and Jackie (Gibson) Alper singing rounds at a hootenanny with Pete Seeger accompanying on banjo, New York City, c. 1947.

4. Pete Seeger (seated), Fred Hellerman, Ronnie, and Lee Hays at the Village Vanguard, posing for the Weavers' first publicity photo, Greenwich Village, New York City, 1950. (Photo by Sonia Handelman Meyer)

5. Ronnie dressed for stardom, according to the Weavers' early manager, Pete Kameron, 1950. (Photo by William "PoPsie" Randolph)

6. Wedding portrait, Ronnie and Marty Weg, June 25, 1950.

7. Ronnie and baby Lisa at home in North Hollywood, California, 1954.

8. The Weavers' reunion concert at Carnegie Hall, with the three post-Seeger tenors— Bernie Krause, Erik Darling, and Frank Hamilton—and Ronnie, Lee, Fred, and Pete, 1963. (Photo by Norman Vershay)

9. ▶ Ronnie in a scene from the Open Theatre's production of *America Hurrah,* by Jean-Claude van Itallie, at the Pocket Theatre in New York City, directed by Jacques Levy and Joseph Chaikin, with (clockwise from left) Bill Macy, Conard Fowkes, Cynthia Harris, Brenda Smiley, James Barbosa, Joyce Aaron, and Henry Calvert (with glasses), 1966. (Photo by Phill Niblock)

10. ▶ Joe Chaikin, founder of the Open Theatre, 1978. (Photo by Terry Stevenson)

11. Director Jim Brown filming the documentary *The Weavers: Wasn't That a Time!*, New York City, 1980. (From left) Pete Seeger, Lee Hays, Ronnie, and Fred Hellerman. (Photo by David Gahr)

12. Ronnie and Will Patton in the Winter Project's production of *Tourists and Refugees*, New York City, 1980. (Photo by Nathaniel Tileston)

13. Ronnie and Holly Near having a great time at the Sisterfire music festival, Takoma Park, Maryland, 1982.

14. Ronnie and Holly Near about to go onstage at the Sisterfire music festival, Takoma Park, Maryland, 1982. (Photo by Susan Wilson)

15. Ronnie as Saint Joan in *Top Girls,* by Caryl Churchill, directed by Larry Lillo at the Grand Theatre, London, Ontario, Canada, 1988. (Photo by Jackie Noble)

16. Life partners Larry Lillo (seated) and John Moffat, 1992. (Photo by David Cooper)

17. Ronnie and her partner, Donna Korones, 1987. (Photo by Joe Abaldo)

18. ▶ Ronnie and Lisa kayaking in Sausalito, California, 1993. (Photo by Jill Davey)

19. ▶ Ronnie with her mother, Sarah (left), and lifelong friends Jackie Alper and Dottie Gottleib, following a performance of *Mother Jones* at the Hasty Pudding Theatre, Cambridge, Massachusetts, 1994. (Photo by Ellen Friedman)

20. ▶ (Clockwise from lower right) Ronnie, Donna, Lisa, and Donna's daughters, Harlene and Alicia Katzman, Hawaii, 1998.

21. Ronnie and Donna with their new grandbaby, Sara Zoë, Berkeley, California, 2001. (Photo by Lisa Weg)

22. Ronnie and Zoë at the zoo, Oakland, California, 2003. (Photo by Donna Korones)

23. Ronnie with singer and San Francisco folk music doyen Faith Petric at a Women in Black silent demonstration for peace in the Middle East. Puppets by Annie Hallatt and Arina Isaacson, San Francisco, California, 2003. (Photo by Joan Bobkoff)

24. Lisa and Zoë, Mendocino, California, 2004. (Photo by Jerry Kashiwada)

25. Ronnie and Donna, Mill Valley, California, 2012. (Photo by Redwing Keyssar)

FOUR

The Weavers

Back from campaigning for Wallace, Pete Seeger found People's Songs barely breathing. The three-year-old organization was choked by past-due bills and unpaid salaries. What was to be done? Why, hold a glorious hootenanny, the best one ever! Pete's trust in the power of music was unshakeable.

The 1948 Thanksgiving hootenanny celebrated internationalism as if the election results and the Cold War itself would melt in the happy flames stirred up by singers, songwriters, pickers, and, special for this night, dancers. Satire ruled the stage:

> The atom's international, in spite of hysteria.
> Flourishes in Utah, also Siberia.
>
> So listen folks, here's my thesis:
> Peace in the world or the world in pieces!

Sam Hinton's "Old Man Atom" was followed by:

> Is there a Red under your bed?

And then Harold Rome's:

> Who's gonna investigate the man
> who investigates the man who investigates me?

Fred Hellerman and I joined Lee and Pete to try out Priority Rambler Tom Glazer's new setting to a familiar Bach chorale:

> Because all men are brothers, wherever men may be,
> One union shall unite us, forever proud and free.

Our voices rang through the old hall, startling us and the audience. Then, riding on that excitement, we whipped out the words to Pete and Fred's medley "Around the World" while a dance group whirled and stamped:

> Sing this song in every land, hey li-lee li-lee lo.
> Dance together hand in hand, hey li-lee lie-lee lo.
> Hey li-lee, Hey li-lee lo-o-o-o.

The audience stood up and roared its approval. "Gosh, we may have something here," said Pete, voicing what we were all thinking. From then on, Lee, Fred, and I trailed peripatetic Pete to his bookings. Before long, we became a feature attraction at progressive events and began regular rehearsals. We cast about for a name, but it would be a while before we found the right one. Oscar Brand had us on his WNYC radio show once or twice while we billed ourselves the No-Name Quartet, and he held a naming contest for us. In the end though, we named ourselves after a nineteenth-century play Fred was reading about a strike of factory workers in Silesia, Gerhardt Hauptmann's *The Weavers*. The name evoked something preindustrial and handmade. It was folky and comfortable, but not too cozy.

PEEKSKILL

It was breathtaking how quickly song arrangements came to us. For an hour or two before an appearance, we'd convene in the basement of Pete's in-laws, Virginia and Takashi Otah (Toshi Seeger's parents). We'd figure out which songs we would perform and work them up right then and there. By September 4, 1949, the date of People's Songs' final major venture, an outdoor picnic and concert near the town of Peekskill, New York, we had hit our stride. Cosponsored by a couple of progressive trade unions, the event featured Paul Robeson and Pete, along with two renowned classical pianists, Rae Lev and Leonid Hambro. Fred and I had summer jobs at a hotel resort in the Catskills, close enough to Peekskill that Pete suggested we come. He said he might even ask us to join him onstage. High with excitement, we all rode in style to Peekskill in Marty Weg's baby blue Dodge. He dropped us off at the top of the site. "I'm going to scout a good parking spot for getting out quickly after the show," he said. "You'll be sitting close to the stage. I'll find you." We started down.

The gently sloped grassy field, surrounded by trees, was a beautiful natural amphitheater. I caught my breath at the scene: on the stage below, a concert grand piano sat, its lid lifted high as if to say, "Welcome, welcome! Wait till you hear what's coming!" A hundred men wearing caps emblazoned with their union logos stood shoulder to shoulder around the periphery of the stage, the very symbol of progressive solidarity. At least that is how I saw it, as a good theatrical idea, not an intimation of trouble; I hadn't heard that an earlier concert had erupted in violence. The day was so beautiful, the sky such a cloudless blue. There were so many of us. Thousands of people were streaming in from New York City and the hundreds of little summer hotels and residences of the Hudson Valley.

I walked down the hill and sat where I could dash quickly down to the microphone the minute Pete gave the signal. Fred had somehow disappeared. I thought he might have gone down to stand nearer to the stage and keep his guitar tuned. Although we weren't called to join Pete, everything went beautifully, and I lost myself in the gorgeous piano music. Robeson sang a short set. When he ended "Ol' Man River" with his change in the lyrics—"I must keep fightin' until I'm dyin'"—I rose to my feet weeping and cheering, along with the twenty-five thousand other lefties and liberals (and however many FBI agents had been assigned there). When he had finished, someone came to the microphone and told the audience to leave the site and go to their automobiles and buses quickly. I hadn't seen Marty for a while and thought he'd gone off to get the car. I couldn't see Fred either, so I headed up toward our meeting place at the top of the hill, climbing through the confused crowd of parents trying to round up their kids and picnickers trying to gather their belongings from under the feet of others who were hurrying away. Apprehension charged the air, but I did not know what was causing it.

The whole area was in turmoil. There was no sign of the blue Dodge. Someone was shouting, "Get on a bus, any bus!" I saw one pull away empty, the driver waiting for no one. Someone grabbed my hand and pulled me up through the rear door of a bus already beginning to move. The door slammed behind me and we fled. But from what? I figured that something must have been happening down at the stage. We weren't going out the way we'd come in. I could see that. A state trooper had directed us onto a narrow, rutted road through the trees. The bus moved slowly, rocking and bumping, those of us in the aisle holding onto whatever we could, grabbing at the shoulders of those with seats. Suddenly, we lurched to a stop. I looked past the taller person standing in front of me. Another state trooper stood in the road in front of the driver with his hand up. "Okay, protection," I thought, and peered out the window. We were in a dark, leafy tunnel, under a canopy of overhanging trees. In the dusky light, a young man in rolled-up shirtsleeves stood at the side of the road, a neat pyramid of rocks at his feet. "Watch out, watch out!" I yelled uselessly as he bent and chose a rock, wound up like a baseball pitcher, and fired it at the bus, straight at us. A window smashed near where I was standing. Everyone was screaming. "Jesus, don't faint," I told myself. The trooper kept his hand up. In no hurry, the man by the road grinned, chose another rock, and fired again. We were jammed in too tightly to duck, so I put a hand up to shield my face. This one, however, missed the windows and slammed into the side of the bus. He bent for another rock. But now the trooper stepped back and let us move, gesturing the driver to go slowly—a joke, I guess. At about five miles an hour, we followed the buses ahead through the gauntlet: every few yards, a policemen or a state trooper would hold the drivers back while the pitcher near him got a good shot. The dialogue was lovely, too: "Kikes, Jews, go back to Russia, you dirty commies!" Gosh, I hadn't heard that kind of thing since before the war, when the American Nazi Party had been on the loose.

Finally, we were out and on the road, headed for the Mohegan Colony summer residences, where the bus I was on had been chartered. We dozen or so hitchhikers spent the rest of the day as guests of the residents, calming ourselves and using their phones to try to reconnect with family and friends. It was late night before Marty found me. He had missed the "fun." He had parked outside the area of attack and been prevented from driving his car back into the site. I soon learned of my good luck to have ridden out on that bus. Some passengers in autos had been hauled out of their cars and beaten unconscious by the "patriotic" Red-haters, both in and out of uniform. Greta, traveling with friends in a jeep, received a gash through her eyebrow, the glass miraculously missing her eye. Somehow, no one died, although several came close.

After "a thorough investigation," the New York district attorney commended the police for the excellent job they had done in putting down "the communists' riot." Here was a lesson in law and order for us nice, mostly white progressives (one that Native and African Americans had been learning throughout American history). My girlish denial disappeared. The potential for fascism in America had not died with the American Nazi Party.

Lee Hays wrote a ballad about that afternoon at Peekskill. In the fall, we recorded it for tiny Charter Records. It was our first recording as the Weavers. "Hold the Line" was part of a dramatic script narrated by the writer Howard Fast. It ended:

All across the nation, the people heard the tale,
And marveled at the concert, and knew we had not failed.
We shed our blood at Peekskill, and suffered many a pain.
But we beat back the fascists, and we'll beat them back again.

Talk about whistling in the dark! The Red Scare had been gathering physical force all across the nation as veterans' organizations lined up to have a go at the commies, replacements for the Nazis as the enemy.

COLD WAR

On August 29, 1949 (two days after the first Peekskill skirmish), the Soviets detonated a nuclear device, stripping the United States of its monopoly on the atom bomb. Would the Cold War get hot? The world cowered while the American eagle and the Russian bear postured with their new weapons of mass disaster. At home, children hid under desks and J. Edgar Hoover ordered a national feeding frenzy on "Godless American commonists, pinkos and their fellow travelers." Soon, every pro-peace group, past and present, was given a place of dishonor on the Attorney General's list of no-goodnik "subversive" organizations. People's Songs was included, of course. Slightly left-leaning groups corrected their posture—even the venerable American Civil Liberties Union. No one could afford to be caught with Reds in their beds. The Taft-Hartley labor law forced unions to name their most militant union builders, officers who were or had been communists. Unions who refused were emptying their treasuries in legal battles. The Smith Act of 1940 made teaching or advocating Marxism a crime. Socialist and Communist Party leaders were tried and jailed for refusing to name other party members. Ten Hollywood screenwriters challenged the constitutional right of the House Un-American Activities Committee to question them about their political beliefs and were sent to jail for contempt of Congress. The times were perilous for dissent of any kind.

Even so, many people held on to the vision of world peace promised by the new United Nations, and they fought back hard. In November, the Weavers were pelted with vegetables while staffing a sound truck in the American Labor Party's campaign for two New York City politicians. At the Labor Party's

Madison Square Garden rally, we squeezed new words neatly into a jazzy blues stomp:

Here we are in Madison Square,
Davis for Council, Marcantonio for Mayor,
In New York City, New York City.
In New York City, you really got to know your line.

Did anyone think these two left-wing stalwarts could win? Who knows. But the best one could do was stand up as long as possible and fight. As for the Weavers' status as important troubadours for the Left, however, the message was writ clear: there was precious little Left left to sing for. We hunted for ways to stay alive. A benefit performance for the left-wing Photo League netted us the use of their clubroom at the Hotel Albert for informal Sunday afternoon drop-in sessions. A handful of *Daily Worker* or *People's Songs Bulletin* readers showed up and paid the one to five dollar admission, but no one could live on that take, far less four of us. Pete recommended the Weavers to academia, writing to thirty colleges with good music programs. "It's been our feeling that American folksongs have not been done justice to either by conservatory-trained glee clubs or ensembles. We can perform either for classes or more general audiences, always with brief narration to explain the material.... Sample repertoire is enclosed." I don't know if it was the critical tone of the letter or the signature Pete Seeger care of People's Songs that scared off the professors, but we received not one response.

Finally, we had to face it: there was no future for the Weavers. Lee Hays was penniless. Fred Hellerman, living at home with his parents, was considering graduate school and donating his share of the Hotel Albert Sunday afternoon admissions to Lee. My unemployment insurance had run out. I had to find work.

But our music was so good. How could we give up? It was Toshi Seeger who convinced a discouraged Pete to give it one last-ditch try. Pete had successfully worked solo at the Village Vanguard. He phoned proprietor Max Gordon with a deal that at least had to be intriguing: all four Weavers for what Max had paid him alone—$200 a week. Max said he'd give us a listen.

THE VILLAGE VANGUARD

The Village Vanguard of that time was a long way from the legendary international jazz venue it is now, although it did have a fascinating history. In the midst of the Great Depression, barely two years after Prohibition had been repealed, Max, then a nerdy young Reed College literature graduate with no way to make a living, had fled to downtown New York. There, he rented a padlocked basement speakeasy and turned it into a stomping ground for New York's wild bohemian poets and their admirers. It survived week to week for years to become a Greenwich Village standby. By the 1950s, however, it had evolved, via Max's savvy taste, into a hip venue for emerging comedic and musical talent, including folk music. Josh White and Richard Dyer-Bennet had played there, as had Pete.

As I opened the street-side door at 178 Seventh Avenue South on the afternoon of our audition and descended the steep, narrow staircase into the lower depths, I thought poets' ghosts might still be creeping around inside the cracked walls of the shabby triangular room. You encountered the bar first, on the near wall, then a lot of slightly beat-up black tables and mismatched chairs, and a tiny stage at the tip end. I was disappointed; this place bore no resemblance to all the nightclubs I had seen in the movies. Prematurely white-haired proprietor Max Gordon—short, slightly paunchy, and smoking a cigar that looked too big for him—turned a piercing eye on me while he greeted Pete, and he continued to stare for an extra silent second. Okay? Not okay? "Uh-oh, this is a bad idea," I thought. "He hates us already. Well, it'll be over soon." He waved us to the stage. Pete started us with a Bahamian gospel song, "Go and dig my grave both long and narrow." "Very appropriate, Pete," I thought. No comment from Max. We launched into an Israeli dance tune in Hebrew. No comment. Finally, we sung a couple of Christmas carols. "Very nice," said Max, lighting his cigar, and he booked us to cover the Christmas season through New Year's Eve at $200 a week ($50 each), plus make-your-own sandwiches! Singing what we loved and getting paid a salary for it? And in a nightclub? I was giddy with excitement! Max seemed positively avuncular to me now.

On opening night, the 123-seat room was lit up and looked warm, intimate, and very lively. Friends and fans who knew us from benefits, hootenannies, and Oscar Brand's WNYC radio program jammed the place all weekend, grabbing at our hands as we walked through the tables on the way to the stage and applauding, cheering, and singing along with us. During the week, it slowed to a trickle. By the weekend, I gloomily pondered January 2 and my hunt for hated office work. But Max liked our music and he liked us—and we were cheap. He gave us a new deal—a raise in salary to $250, but no sandwiches. He had discovered that Pete and Lee were taking half-pound or more helpings of hamburger. Lee complained, but I was forever on a diet and not eating sandwiches, so I was fine with the extra $12.50 a week. Max kept us on and on, even through times when we threatened to outnumber the customers. The Village Vanguard was the Weavers' incubator. We hung out in the kitchen between shows, learning songs, reworking lyrics, and developing a repertoire. We evolved a kind of choreography for four klutzes on the Vanguard's tiny stage. Pete displayed his virtuosity with the banjo, raising its long neck over my head to avoid hitting Fred in the eye as we exchanged positions at the single microphone. The Weavers had no musical arranger. There was no standard lead singer or backup. Someone might start with melody but then move to harmony, vocal lines crossing. Anyone could lead. We'd take turns close to the microphone and then back off, working our way around Lee's sometimes firmly planted largeness, leaving room for frequent instrumental phrases. We were happy vocal acrobats.

Playing the Vanguard night after night for months made us comfortable performers. Anyone who has attended an acoustic concert with strings knows about the "tuning beast." A hootenanny audience in a big hall might expect interminable pauses between songs while a player battled a wayward string, and there would usually be someone else onstage to step in when things got too bad. But the nightclub audience sat two feet away from us, literally at our knees, and every expression, drop of sweat, and confused moment was visible to them. Alcohol was another variable. We made some changes. It was assumed, for instance, that Pete, the driving force of the group, was the logical person to lead off each set. "Friends," he would begin. It was an unwarranted assumption, I would often think; suppose this audience wasn't feeling so friendly for some reason? Doesn't one have to win their friendship? Fortunately, they always seemed to warm to the music. We followed Pete's musical or philosophical mood. He had brought us most of the songs, and we figured that if someone ought to talk about them, who better than he? Actually, anyone better than he, at times. Honed over decades, Pete's introductions were an enjoyable part of his later appearances.

But in 1950, Pete would often talk and tune at the same time. As Lee pointed out, his internal rhythm was twice as fast as that of most living human beings, and he would often enthusiastically launch the next song while Fred was still struggling with his guitar strings. Other times, Pete's tendency to lecture led him on and on. And on.

With his roots in the story-telling south, his background of rural union organizing, and his sharp intellect, Lee eventually seized the reins and turned the tuning beast into a highly useful aide-de-camp. His deadpan deliveries of sociopolitical homilies couched in absurd rural narratives delighted the audience:

> Two newly hatched maggots went out into the world to seek their fortunes. The first fell into a crack in the sidewalk, the second into a dead cat. Toward the end of their lives as maggots, they chanced to meet. "Old friend, you don't look well at all," said the second maggot to the first, "how thin you are."
>
> "Yes, it has been a hard life," said the first. "You, on the other hand, are fat and sleek, clearly prosperous. To what do you ascribe your success in life, my friend?"
>
> "Why, brains," the second answered. "Brains and personality."

.   .   .

Two or three months into our extended stay at the Vanguard, we had a clothing crisis. Fred's look was unremarkably collegiate, Pete wore whatever he had on during the day (often jeans and a work shirt), and Lee had nothing presentable. So Toshi took the guys out shopping. It was not an easy job finding duplicate coats for two slender fellows and a larger one at a big man's shop. But they came back from the adventure with their first group garb—matching green corduroy jackets. Their responses were far from positive.

"I hate this," Lee complained. "I'm so uncomfortable."

"Yech," Fred agreed. "The bilious color, and why must we wear uniforms anyway?"

"I'm not sure it's a good idea; where will all this lead?" Pete wondered.

"It will lead to our being taken seriously as musicians and singers," I insisted, "and not as a bunch of amusing characters who accidentally wandered in off the street. Can we please just try to look like a professional singing group and take the focus off the clothes?"

Actually, I was sick of the references to my own attire—for example, the "sweaterish girl singer." Expensive grunge would be the costume of choice two decades later, after Woodstock, the Summer of Love, the Grateful Dead, Jefferson Airplane, and the deification of Woody Guthrie. But in the 1950s, any attempt to countrify ourselves was sure to bring some "cornball" responses. So they wore their outfits, and our first promotional photographs resemble a casual group comfortably in agreement about something.

For me, the Weavers' Vanguard days were treasure undreamed of in my catch-as-catch-can, childhood-through-youth musical life. The resonance of our combined voices thrilled my soul night after night. Our musical leaps from genre to genre, fully embracing each, kept me in a state of high excitement. The beneficent power we wielded over the audience amazed me. In her biography of Lee Hays, Doris Willens wrote of the time:

> Here were these four rather oddly assorted people, with an unlikely combination of voices, singing this weird collection of songs— African chants and Israeli horas and hymns and Christmas carols—and when they finished you felt as if you'd been through some kind of religious experience.... Their music soared. It blew

you right out of your seat, with its passion and integrity, its strength and clarity and simplicity. They rarely sang a song the same way twice, but somehow every chord and harmony they hit was right—never a word that rang false.

It was true. For the time, our choice of songs was "weird." We had the huge wide world of folk song to work with. A scrap of a song, a piece of an old hymn, or a verse or two of something that had been collected at some time would become the foundation for a new piece. In those early days, it was assumed that any folk song was by its nature in the public domain, game for anyone's creative use. One day, Pete came to rehearsal full of enthusiasm about a choral song from South Africa that he'd been listening to on a record Alan Lomax had given him. "It's easy," Pete said. "The parts are just one word repeated over and over—like this, see? And the bass goes ... and the tenor goes ... and there's a sort of middle part that goes ... You could sing that, Ronnie. And over that, there's a kind of shout, like this: 'doooo da doo da da da.'" There was nothing quite so bloodcurdling as Pete straining his vocal chords to sing four parts at once. "Pete! Bring in the record!" we pleaded in unison. He did, and he also brought out an envelope with vocal parts sketched out on it. (It may not have been an envelope; it might have been an unused half-page torn from a notebook, the back of Toshi's shopping list, or a paper napkin—any of those are likely to have been correct. After all, what was the point of keeping a supply of music paper for a group that did not read parts? Not that we couldn't, but generally we improvised.)

But after hearing it, I was thoroughly confused. Where was the song? As Pete had said, a male chorus repeated one word again and again, but what was the word? The record label gave the record's title as *MBUBE,* a set of letters that didn't seem to resemble the word the singers were singing. No one could come up with any word better than what Pete thought he heard, so, casting aside confusion, quelling the giggles, and cleaving close to the recorded rhythm, we three took up the simple harmonies and obediently began chanting, "WimoWEH, wimoWEH, wimoWEH, wimoWEH." Then, after a few measures of that, Pete came in high over us, singing something between a yodel and a holler, and—a musical miracle—whatever it was we were singing took on a mysterious force from … South Africa? Folksong heaven? Outer space? Whatever it was, we were carried away together, sailing on waves of sound, measure after measure, the music meaning nothing and everything, until finally, sensing the end of Pete's phrase, we raised up our chant to meet his call and finished together with one last "WI—MO—WE—EH!" The song became a high point of our programs.

We would later learn that "MBUBE" wasn't a folksong at all, although the style of singing was indigenous. In fact, the Zulu singer Solomon Linda and his group Solomon Linda and the Evening Birds had created it years earlier, invoking a Zulu legend about a mighty sleeping warrior chieftain, Mbube (The Lion).

In 1950, it didn't take much imagination to think of Linda's song as a shout for freedom, for the lion to awaken. Racial discrimination against the black majority in South Africa had just been codified by the government's unspeakable apartheid laws, while at home, the obscene winds of what would soon be called McCarthyism were gathering force. I thought of "Wimoweh" as a lesson from black South Africa and felt that we sang it as an example of the power of joy over dark times. The furor over the copyright was far in the future.

The Vanguard was home. It was where I felt secure. We belonged there. However, we discovered that discount liquor, available at the bar, was a prime cause of throat trouble in bass singers from Arkansas. Lee Hays began to have frequent bouts of laryngitis, preventing him from performing. His bouts began to last a week, then two, then three, and I expected the axe, but amazingly, Max kept Pete, Fred, and me on as a trio. Musically, however, we needed that bass part. And where was the humor, the wonderful stories that lifted our performances out of the ordinary? Lee was irreplaceable, but he was forcing us to talk openly about searching for a substitute. But then, mysteriously, Lee's laryngitis disappeared.

Meanwhile, we continued to appear at hootenannies and benefits whenever we could. Defunct People's Songs had morphed into People's Artists, a booking agency providing entertainment for the Left. A new folk song magazine, *Sing Out!*, edited by Irwin Silber, had taken the place of the *People's Songs Bulletin*. On the commercial side, the Weavers even recorded a children's record, for which we were paid a modest flat fee but not credited. It was called *Train to the Zoo*. It became a much-honored favorite in the children's-music world. In March of 1950, we were invited onto the relatively low-profile Abe Burrows TV show. I felt that we were normal entertainers, doing what normal entertainers do. The response to the Weavers' TV debut was unremarkable. A viewer wrote us wondering if we would be interested in entertaining at her local Hadassah donor affair. One reviewer wrote, "Down at the Village Vanguard is the folk-singing group called the Weavers, who go about their business of singing folksongs without any foolishness about art."

· · ·

Doubtless reassured there would be no art to disturb them, uptown audiences began wending their way down to the Village

Vanguard to see us. One night, Carl Sandburg came in to check us out, and he gave us a Walt Whitmanesque imprimatur, which journalists loved: "When I hear America singing, the Weavers are there." I felt quite proud. Sandburg's biography of the young Abraham Lincoln had opened the door to nonfiction for me when I was a child, and when I began to read poetry in my teens, his *The People, Yes* was accessible and exciting. Lee Hays, however, threw sly little barbs at Sandburg's importance as a folk song collector, referring to his book *The American Songbag* as "Carl Sandbag's Songburg." We began to attract "show biz" types. "Hey," said a dapper fellow after a set, "you Weavers are really good. Do you have a manager? You've got a great act." "It isn't an act, it's real," was Lee's annoyed riposte. Another man assured us he could get us a major TV show. "You'd be terrific!" he exclaimed. "The boys would wear farmer clothes and the girl would wear an apron, and when you sing the Jewish song, she'd pull bagels out of her pocket and toss them to the audience." I looked hard at his face to see if he was being sarcastic or if he really meant it. He meant it.

Leery of the weird world we were stumbling into and our lack of know-how, we sought a manager who knew what the Weavers were about and could help us find our way safely around. We found two. One of them was Harold Leventhal, a childhood acquaintance of Pete Seeger's who had worked for the Irving Berlin publishing house and even plugged songs for them. Now, he ran the accounting department for his brother's large manufacturing company. We all liked Harold from the first; he was easy to like. As Doris Willens wrote, "his eyes twinkled with humor rather than dollar signs." Toshi, who had been taking care of the Weavers' accounts, was more than ready to put the increasingly burdensome business into Harold's capable hands. The other was Pete Kameron, a boyhood friend of Harold's, who had been road-managing an African American female jazz band, the Sweethearts of Rhythm, through a grueling tour of the segregated South. He was not sure about continuing in the music industry. But, living near the Village Vanguard, he began to spend his evenings watching us and brought friends from the industry down to show off "his find." Harold Leventhal and Pete Kameron, both lifelong lefties like us, seemed like a good combination. Harold was modest, funny, soft-spoken, and very good with numbers and Pete was a brash smoothie, full of ideas and "connections."

DISCOVERED

One night, Gordon Jenkins, the managing director of Decca Records, introduced himself to us. Strangers to the mainstream music world, we didn't recognize the brilliant songwriter, arranger, and conductor. But I should have; his hit recording "Manhattan Tower," a choral-orchestral love story to New York City, was the present I bought myself when I returned to New York from DC. During at least two or three performances, we recognized Gordon's voice in the audience, heartily laughing at Lee Hays's stories, sometimes at the same ones. Gordon was from Webster Groves, Missouri. He was the banjo-playing son of the church organist and had been a teenage ukulele contest winner in his youth. He arranged an audition for us at Decca. As we clumsily trooped into the office, I felt embarrassed to be paraded before some record execs. Dave Kapp, one of the two owners of the company, introduced himself. Milt Gabler, a chubby, balding fellow with a too-ready smile, confronted us, leaning back in an executive office armchair. Fred Hellerman's recollection of the experience is more elaborate than mine. He remembers various heads of Decca departments walking out of the room, shaking their heads at our performance and saying we didn't fit into their projects. He remembers Dave Kapp shouting that he wouldn't know what to do with us. I remember standing there with no mic, as if in someone's living room, singing "When the Saints Go Marching In," "Wimoweh," "Goodnight Irene," and "Tzena Tzena." I recall Gabler saying, "Oh yeah, I know you, Pete. Always liked you." And I wondered if his "knowing" Pete meant that he knew about Pete's left-wing identity, or if he had seen him when he soloed at the Vanguard. "Your group is good, Pete, very good." I had never thought of us as "Pete's group." Perhaps that's really what we were, but it sounded patronizing. I remember Dave Kapp striding to the door, saying flatly, "They're not commercial," and leaving, Gordon silent and Milt Gabler smiling.

"See, you're good," Gabler repeated. "But you have to decide if you want to be good or commercial."

Lee spoke up, "We hoped we could be good and commercial."

"Yes, but you see, the lyrics, for instance ... "

I don't remember how long Gabler talked, only that we listened politely, said thanks very much, took our leave, shrugged our shoulders, and went our separate ways. At the Vanguard later that night, Pete told us that Gordon whispered to him not to worry, that he'd get us on his next record if he had to pay for the sessions himself. I was hardly worried. To me, the whole thing seemed somewhat absurd, as in Shakespeare's *The Tempest*—an insubstantial dream, soon to dissolve, leaving not a trace behind.

Meanwhile, wheeling and dealing, Pete Kameron went to Columbia Records and told them Decca Records was interested in signing the Weavers. Columbia then offered us a contract.

Pete Seeger, feeling loyal to Gordon, called him in California. "Hold everything!" Gordon said. At that point, Decca decided they had to have us. Isn't it wonderful to be loved? We signed with Decca.

We recorded most of our repertoire in a small Decca studio, with bass player Sid Weiss helping Pete and Fred pin down their errant tempi. A week or so later, in June 1950, we were called to the big Decca studio, where Gordon Jenkins's orchestra and chorus were recording two of our good but uncommercial songs. "Where's the melody?" pleaded a balloon over a representation of a ten-foot tall supplicant Native American woman, which hung on the wall opposite the front door of Studio A. Six or eight attractive young men and women looked up from their vocal scores of "Tzena Tzena" and flashed us friendly smiles as we walked in. Musicians seated in another part of the room gave us a once-over and went back to their music. I hadn't been in a first-rate recording studio since I stopped singing in the Rainbow House Choir. All my juvenile thrill at being part of a big, important process with lots of competent people busy with their individual jobs in the service of the broadcast came back in a wave. And when Gordon raised his baton and ran the terrific singers through their parts, I was in heaven. Tape was not being used at that time—the music was recorded directly to the master disc. You did the whole thing from start to finish, in proper balance and without mistakes, or you did the whole thing over, as many times as it took. With all the checking and rechecking and the placement and replacement of microphones for us, the chorus, and each of the various instruments, there was very little required of us over the long, complicated process. After two or three hours, Pete Seeger just dropped to the floor, stretched his long self out, and had a little nap.

Embedded in Gordon's rich arrangements are the Weavers singing the songs exactly as we sang them at hootenannies or at the Vanguard. All that had changed were the lyrics to "Tzena Tzena," which were originally in Hebrew; Gordon had written a new English version of them for us.

> Tzena, Tzena, join the celebration.
> There'll be people there from every single nation.

Gordon's lyrics capture beautifully the feeling of the song and the internationalist impulse for us to be singing it, whereas the original Hebrew, written by two young Jewish soldiers in the British Army in the 1930s, was a kind of hiss at the girls to come out and dance with the soldiers.

COUNTERATTACK, 1950

With the record to be released that summer and our reputation as popular entertainers blooming, Pete Kameron went about garnering work for us, which included appearances on major television shows. The first was a guest spot on *Broadway Open House,* NBC's new, highly publicized late-night variety show (a program several notches up in industry importance from the Abe Burrows Show, which we had appeared on several weeks earlier). NBC's announcement of our upcoming appearance initiated the anti-Red inquisition's opening salvo against the Weavers by *Counterattack,* a weekly newsletter of "facts to combat Communism," which was issued by American Business Consultants, a small group of former FBI agents engaged in the lucrative business of selling information. The group sold its pricey newsletter by subscription to "security officers, personnel directors, employment managers, and all sorts of people whose businesses required them to know the facts." Broadway Open House with the Weavers aired on May 29, 1950, just in time to make the June 6 issue. "This folksinging quartet, composed of Pete Seeger, Fred Hellerman, Lee Hays and Ronnie Gilbert, is well known in Communist circles," said the newsletter. "The folk songs they sang for Broadway Open House are not the 'folk songs' they sing for the subversive groups they frequently entertain. On such occasions they usually sing the fighting songs of the Lincoln Brigade (which fought for Stalin in the Spanish Civil War) and other Communist song favorites."

An appearance in *Counterattack* was sufficient to block anyone's employment anywhere. Another network TV spot that we had booked, one of Kameron's prizes, was immediately canceled. It was true that we sang the fighting songs of the Abraham Lincoln Brigade. "Venga Jaleo" was one of the highlights of our repertoire. I sang the line "Franco se va paseo!" with all the fervor I could muster, thinking of the infant social democracy that had been murdered under Mussolini's bombs, of Picasso's great painting *Guernica,* and of La Passionaria, Loyalist Spain's great woman leader. We loved that song. "Wasn't That a Time!" Lee's and Walter Lowenfels's brilliant answer to the McCarthyites, had been practically our signature song. Fortunately, the liberal, progressive, left-wing audiences of that time got to hear the Weavers sing these great songs. But I pitied the radio and TV audiences who couldn't because of the manufactured hysteria over "communist infiltration."

MARRIAGE

June 25, 1950, was the hottest day on record for New York City. It was also the day the Korean War broke out. In mid-June, the un-air-conditioned Vanguard closed down for the summer, and the Weavers took a break. Marty Weg had completed his residency in dental surgery at Mount Sinai Hospital, and we decided to get married. We'd been a couple for almost three years, as everyone knew, and the thought of a big, fussy wedding repelled me. To celebrate, though, I bought a filmy, pale-green dress and a hat to match. We signed papers at City Hall and religious ones at a rabbi's apartment, and then we partied at the Vanguard. Everyone we knew who was in town came, and we all played and sang; it was a fine hootenanny. We served hors d'oeuvres because Mother insisted that there be food at a wedding. Steve Gardner, the club's genial bartender, took charge of drinks. Marty and I started our wedding night at the grand Essex House hotel but ended it in Mount Sinai Hospital. Marty had self-medicated with penicillin against the flu and had had an allergic reaction. After greeting the fifty relatives my father had invited to the reception, whom we had hardly even met, Marty's hand had swelled hugely.

We emerged from the hospital none the worse for the experience—save for a lot of ribbing from Marty's Mount Sinai buddies—packed up the big trunk of Marty's Dodge, and set off across the country to explore national parks and visit my mother, who was now living in Los Angeles. Our friend Greta Brodie came along for part of the way. Novice campers, we forged Bryce and Grand Canyons, Yosemite, and Death Valley, equipped with a pup tent and an innerspring mattress with holes punched at each end for the tent stakes. We assured each other we'd know better next time as we dug ourselves out of the snow in Yellowstone Park on July 4.

Somewhere in America, a wedding present caught up with us, delivered by a radio disc jockey: "And here's a new group, the

Weavers, with a tune from, uh, Israel, yeah, the new state of Israel. Hey, that's in Palestine, right? Somewhere in the desert? Anyway, here they are, a new quartet, the Weavers, with 'Tuhzeena, Tuhzeena!'" In 1950, an Israeli tune spilling out of a jukebox in Ogalalla, South Dakota, seemed an improbable cultural warp, but "Tzena Tzena" preceded us all the way across the country. When we reached Los Angeles, we found a telegram from Pete Kameron, telling me to please rearrange my schedule so that I would be back in New York by August. He had booked us to play the stage show at the Strand Theatre and double at the Blue Angel, Max Gordon's sophisticated nightclub uptown.

A Chicago disc jockey had turned the recording of "Tzena Tzena" over and discovered another uncommercial song on the other side—"Goodnight Irene." "Irene" was on every jukebox we encountered all the way back to New York. I came home a recording star, or more accurately, one fourth of a recording star. "Goodnight Irene," a folk song that had first been recorded by Huddie Ledbetter, racked up a sale of two million records for Decca—which was quite a few in those days. It became the most-featured song on TV and radio for weeks and was covered by an array of popular singers, including Frank Sinatra and Vic Damone.

HEADLINERS

Vaudeville was not quite dead yet, and it almost killed us. The Strand Theatre on Broadway, one of the last of the big movie palaces, featured stage shows between movie screenings. We did four, and sometimes five, short shows daily, on a bill with the Harvest Moon Ball dancers, an animal act, and I don't recall what else. After the last show, we would cab to the Blue Angel on East

Fifty-Sixth Street and do two full sets there, sharing the evening with the beauteous young chanteuse Barbara Cook in her professional debut. Our first uptown audience was perfectly congenial. They loved Lee's stories and applauded everything we felt like singing. Even if the place was posh, I must say I enjoyed it. Marty and I dined frequently on the chef's specialty, Shrimp à la Jake (five decades later, Marty couldn't forgive me for failing to remember the recipe). Even Pete seemed at ease at the Blue Angel. After meeting Tennessee Williams, his partner, and their friends, who were regular visitors to the Angel, Pete inquired, "Is it the custom here for young men to go out in couples?"

Though the *Counterattack* article affected bookings, Pete Kameron was not about to let us quietly fold up our tents and disappear into the nebulous Left. A tough kid, who tended to get in serious trouble in boyhood, he had somehow become skilled at loosening up tight situations without violence. Kameron approached the editor of *Counterattack* with absolute faith in his powers of persuasion. He introduced himself as the Weavers' new manager, a businessman faithful to the capitalist system, who was concerned with the loss of his revenue. His singers were good people, he told the editor, well-meaning but naive. Now that they were making good money, they were losing their interest in politics. As their manager, he would see there would be no more appearances for communist front groups. According to Kameron, the editor had laughed and even kibitzed about a donation to his organization if we did well financially. After the visit, Kameron's evaluation was that if we were to forego our usual appearances for the Left (the hootenannies and such) for the time being, *Counterattack* would probably lay off, at least for a while. CBS offered what was becoming the American hiring modus operandi: we could work for them if we signed a loyalty oath. That demand, begun against federal employees, had spread throughout industry, academia, the media, and wherever else it could be made useful. Refusing to sign the oath was a clear choice for us, but foregoing appearances for the Left was not.

I was ambivalent about TV work in general. It struck me as a repressive, alienating process. I felt silly being moved quickly into place in front of the camera, showing off for a number of minutes, and then quickly being shoved out of the way to make room for the next showoff, which broke the connection between us and whoever had been out there watching. But paramount to me was to keep on selling records so we could afford to keep on singing. If TV could secure that for us, I was for it. No doubt, the work itself might become more interesting if we were to get our own show. But if we didn't, I wouldn't cry, assuming we kept on singing and recording. Pete, however, had wished fervently for us to be on television because of the medium's potential to reach the American people with folk music. He faced a dilemma: whether to align the Weavers with folk music or with the Left and People's Artists.

The *People's Songs Bulletin* had morphed into the folk music journal, *Sing Out!*, with a radical leftist editor, Irwin Silber. Black America and white racism was a major issue at that time, with the Left quite properly trying to confront its own unrecognized racist tendencies. Irwin climbed on board, writing an editorial that dubbed the square dance tune "Black-eyed Suzie" racist and inferred that, since the Weavers borrowed from black culture, we ought not be an all-white group. We were good Lefties, and we took it seriously. I blush to recall our foolish, embarrassing, and, in my opinion, patronizing attempt to re-form ourselves through recruiting a black singer, beautiful Hope Foy. After a few rehearsals and one or two appearances, Hope wisely decided to follow the road her operatic soprano took her instead

of letting us try to mold it into Weaver shape. We continued on
our politically incorrect way.

Should we—and could we—break out of our symbiotic relationship with People's Artists, which was slogging on, trying to
be culturally useful to the needy Left? *Sing Out!* offered its editorial opinion that commercialism was affecting our music.
They felt that singing for "upper class" audiences was robbing us
of our real strength, our hootenannies. Pete, quite concerned
himself about where success was taking us, exploded at the gross
heavy-handedness of the editorial. Fred was furious. I sneered;
since when did being an occasional square dance caller (Irwin's
sole musical background) qualify him to assess anyone's musical
development? Lee averred that there was nothing humiliating to
him about being commercial and that we ought to try to beat the
blacklist. If avoiding controversial appearances would help, we
should avoid them. In a painful final meeting, we all agreed to
follow Pete Kameron's advice, with Pete announcing, "I'll go
along, but I will feel like a prisoner." He was true to his promise,
reminding us of it every step of the way.

On the bright side, our "commercialism" was certainly opening a crack in American mainstream culture for folk music. As
we had been pondering which path to take, our recording of
Woody Guthrie's Dust Bowl ballad "So Long, It's Been Good to
Know Yuh" had been released, and it took off and hit the charts.
Meanwhile, the *Counterattack* boys, using their access to FBI files,
were about to publish their prize, a volume called *Red Channels:
Communist Influence on Radio and Television,* a virtual encyclopedia
of black-listable actors, musicians, directors, producers, journal-
ists, writers, and others. To have signed a petition supporting
Henry Wallace for president was enough to be included. Pete
Seeger was listed. Strangely, the rest of us weren't.

Pete Kameron told us we were about to be offered a contract to star on a summer replacement TV show sponsored by Van Camp's Beans. We played with the notion—how much talk would there be, how much singing, which songs—but it never happened. In September, we appeared on *The Art Ford Show* on WPIX-TV. The next issue of *Counterattack* urged readers to send protests to the station manager for featuring Pete Seeger, claiming he entertained for Communist causes. After that, Van Camp's canceled our show. I kidded Kameron about his claim that he had charmed the snakes. According to Fred, "They were sending us all cases of their goddam beans!" I wondered where the beans went. I never got any.

For the rest of 1950, our name went up in lights on the marquees of several more big movie houses during a whirlwind tour of stage shows. These engagements were hard work, but I enjoyed them. Having spent many hours of my teens at the movies instead of in school, I identified with the big, unknown, appreciative audience out there in the dark theater. I liked feeling like I was part of an old-time traveling community of players—although that was a complete fiction, of course. As headliners, we were pretty much isolated from the other performers in our private dressing rooms. Still, I liked the bits of showbiz lore that got through. It pleased me to learn from a member of the Baltimore Hippodrome pit band that the rapid fanfare they played to goose the acts on and off the stage was called "B Bows," a carryover from burlesque. The Weavers never quite ran on and off stage in the manner of seasoned vaudeville players, but we did learn not to saunter.

We also saw a lot of the Decca studios as we recorded follow-ups to our hit records, all of which seemed to follow each other right up the Billboard charts like mice let out of a cage. Our suggestion for the single to follow "Tzena" and "Goodnight Irene" was Woody Guthrie's "So Long, It's Been Good to Know Yuh," which Woody obligingly bowdlerized himself to meet Decca's concerns about content for radio broadcast. He took out the verse about the high cost of groceries—"one pound of butter for two pounds of gold." Woody was practical, not a purist. In his *Posthumous Memoirs,* Lee wrote that in the Almanac days, Woody had fumed over the song "I Don't Want Your Millions, Mister," insisting, "By God I DO want their Cadillacs. I DO want their diamond rings."

The year 1950 ended with our first Christmas concert at New York's prestigious Town Hall. I was gowned in sparkly white and the "boys" wore tuxedos, which they agreed to only when Lee presented them with a photo of Paul Robeson singing in Moscow, dressed in a tuxedo. The staid *New York Times'* music reviewer wrote, "About the authenticity or scholarship of their material, this listener cannot vouch; but about their showmanship and effect upon an audience, there can be no doubt."

ON TOUR

We were now national celebrities, and Pete Kameron booked us at the most notable venues in the country. In January 1951, we left for a six-month tour of glitzy nightclubs and hotel ballrooms, accommodated from city to city in hotels consistent with our new status as headline entertainers. Nothing highlighted our personal differences so much as how we each lived our lives on the road. For me, touring was an education; confusion, wonder, and guilty pleasure were all part of my enlightenment. I, who could have spent perfectly happy hours in a free museum or a movie, suddenly had discretionary money. I soon discovered recreational shopping. I found one day that I had actually bought what I liked rather than what I really needed— an extra pair of shoes and a dress that looked good but that I wouldn't wear much. Soon, I even began to buy things I would probably never wear. How many occasions would I have to sport long black kid gloves? Within a year, I knew the layout of every major department store of every city we played in. But each dollar spent frivolously bought a childhood memory of my mother bending over a power sewing machine in a factory. Even though years had passed since she had been in that position, I imagined the disapproval in her eyes. And then there was our tarriance in first-class hotels. I loved them. Every day, a chambermaid made my bed, cleaned the bathroom, changed the towels, and vacuumed the rug. I'd find my sheets neatly turned down in the evening, with a little wrapped piece of chocolate on my pillow. It was hotel routine, but I enjoyed the illusion of being cared for. Nevertheless, I could not shake my self-reproach over someone "drudging" for me. Didn't that make me an exploiter of workers, a member of the despicable bourgeoisie? At an elegant hotel where we stayed for a month, a cheerful maid asked why I made my bed in the morning. I had thought I was being considerate, but it turned out that she had to go to the trouble of undoing it to remake it in the manner the hotel required. She let me know that she didn't find it at all demeaning to make beds and clean rooms. Rather, she was glad for the work and the tip I'd be leaving. I saw it was not the bed but my point of view that needed changing.

Lee Hays took shelter in his hotel rooms during the long weeks, reveling in his discovery of room service, the ultimate ally of his sedentary style. The telephone at his bedside now brought him all the food and drink he had dreamed of in his not-so-distant deprived days. Unless we were rehearsing, the television and typewriter absorbed most of Lee's waking hours, and we rarely saw him in the daytime. Lee would appear shortly before show time, bristling with the latest news: bloody battles over the 38th parallel in Korea; the Army beginning to detonate nuclear bombs in Nevada; old Dr. W. E. B. Du Bois dragged into court in manacles, charged with being a foreign agent. It wasn't Lee's fault that the news at that time fluctuated between bad and worse. Certainly the most terrible and ominous story of the time was the conviction and sentencing to death of Julius and Ethel Rosenberg.

At the other extreme, Pete, ill at ease in the upscale hotels and propelled by his inexhaustible physical energy, would light out almost the minute we landed to dig up old friends from the Almanacs' traveling days, explore historic sites, parks, and working class neighborhoods and search out stores that sold art supplies to work up crafts projects in his room. One month, he designed and printed his family's holiday cards on a hand press he bought. In another hotel, he made plaster of Paris casts of some Arctic artifact, creating havoc with the housekeeping department. Pete stayed busy to keep his head above "the big muddy" of boredom.

Life on the road was apparently as challenging for Fred, who was the unattached young male in the group, as it was for the rest of us. I used to imagine amusing and literate twenty-five-year-old Fred spending his free hours deep in pleasant conversation (or something along those lines ...) with one or another of the attractive young women performers we met along the way. On the contrary, he later told me, there were the occasional afternoon dates, thankfully, but diversions such as the wonderful Art Institute of Chicago claimed a lot more of his time.

The Weavers' first engagement on our national tour was three weeks at the Las Vegas Thunderbird, which was then a new hotel on a Strip not yet teeming with gambling palaces. The landscape across the road reminded me of the Wild West I revered in my cowboy-besotted childhood. The desk pointed me to a nearby dude ranch, where I borrowed a horse for a few hours. I admitted my inexperience and was given a horse the rancher said was submissive. It came with a cowboy companion who yes-mam'd me for an hour until I proved I really could stay upright. Comfortable on the big Western saddle, so unlike the English saddle I'd learned on, I rode for half a glorious day—which was a big mistake. The skin of my inner legs went raw from the seams of my new jeans, and that was the end of my riding adventures.

Unable to play cowgirl any longer, what was a poor girl to do at the Thunderbird but try the slots? There was no escape from them. They were everywhere, rows upon rows of them, with people shoveling in coins like moms late for work, frantically shoveling oatmeal down the kids' throats. One day, there in my pocket were three shiny silver dollars, change from a five I'd used to buy cigarettes (one never received paper change). Just for the joke of it, to see how it felt to fly in the face of my own values and common sense, I fed my coins into the nearest slot machine. The second one hit the jackpot. Players crowded around me, screaming with pleasure as they helped me pick up the shower of coins. Someone brought a paper bucket. Stunned at the vicarious pleasure people took in my success, I followed the kindly instructions of the crowd and presented my bucket to a teller's window across the floor, only to receive—chips. My winnings weren't money; they were little round pieces of cardboard. So I wandered over to an unoccupied blackjack table and, with the quiet encouragement of the dealer, learned the game of twenty-one. I played several rounds, winning some, then losing, and then winning again. When I had a tidy profit of twenty whole cardboard dollars, I walked away, as pleased with myself for my self-control as for winning. Alas, the former turned out to be as unreliable as the latter. Before long, the mysterious liveliness of the craps table claimed all my chips.

Marty came from New York to share the Las Vegas experience with me. He favored roulette. One night, I stood at his shoulder, calling numbers for him to bet. The wheel kept stopping on them, until he had nearly a thousand dollars he hadn't had a few moments before. Lacking complete faith that chance had been the sole operative, especially since I had seen Marty exchanging mischievous winks with the croupier earlier, I suspected him of fiddling with the wheel somehow for my benefit. When I sensed that either chance or the croupier had been kind long enough, I urged Marty to walk away. He couldn't. I went off to watch some exciting play at a dice table, and he lost it all and then some. It was the kind of public gambling drama that was repeated hundreds of times daily for huge stakes, not just for tiny ones like ours. Frankly, I was saved from profligate gambling not by personal principle but by personal idiosyncrasy: I just plain hated to lose even more than I loved to win.

Pete could hardly contain his contempt for the place, the ugly greed for personal riches it encouraged, or his disappointment in Fred and me for falling in with the games of chance. When we attempted conversation, Pete's words would come clipped and icy through tight lips, a fine study in pure New England disdain. Forbearing to scold, he stared down at us with cold eyes, seeming even taller than usual. One evening, as we were all walking by the pool, Pete tossed a silver dollar into it with deliberate carelessness, showing us by example the error of our ways.

Unfortunately for the lesson, Marty was a good swimmer. He dived in, retrieved it, and pocketed it.

It was at the Thunderbird that the extent of Lee's drinking became clear from the large aluminum bucket bristling with the necks of empty beer bottles that would appear outside his room every morning. Lee developed a phlegmy cough, claiming it was a touch of flu. Elegant actor Arthur Treacher, another performer at the hotel, called him on it: "Come off it, old boy, I know bourbon when I hear it." But neither that nor disapproval from Pete deterred Lee from his pleasure.

February took us to Ciro's in Hollywood, where at first the crowd appeared more interested in each other than in who was on stage. They warmed up eventually, if in that somewhat distracted way peculiar to Hollywood. We won crass kudos from LA gossip columnist Florabel Muir, who attempted to explain how the heck the Weavers had gotten into Ciro's:

> Nobody knows all the answers in show business. Not many would have bet their dough on the success of an act cooked up by three guys and a gal who ... gravitated toward each other because they all liked to warble folk songs ... but the [Greenwich Village] hepcats took a liking to the corn they dished out and their fame spread uptown.... Before long Gothamites were all talking about The Weavers and humming their songs. Their Decca record of "Goodnight Irene" sold like $5 gold pieces going for a dime and their next one, "So Long" was just as hot.... I think the answer to The Weavers' success is that the American public likes corn—corn on the cob, popped and in their entertainment.... Herman Hover [the owner of Ciro's] is to be congratulated, I think. The gang last night kept crying for more.

We were kept busy in LA, doing big-band record sessions for Decca and becoming movie stars. Well, not really stars. And not exactly for the movies, either. We made four or five "telescrip-tions" for an outfit that supplied three-minute videos to TV sta-tions as fillers for their programming. Seeing yourself for the first time as the camera sees you can be daunting. Upon viewing a clip years later of the 1950s Weavers all dressed up in our recording-star finery and singing "Tzena Tzena," Lee Hays guf-fawed: "Would you look at that! Barbie Doll and three stuffed dummies. If I'd known how foolish we looked, I swear on Pete's chin whiskers that I'd have given this up for something socially useful, like plucking chickens." I enjoyed doing the TV spots. A Hollywood makeup professional readied us for the camera. As he painted on my makeup, he made flattering comments about my eyes and lips. "Oh, wait, just wait," he pleaded when we were called for the camera. "I'm working on something really nice here." Watching the videos, I realized, alas, they were his eyes and lips that he had been admiring. They certainly weren't mine.

Marty was able to join me again for several days during the Ciro's run. We lived in a studio room in the home of former film star Francis Lederer and his wife, Marion, somewhere just above the Hollywood Strip. An import from Czechoslovakian films, Lederer, dark, romantic, and mysterious, had been one of my favorite movie actors. I hadn't seen him in a movie for a long time. Was their garden decor, row upon row of burned out light bulbs, a rueful jibe at life as a Hollywood actor?

Deplaning in Houston for an engagement at the grand Sham-rock Hotel, we were greeted on the tarmac by six enthusiastic Texans in full garb—Stetson hats, cowboy boots, the whole deal. It was a relief to be so heartily welcomed by the natives. With the Red-hunt ever threatening, we never knew what kind of political jungle we might have landed in when we got off a plane. And Texas was especially scary, even then. "There you are, Slim, I'd know you anywhere!" called out an older woman, clapping her hands and hurrying up to Lee Hays. She was as tall as he was, her pouffed-up gray-blond hair making her appear even taller. "And here's Elviry!" she said, wrapping me in a great she-bear hug, pressing my face against her bosom, which it just reached. It was a case of mistaken identity! We had been taken for the Weaver Brothers and Elvira, a group of country singers well-loved in those parts. But if the greeters were disappointed at their mistake, they didn't let on. What would happen, I wondered nervously, if everyone were to realize we were there under false pretenses?

But in the Shamrock's Emerald Room, following an elegant magician from Spain, who called out "*Chispitas, chispitas!*" while doing remarkable things with sparks from a cigarette, we sang our mixed repertoire of American and world folk songs for an appreciative audience of Texas oilmen and their consorts. One night, the heads in the audience swiveled toward a man making his uncertain way to a table, escorted (held up, really) by an exquisitely gowned woman on each arm. A whisper went around the room: "H-h-ewss! H-h-hewss!" I heard. People kept staring as they crumpled into their seats.

"That's Howard Hughes," Fred whispered.

"Who's Howard Hughes?" I asked.

"Oh, you know," he said, "that aviator."

Marty was on the tour with us while we were in Texas. We went car hunting with my "Goodnight Irene" share and captured a brand new shiny red Pontiac convertible. We drove away from the dealer in a cloud of euphoria, paying no attention to either the speedometer or the rear view mirror, and thus failed to notice the police motorcycle following us. The patrolman handed us our speeding ticket politely, with a grin of pure Texas amusement on his face.

The entertainers we met on the road, and the women especially, fascinated me. Who were these people behind their fabulous costumes and polished acts? How had they gotten into what they were doing—had it been by choice, by training, by accident? I wanted to think of myself as one of them, but the Weavers were just the Weavers, offstage and on. We played a fancy dinner club, where I became friends with a dancer named Jean, a quiet woman with lovely, natural cornsilk hair. It felt comforting to exchange ordinary female talk. Jean carried a small portable sewing machine with her on the road. She liked to make clothes for her brother's children during the many long days. She helped me pin up the hem of my costume, which had torn as we came offstage. I told her that my mother had been a factory dressmaker in New York City and had made all my clothes when I was growing up. We exchanged stories about our impossible girlhood crushes and giggled to tears about our early disasters at dancing school. At the end of the run, we exchanged addresses, promising to stay in touch. A year later, when I tried to reconnect, I discovered a tragedy: this sweet woman had recently jumped from a hotel window.

During a run in a hotel ballroom, we shared the bill with a sexy dance troop, Chandra Kali and His Hindu Dancers. In their act, a sleek man wearing a jeweled necklace over his bare chest divided himself among three pulchritudinous women in diaphanous pajamas, who demanded his attentions, each in turn. The most exotic of the women had a supple, sinuous body and catlike eyes, resembling a glossy jungle animal—a panther, perhaps. She was reputed to be a girlfriend of Marlon Brando. I felt a little afraid of her, so I thought I ought to get to know her, but she seemed unreceptive, responding with only a quick nod and no smile to my greetings. The program note explained that the dancers were re-enacting the legend of Shiva and Paravati, the goddess Paravati being the benevolent side of the goddess Kali, the destroyer. Backstage after their set one night, I heard a pure Brooklyn accent—it was the Panther snarling at a cohort: "I'm tellin' ya, y'betta watch it or y'gonna find lye in y'douche bag!"

Closing our tour of high-end commercial bookings was a four-week engagement at the elegant Empire Room of Chicago's Palmer House. In lively Chicago, we got to tour Lake Michigan twice, once as Purple Hearts money-raisers for wounded veterans and once as guests of Pete and Lee's old friend Mandel Terman, who took us out on his luxurious motor launch for a glorious sunshiny spin.

Chicago is about the blues—I always think of it that way. At the Blue Note, another venue we were playing at, the Weavers were on the bill with jazz pianist Slim Gaillard, who tickled Lee Hays's funny bone mightily every night. (According to some, the Blue Note used to be Lip's Lower Level in speakeasy days.) One night at Lorraine Blue's great Old Town club, Mother Blues, I fell off the stage twice, not because of alcohol, but rather spike heels. (I gave them up after that.) But what stamps Chicago forever on my memory was the benefit for the Old Town School of Folk Music, the bastion of folk culture in the Midwest. Studs Terkel emceed that evening, which we shared with Big Bill Broonzy's blues and Mahalia Jackson's gospels. Had I known that the event was going to be history, I'm sure I'd have paid closer attention to details. As it was, my brain was utterly bemused and dumbfounded by one thing: the fact that I was actually sitting next to and getting to sing with one of my musical idols, Mahalia herself! I felt at that concert that I'd truly "moved on up a little higher" than I could ever have expected.

WEAVERS NAMED REDS!

We had not done any hootenannies or left-wing performances for six months. Hard as that had been, especially for Pete Seeger, Kameron's strategy seemed to be working. As long as we stuck to live performances and stayed off TV, *Counterattack* left us alone. Was that the bargain? It seemed to be. But it wouldn't last.

To publicize our opening at the Empire Room, Kameron arranged a guest appearance on an innovative Sunday afternoon radio show hosted by Dave Garroway, a popular Chicago media personality. We were also scheduled for *The Dave Garroway Show* on NBC later in the month. However, the radio appearance alone was enough to galvanize *Counterattack*. Their June 1951 newsletter urged readers to contact the sponsor of Garroway's show, the president of NBC, and Conrad Hilton, owner of the Empire Room, and ask them why they would feature the Weavers as entertainers. The American Jewish League then coordinated a call-in campaign to protest our appearance on NBC, led by the McCarthyite rabbi Benjamin Schultz. NBC immediately withdrew its invitation to *The Dave Garroway Show,* citing the Weavers' "conflicting rehearsal schedules." It seemed more to our advantage at the time to allow this lie to stand than to make the situation public. Lee was especially disappointed. An avid TV watcher, he greatly admired the artistically liberated Chicago School of TV productions—such as *Kukla, Fran and Ollie,* Studs Terkel's *Studs' Place,* and *Garroway at Large.* "Damn it, the Weavers belong on it!" he grumbled. Adding significantly to the disappointment, of course, was the suspicion that the worst was yet to come in our tug of war with the witch-hunters.

In the meantime, coins in jukeboxes all over the country were going jingle-jangle-jingle for our records: "On Top of Old Smokey," "The Roving Kind," and "So Long, It's Been Good to Know Yuh." After the Empire Room date, we returned to New York to put two more big band singles, "When the Saints Go Marching In" and "Kisses Sweeter Than Wine," onto the charts and into the Decca cash register. *Counterattack* was clearly determined to kill the Weavers' potential for TV. Still, we were making a reasonably good living, sought after by nightclub owners and show producers. We looked forward to a major appearance in August at the Ohio State Fair. But when Ohio governor Frank Lausche received copies of *Counterattack* from a patriotic Knight of Columbus, the unpleasant odor of June ripened into a much more potent stink. It was illegal for a private citizen, even a governor, to see confidential FBI files, but Lausche requested ours, and J. Edgar Hoover sent them. Firing the "commie" Weavers from their major live entertainment event would make political news, worthy of both the governor and the FBI. The broken contract was already local news on August 25 as we deplaned in Columbus. Pete Kameron had been adamant that we not give the fair any excuse to claim we never showed up. They owed us nearly four thousand dollars, not a negligible sum in those days. Several reporters surrounded us, Pete Seeger their primary focus. I walked away, and when one fellow followed me, notebook in hand, I played the role usually assigned me by the press—"I'm the girl in the group; what do I know?"—and he soon lost interest. Governor Lausche then shared with the press the FBI material that the *Counterattack* fellows had been helping themselves to: lists of "Red front groups" we'd sung for, reviews from the *Daily Worker*, reports by FBI infiltrators at public fund-raising events and hootenannies, and personal evaluations of the group's Redness by FBI agents. It wasn't such heavyweight material, but in those days it was enough to smash commercial support. The *New York World-Telegram* printed the story under the headline "Exposed!" written by the well-known Red-baiter Frederick Woltman, to be carried by Scripps-Howard subsidiaries. Local papers picked it up. Public-spirited patriotic organizations—such as the Knights of Pythias (more Knights), the American Legion, and the Catholic War Veterans—quickly saw it as their duty to rally and save America from the Weavers.

"While my husband is fighting communists in Korea," an invited speaker from Vassar College testified at a Kiwanis Club dinner, "I'm fighting communism here at home. I have come to you for aid and advice." It was disingenuous. She needed no help or advice from the Kiwanis. Her information was straight from the *World-Telegram* and *Counterattack*—in other words, straight from "confidential" FBI Weaver files. Her point was that it was not "Moscow gold" that was financing communism but rather the salaries of left-wing performers. To show what sort of people we were, she revealed the lyrics of our song "Banks of Marble," which *Counterattack* had printed:

> The banks are made of marble with a guard at every door,
> The vaults are stuffed with silver that we have sweated for!

She asked people to imagine how their local banker would feel about that. "Think of the money Pete Seeger and the Weavers have raised for Communist fronts," she continued. "Think, too, of the boys who used to collect records before they were sent to Korea to be struck down by Communist shells bought by

Communist money!" She went on and on. The Vassar lady's passionate plea to deny us the right to make a living was soon answered in full agreement by the Syracuse, New York, American Legion Post #41, who wrote Decca, terming the Weavers "undesirable characters." "We have passed a resolution in this Post hitting at the Weavers and are contacting all radio-TV stations, juke box distributors and record shops giving them the information that we have in our possession." The damning information was that we had released "Banks of Marble" on Hootenanny Records, a People's Artists Production.

This was a moment for decision. TV was dead to us, but we had a year's worth of touring lined up. Decca had released *We Wish You a Merry Christmas* for the upcoming holiday season. It was an unorchestrated ten-inch beauty containing some carols never before recorded and some of our best singing. It could take a while before the blacklist could completely close us down. Personal appearances helped keep the records selling.

Pete was ready to call it quits. He had never been happy with rich audiences in plush places, but his problem was more than philosophical; touring for weeks kept him away from Toshi and their kids and from working on the primitive log cabin where they lived year round. Lee was for going the distance in the race with the Red-hunters. A complete blacklist might come, but Lee thought we should resist, resist, resist as long as possible by staying on the job. Fred and I agreed. We decided once more to keep on keeping on, taking as much work as we could get in the service of moving our recordings, as long as Decca would make them. I said that I thought of this as "singing for the people," but I was firmly corrected by a leftist cultural pundit, who replied, "But I thought we were all developed thinkers. Are you speaking of the people of— hmmm—Carl Sandburg?"

Developed or not, the Weavers had a solid accomplishment for our trouble: millions of those "Sandburg-type" people were now humming songs inspired by America's own diverse, home-grown musical culture, such as "Goodnight Irene," "Midnight Special," "Follow the Drinking Gourd," "So Long, It's Been Good to Know Yuh," "Trouble in Mind," "Across the Wide Missouri," "Easy Rider Blues," and "On Top of Old Smokey," and they had been introduced to other world cultures through songs like "The Roving Kind," from England; "Tzena Tzena," from Israel; "Suliram," from Indonesia; and "The Wreck of the John B," from the Bahamas.

In October 1951, the Weavers met again with Gordon Jenkins and his orchestra and chorus to record Lead Belly's "Midnight Special" and Gordon's exciting arrangement of the South African song "Wimoweh." Also, I signed a contract with Decca to record four solo singles with orchestra: one torch song from my unfathomably sloshy teens and three contemporary takes on old ethnic pop songs—one Jewish, one Italian, and one quasi-Spanish. Recording them was fun, but the records weren't. They weren't awful, just a trifle boring. They passed into oblivion, which is where they belonged.

In November, Decca received a telegram:

> Listeners have called to our attention that the Weavers were cancelled from their Ohio State Fair engagement after allegations were made that they ... had recorded for a communist front a party line ballad called "The Peekskill Story." What is their comment and what is Decca's comment? Tom McCarthy WKRC

Then came another letter of concern, this one written to the president of a newspaper company, which owned an important radio station in Tampa, Florida: the writer was "distressed to think the disc jockey has overlooked the important matter … " The "important matter" that distressed the informant was the very same cited by the Vassar lady to the Kiwanis Club. Her plea for help was traveling.

Under the gathering clouds, we played on, ending 1951 at home with our second annual Christmas concert at The Town Hall venue in New York. We got to play all the songs we loved. What a pleasure. The energy we absorbed from that performance powered us on into 1952 to face a series of dates in places like Daffy's Starlight Room on the outskirts of Cleveland and the Blue Note in Chicago. Most were a far cry from the Empire Room and the Blue Angel, but they were still quite good venues, where we might alternate with great jazz musicians as we had in the old days at the Vanguard. Some, like Daffy's, owned by folks with access to well-organized protection, were not much disturbed by threats from the American Legion. But in March, Harvey Matusow, a former communist turned government informer, who had been working his way up the ladder of anti-Red success with the help of Roy Cohn (Senator Joseph McCarthy's handler) and the *Counterattack* fellows, testified to the House Un-American Activities Committee that he saw us at Communist Party meetings.

Clubs canceled their contracts with us, the owners scared of property damage by vigilante veteran's groups spoiling for a fight. One tough fellow with "connections" offered a renewal, swearing that no one was going to tell him whom to hire. But when he was threatened with the loss of his state liquor license, he had our encouragement to back out, and he did. We finished out the season without too much trouble apart from a few drunks requesting "The Star-Spangled Banner."

I heard with glee that when Joe Glazer, our booking agent, was approached by two FBI agents, he kicked them out of his office and down the stairs. Walking to work at an Akron club one evening, Fred, Lee, and I became aware of footsteps following us an insistent four feet behind. Scared and expecting violence, I stopped and turned to face two men. "Is there something you want?" I demanded. They were silent for a minute. Then, with a sneer, one of them held out an envelope and said, "Will you take them here or on stage?" So, they weren't thugs after all, but process servers from the House Un-American Activities Committee serving papers for us to appear at a hearing. At a hotel, a friendly bellhop warned us to keep the door open when we got together to talk or rehearse in anyone's room to avoid being targeted by the vice squad for hanky-panky. Radio, dependent on advertisers, was now tied up as tightly as TV by the witchhunters. Within a month, Weavers recordings disappeared from disc jockey shows. Oddly, the last work of any financial substance we were offered was a tour of segregated Southern movie theaters. We decided to skip it.

The Weavers' status as mainstream stars, orchestrated by Pete Kameron, had lasted two years. The hard, painful, and worthwhile collaboration was finished, or so I thought.

A HOUSEWIFE

So, carpe diem, I thought. What better time than right now for home and family—motherhood? Why not join the demographics? I would become the typical, cozy American housewife I saw on TV with two-and-a-half children, a super clean kitchen floor, and a martini in hand for her hubby when he came home from work. I didn't ask myself whether I had the talent for that kind of life; the women's magazines I'd been collecting would show me how it was done. Marty and I were intrigued by Southern

California. He was early enough in his career to make a change
and had acquired California licensing. We headed for Los Angeles via a leisurely drive through Mexico.

In our fine red Texas convertible, we traveled dusty roads
and ventured up into pristine mountain villages. Mexico's con-
trasts fascinated us urban New Yorkers. We drove through hours
of seemingly deserted dry miles of desert, with gorgeous bougainvillea flashing from every tiny shack. Local boys in a mountain village without an auto repair shop found us their "mae-
stro," who figured out what was wrong with our stuck car and
fixed it. We saw the known touristic "don't miss" sights and traveled quiet byways. We gasped at both the splendor and the awful
poverty of Mexico City. In Acapulco, we went deep-sea fishing
and water-skiing. Well, at least Marty skied; I couldn't get my
behind up out of the water. I indulged in bits of silver jewelry
and luscious tropical fruits, and I survived the turista.

My sadness over the Weavers' demise began to give way to the
adventure that was Mexico. Nagging thoughts about the folk
song world in New York carrying on without the Weavers—
without *me*—began to fade, as did my resentment at Fred Hellerman, now known as "Fred Brooks," for getting his pop-folk tunes
recorded (two of them based on songs I'd brought to the Weavers
from my Priority Rambler days) and my envy of contralto Martha Schlamme for recording German folk songs, accompanied by
Pete on recorder and banjo. We were so enchanted with Mexico
that we even mused a bit about coming back to live there, à la
some of our old left-wing friends, like Mary and Cedric Belfrage.
But before we reached Los Angeles, I knew I was pregnant.

We found a pleasant tract house on a quiet street in North
Hollywood, bought a dog, and waited for our baby. I registered
for a music theory and composition class at nearby San Fernando

Valley Junior College, had my old piano tuned, and joined an a cappella choir. A recording of the calypso song "Matilda," sung by upcoming star Harry Belafonte, caught the public ear. It caught mine, too, and I spent many hours of my pregnancy in the University of California's music library with their small collection of delightful West Indian songs.

Lisa was born at the end of 1953, the year they electrocuted Ethel Rosenberg, the mother of two little boys, for being a spy because she was accused of having typed something for her husband, Julius. We burrowed into suburbia: snapdragons in the yard, a pet turtle that ate only lox, and dinner on the table each night. But it turned out that my singing career wasn't quite finished yet.

. . .

In 1955, Harold Leventhal wrote from New York suggesting I come there for a possible Town Hall concert. "He's got to be kidding," I said to Marty. It was like Don Quixote challenging windmills. Senator McCarthy had been doing himself in publicly, causing his popularity to wane, but the era that borrowed his name was at its height. McCarthyism had dug the Weavers' grave; I was still mourning, but I was getting on with life. I said no. Harold persisted. The following fall, another letter came. Harold insisted that there was still a loyal audience in New York City and that we ought to encourage them: "I'll book Town Hall. Come. You'll see." Our friends Jane and Jack Rollins offered us a haven in New York with their two toddlers, so I packed up Lisa, who was just shy of her second birthday, and flew east. Marty would follow when he could. As it turned out, the 1,500-seat Town Hall, fearful of trouble, refused the concert. But stubborn Harold booked us into Carnegie Hall.

On Christmas Eve 1955, the McCarthy era still at its peak, three thousand people jammed Carnegie Hall to the rafters to hear the Weavers sing. Some came from across the country, some from across the sea. Hundreds were turned away. And we sang—oh yes, we sang up a storm.

> Pace! Friede! Salud! Shalom!
> The words mean the same, whatever your home.
> Why can't we have Christmas the whole year around?
> Why can't we have Christmas the whole year around?
> We wish you a Merry Christmas
> And a happy new year.

RESURGENCE

Harold booked Carnegie Hall for a repeat performance in the spring of 1956. I flew to New York alone for the show—it would be a quick trip, and then I would go right back home to Lisa. Just as at Christmas, the demand for tickets exceeded the capacity of the auditorium. Buoyed by the response and looking forward to the next night's celebratory concert, we all sat down to enjoy dinner at Natalie and Harold Leventhal's apartment.

"Oh, by the way, Ronnie," Natalie said, handing me a slip of paper with an unfamiliar name, "this woman phoned here asking for you. I told her you'd be here this evening." Probably someone hoping for a ticket, I thought. But who would have this phone number?

"Mrs. Scatti? This is Ronnie Gilbert. You phoned. What can I do for you?"

"Ah, yes. Miss Gilbert. Hello. You see, my dear, even though you're married, we found you. We can always find you."

Married? What was this, some kind of crank call? I thought about just hanging up. But then it occurred to me—could it be the House Un-American Activities Committee? Was it legal to hang up on HUAC?

"Now, Miss Gilbert, the Counselor wants to meet with you."

"The Counselor … ?"

"Yes, for the Committee, of course. It will be an absolutely confidential interview, I can promise you that. It's understood that girls may not want their husbands to know everything about their earlier life."

Who was this weird woman? One doesn't get invited to HUAC subpoenas. Did this mean that there was a subpoena coming?

"I need to think about this, Mrs. Scatti. I'll call you back."

"There's nothing to think about, Miss Gilbert, the Counselor is expecting to meet with you!"

"Yes, I understand. I will call you. Goodbye."

Why would HUAC be after me now, after all this time? Pete's trial for contempt was coming up. Did they hope to get something incriminating out of me? Harold furnished me with an attorney's phone number, but the lawyer's guess was as good as mine. If there were a subpoena coming, he told me, it might miss me since I was flying home to California the morning after the concert. He instructed me to wait to phone her until I was at the airport and about to board the plane. The evening passed at Carnegie without a summons. The next morning at the airport, I followed the lawyer's advice.

"Mrs. Scatti, I'm sorry, but I can't manage a meeting with the Counselor just now. I need to get home to my daughter. By the way, the Committee can easily find me; my name is listed in the Los Angeles phone book." Weeks passed, then months, and I heard no more. Couldn't the FBI figure out which LA phone book I was in? Some time later, an actor friend remembered the name Scatti as belonging to a strange woman who had tried to stir up HUAC's interest in the New York theater community. She had failed, of course. HUAC wanted headliners like us, not ordinary working actors.

As news of the Carnegie success spread, many concert halls across the country decided to brave it out with the picketers from the Veterans for Foreign Wars in favor of democratic principle, potential profit, or both. Harold organized a Weavers Reunion Tour. We played to jam-packed audiences in San Diego, Los Angeles, Salt Lake City, San Francisco, and Toronto, gathering rhapsodic press reviews. At Chicago's Orchestra Hall, a stink bomb exploded, causing a slight delay in starting time. This in no way dampened the enthusiasm of the five thousand people in the audience. In those dark "scoundrel times," as Lillian Hellman termed the ongoing McCarthy era, such public expressions of approval were exhilarating—and ironic. TV and radio blacklisting had "limited" us to our favorite form of performance—concerts.

The progressive Solomon brothers, Maynard and Seymour, owners of Vanguard Records, which was known for its prestigious Bach Guild recordings, picked up the produced concert tapes. *The Weavers at Carnegie Hall* was released in April 1957, and even without the benefit of radio play, it reached third place for national album sales by September, according to industry charts. It seemed the Weavers were out of purgatory; we could be back in business if we wanted to be.

Harold said we owed our return to our supporters, who would see us as a hopeful harbinger of better political times. Were we? Pete was awaiting trial by the federal Justice Department for ten counts of contempt of Congress. He was out on bail, but his travel was confined to the Southern District of New York, where he played in summer camps, private schools, and local colleges whose directors didn't mind a "felon" teaching children. A generation of youthful folk fans and future singers and players developed under Pete's tutelage.

Every trip with the Weavers required hours of nerve-wracking negotiations with the authorities by Harold and lawyers, and there was never any certainty that Pete would be allowed to participate. There were other problems engendered by our resurgence. I was now the mother of a three year old, and I lived across the country from New York City, which was the center of Weaver operations. Fred had an independent professional musical life teaching, arranging, and song writing, with responsibilities to a publishing partnership with Harold Leventhal. He had sold a couple of his own songs to a new, exciting personality in the folk scene, Harry Belafonte. Lee Hays, prodded away from day-long binges on TV followed by beer chasers, claimed that resuming work with us would be too "taxing and insufficiently rewarding" for him. Adept at dismantling Lee's resistance to change, Harold, who was his loyal manager and protector, soon had him moving, but he knew it was a portent of crunches to come. In an interview years later, Harold confessed that Lee was "a great guy but on the other hand a pain in the ass." As a fellow worker, brilliant, funny, and colorful Lee Hays made excessive demands on everyone's comradeship and compassion.

The Weavers carried on, reinspired by the music we made and the happiness of the audiences we played for. We got along mainly by respecting each other's quirks and taking care of our individual lives. We traveled on weekends at first, visiting one or two cities at a time. Lee, physically uncomfortable and anxious in planes, balked at more frequent flying. I didn't mind the moderate degree of activity. The disturbance to my family life was manageable in short spurts. Moreover, my marriage had not been going well, despite my efforts to emulate *Better Homes and Gardens,* and working was something of a relief. I was happy to be earning money again, little as it was. Fred, on the other hand, complained bitterly that the routine enriched only the airways. Later, with demand for appearances increasing, Harold booked a schedule of mini-tours—four or five days every couple of months. Lee, complaining all the way, took solace in the familiar comfort of high-end hotels. Initially, Harold came on the road with us, largely to look after our high-maintenance partner. Then he hired a road manager to do it.

Lisa, who was moving on toward four years old, and Marty seemed to do all right during my absences, with the help of a daily housekeeper. I'd tie together a string of pennies for Lisa's piggy bank, one for each day I'd be gone, hoping that the shortening string would reassure her that I'd soon be coming home. My teacher friend Sarah Abelson had suggested chocolate kisses, but Marty, DDS, put his foot down; pennies would be good enough. Lisa seemed to get it. I needed to think so.

With the success of *The Weavers at Carnegie Hall,* the Solomon brothers were eager for another album and suggested other potential projects, as well. Lee, reenergized and hugely excited, especially by the prospect of a possible children's album, wanted us to drop everything and gallop ahead with their ideas. But finding a time for rehearsals when all of us were free was a challenge. Pete and Toshi offered to let us use their Beacon home for a week in the summer. I could stay there with Lisa, and it was accessible by commute from New York City. Lee was incensed. A week? "Tell them to rehearse what they want to sing and I'll add my part later," he wrote to Harold. "It's not worth my time to work on only four songs." Nevertheless, the jacket cover photo of *The Weavers at Home* showed the four of us, relaxed, singing to my daughter and the Seegers' kids at their place. The rural, laid-back atmosphere helped to reconnect us. Lee was at his best in sylvan surroundings and especially with children. Lisa had a great time. A suburban child, she followed the tree-climbing, physically adventurous Seeger kids admiringly. One day, she called to me from a platform high above the ground: "Mommy, mommy, watch me slide down the pole with nobody looking!"

PETE LEAVES THE WEAVERS

In 1957, things were moving along modestly well for us. The next recording project, *The Weavers' Almanac,* our first prestigious studio album for Vanguard, was coming together slowly. Then, one day, Harold had a remarkable call from a major ad agency: would the Weavers do a commercial? Imagine that! Had this agency decided to defy the industry blacklist against us? Good for them! What was the product? Uh-oh … L&M Cigarettes. Pete, the nonsmoker among us, was utterly opposed. Lee argued that we owed it to fellow blacklisted performers to take advantage of the possible thaw. Fred voted yes. I'd been smoking since age fourteen and was a pack-a-day smoker by that point. I voted yes. We would do the commercial.

That very night, Pete called a meeting and quit the Weavers—he refused to discuss it, but I could imagine his reasoning: we'd accomplished our goal of bringing folk music to the mainstream. What was the point now, just making money? Pete never had any interest in money; the very subject was verboten among us. The harmfulness of cigarette smoking had been revealed, and

I half-agreed that we had done something not very admirable. But I could not afford to position myself above financial interest. Unlike the others, with their independent writers' royalties, performing was my entire income—save tiny, shared earnings on Weavers' material. I had heard that commercials paid well, with something called "residuals."

Fred and I were shocked at Pete's departure. Lee was devastated and bitter. In an interview for her biography of him, Lee told Doris Willens: "[Pete's resignation] came out in the guise of going ahead to do something pure and noble.... He just walked out on us, and it was a terrible blow.... I hadn't expected it." Doris also quoted Pete: "For a couple of years I felt I just couldn't keep on going.... I wasn't giving it my full attention and I didn't feel particularly happy about just coasting along." And did the commercial signal a breakthrough for blacklisted performers, as Lee had suggested? Hardly. It was never even aired. We were probably brought in by the agency to furnish musical ideas; safer singers were available to carry them out. In any case, when we were finished with the album, Pete was through with the Weavers. Loss of income aside, I was deeply angry at the probability of our demise. We had fought the McCarthyites with dignity. To give up now that we had popular approval to be onstage seemed to me like a slap to the public's face. Depressed and shaken, I even mused on whether the phenomenon of the Weavers had ever really been what our cheering audiences believed it to be.

Regardless of the feelings behind the scenes, the four of us had an obligation to finish *The Weavers' Almanac*. Unsurprisingly, it just wasn't coming together. Pete suggested we invite another performer to join us, recommending a former student of his, Erik Darling of the Tarriers, a fine singer and banjoist. Erik agreed and was introduced in 1958 on *The Weavers' Almanac* recording as a guest artist. Working with Erik on the album proved that we could survive musically without Pete, something I'd never considered before. We invited him to join us permanently. I loved singing with Erik, blending my alto with his high, thin tenor, and listening to him play, admiring his profound take on blues and his accurate feel for songs of other cultures. Erik's musicianship was buoyant and contemporary, stylistically in tune with the rising generation of good players and youthful audiences trained, ironically, by Pete to look beyond him for inspiration and education. We toured and recorded with Erik for the next three years. In the summer of 1959, our former manager Pete Kameron suddenly emerged from silence with an offer from an Israeli promoter for a tour in Israel. I was thrilled to go. But first I had to untangle my personal life: Marty and I were divorcing.

DIVORCE

The divorce should have been simple. We had been separated for months. There was no need for alimony, I thought, since I would have a source of income with the Weavers. But Marty's notice arrived—countersuing for Lisa's custody! I went into an emotional tailspin. In a legal battle over Lisa, would my name as a blacklisted singer stand up against the "Dr." in front of his? At our hearing, the judge said he wanted a few days to make a ruling. Why a few days? Was it the blacklisting? The Weavers' departure date for the overseas tour was imminent. Back in court, I heard the ruling. I would be given occupancy of the house and a stipend for child support, but I would not be allowed to remove Lisa from the jurisdiction of the court without Marty's express permission. The humiliation of having my worth as an independent woman struck down by a court of law filled me with fury; it was far worse than the realization that I wouldn't be able to go on tour. Hardly able to see for my sobbing, I drove home plotting how to escape this prison. In the morning, I would pack a suitcase with clothes for Lisa and me, and we would fly to New York and then on to my relatives in London. If they couldn't or wouldn't help us, there were cultural workers in Paris, leftist refugees from McCarthy, who would surely recognize me.

Who knows whether I would have had the courage to follow through on those plans. Marty called the next day offering to let us go if I agreed to sell the house immediately. So much for his fatherly concern for Lisa's well-being, I thought bitterly. My best friends, Ruth and Alec Cowan, made an immediate offer on the house, and it was done. But fury at Marty traveled overseas with me like an extra suitcase. It would be many moons before I could empty the closet of that piece of heavy luggage.

ON TOUR WITH THE WEAVERS

To me, London was names out of books: the Thames, the Tower, Buckingham Palace, Westminster Abbey. The prospect of walking the actual streets tickled me. We were booked at a downtown hotel, and a stroll around Piccadilly Circus beckoned, but the thought of creeping around London at night by myself held me back. How could I release myself from the emotional prison of being a Mrs.? I got myself dressed to go outside, and whom should I meet downstairs but Fred, restless like me and ready for a long walk. I can't recall any details except finding our way across the Thames to the Albert Hall.

A few radio appearances and a short bus tour through the Midlands with Sonny Terry and Brownie McGee filled the

Weavers' working time in England. And I met the English sub-
jects of my mother's old family photos. My Aunt Rose, widow of
a Sussman half-brother, and my schoolteacher cousin Bella lived
in an apartment in an old building on Baker Street. "What fun,"
I thought. "Shades of Sherlock Holmes!" There was my cousin
struggling with a stuck window against pouring rain: "Ah yes,
Ronnie, the joys of the antique . . . " while Aunt Rose urged, "but
Ronnie, wouldn't you like a nice buy-gull?" It was some minutes
before I recognized what was being offered: the Jewish chewy
bread with a hole in the middle. Bella was amused at my surprise that bagels were available: "Yes, Ronnie, even in London,
on Baker Street." Bella was delighted with Lisa and took her to
her "infants" (kindergarten) class.

· · ·

"Ha Orgim," the literal Hebrew translation of our name, was
what the Weavers were called in Israel. You would never have
known we were pariahs in our own country. It seemed that
nobody gave a damn about America's blacklist outside of the
United States. We were welcomed with great excitement as the
American recording stars who had introduced young Israel to
the United States. Concert halls in Jerusalem and Haifa filled to
overflowing. At an outdoor Tel Aviv auditorium, mobs of young
people who couldn't afford tickets climbed over the walls to get
in, causing a near riot.

In a caravan of three or four autos, which carried our crew,
lights, and sound system, we toured "from Dan to Beersheva," as
Lee Hays, familiar with scripture, loved to say. We were welcomed to crude dressing rooms with armfuls of flowers in primitive halls and amphitheaters. Kibbutzniks fed us proudly on
tomatoes, bell peppers, and other gorgeous, healthy produce

from their gardens, as well as the ever-present sour cream, a familiar food to us all. In the open, unstinting Israeli manner, we were offered the best of everything that was available or could be procured. An especially gracious woman, thinking we might be homesick for American food, served us bacon with lunch— raw slices draped on lettuce leaves. Astonishing. Where in Israel did she acquire bacon? We didn't ask; it might have been a touchy question. Her attractive presentation of our treat was also pretty touchy. I thought Lee was about to pass out. Everyone knows that refusing food in someone's home is tantamount to insulting the host, especially when visiting a foreign country. But eating raw bacon from an unknown pig on a broiling hot day would be an invitation to botulism, listeria, and God knows what else! I decided that Israel, or at least the familiar Jewish home we were in, was not all that foreign, and I gave our hostess a private American cooking lesson. When the bacon made its appearance again, crisp and un-toxic, Lee, the color back in his face, cast me a deeply grateful look as we sat down to a delicious meal.

At one kibbutz performance, we were told that our concert would be heard by soldiers in a Syrian military encampment just over the hill.

"Marvelous," I said. "Sharing music is a civilized approach to peace."

"Sure," said one of our hosts wryly, "It also warns them that the flashlights coming up the road at night are concertgoers, not the Israeli army."

Once, driving between appearances, one of the cars had a flat. Horns honked; the cars stopped. Drivers and crew leaped out. The concert producer reached into our glove compartment and took out a pistol. I had never seen a tire changed so fast. As we roared away, the producer explained: we had been caught in a narrow stretch of land between Israel and Syria, which was apparently "a favorite spot for Arab infiltrators."

In 1959, I did not have the vaguest idea about the recent history of Israel and could not fathom the animosity of the Palestinians for the Jews. Didn't they each have their own territory? Hadn't the Israelis been doing a fine job of "modernizing the wasteland"? When I raised the question to a crew member, I was met with an impatient shrug: "Oh, they're crazy, the Arabs." His friend added, "Don't you know? They'd like to drive us into the sea. We're going to drive them." I didn't press for an explanation, and I went home with my ignorance intact.

ANN SHEPHERD AND THEATER

Once we were back from Israel, Lisa and I settled into an apartment on New York's Upper West Side in Manhattan, near my friend Ann Shepherd. Ann and I had become friends during the early 1950s, when we were both casualties of *Counterattack*'s rout of Reds and liberals from TV and radio. We were both recently divorced, and our kids were the same age. The Weavers were able to work in 1960, thanks to concerts, but Ann, who had been an actress in soap operas, lost her entire employment. Her crime was that she'd studied and performed with the Group Theatre, a revolutionary leftist stage company.

Ann had never stopped training for her craft. She was a devotee of Method acting and was planning to teach. A Chicago theater friend offered her an opportunity to test the waters for a few weeks via a program she ran in Gary, Indiana. Ann agreed and invited me to join the adventure. We took our kids and all shared a bungalow in the awesome Indiana Dunes State Park. While eight-year-old Lisa and Josh and their dogs, Nosey and Pokey, chased each other along the Lake Michigan shore, Annie and I compared our personal and professional histories, weeping, guffawing, and commiserating, forging the kind of woman-bonding I'd known before the Weavers—and had very much missed.

Naturally, we talked theater endlessly. I contributed my embarrassing memories of the Brighton Beach Players' hilariously fumbling productions of the Group Theatre's first great triumphs, *Waiting for Lefty* and *Awake and Sing!* Annie filled me in on the Group's painful struggle with the contradictions of commercial success. She could have been talking about the Weavers' conflicts. I greedily read her copy of director Harold Clurman's *The Fervent Years,* a history of the Group Theatre during the Depression, which included an account of the opening night of *Lefty,* which was a drama about a union meeting. The audience had leapt to its feet spontaneously at the end of the show, screaming with the actors, "Strike! Strike!" Clurman called it youth finding its voice: "the birth cry of the thirties."

I thought of the passionate young singers who were becoming the voice of the sixties, many inspired by the Weavers: Bob Dylan, Joan Baez, and Peter, Paul and Mary. But what was happening to us? Where was our passion? I thought of our fervent years: the joyful noise of the Wallace campaign, the fiery 1948 Thanksgiving hootenanny that gave birth to the Weavers, and the triumphant Carnegie Hall reunion at the height of McCarthyism, only a few years previous. To our audience, we were the embodiment of courageous social action, but I knew we were running on icon-energy, being honored for having stood our ground in the past, not for what we were doing now. We sang our concerts, received our accolades, and went home to our completely separate lives. My own personal activism had been limited to safe street demonstrations. I even gave up tracking the momentous Civil Rights Movement on TV. As a single mom, getting jailed was out of the question. Lee Hays accused me of being "practically unpatriotic." In reality, watching and having no part in the events that were shaping our nation made me feel useless and envious.

In that sunny summer of 1960, when the Lake Michigan sojourn was over and I'd sent Lisa off to her annual visit with her father, I joined my singing partners for our stint at the Newport Folk Festival. The seeds of theater were germinating inside of me, and when we were preparing our next concert series, I thought of a bit of onstage fun we might try. We were working on a set of wonderful old shape note hymns. Lee Hays had told us that in some Southern churches, singers sat facing each other while performing them.

"Let's try that," I proposed. Nervously, my partners humored me, and we sat on chairs and sang to each other. I was quite happy with the result, but there was no interest in continuing.

Lee: "It's very uncomfortable ..."

Fred: "It feels so unnatural ... "

I came across the gospel ditty "S-A-V-E-D" and sang it in the style of a Salvation Army lassie. Lee worriedly showed me a letter from a fan rebuking us for our impropriety toward Christians. Clearly, I had to look elsewhere for theatrical stimulation.

Actually, the Weavers were already winding down, although we didn't know it yet. In 1961, Erik Darling left us, taking with him the creative excitement that had kept my enthusiasm going since Pete's departure. Fred and Lee and I kept working together for another two years, with the help of first one tenor and banjo player, Frank Hamilton, and then another tenor, Bernie Krause. Lee Hays, always problematic, became more demanding and less reliable until Fred, ever short on patience, finally threw in the towel. The Weavers disbanded following a 1963 Carnegie Hall concert, with all three tenors participating, all seven Weavers onstage together. And I started a new career as a solo singer, managed by Harold Leventhal.

LSD

I might have been feeling the Weavers' vitality draining away, or it might have been the condition of the world, or the onset of early menopause, but whatever the cause, in the summer of 1962, I fell into a despair I couldn't shake off. When I finally pulled myself up and into the shower after three days of weeping, I knew I'd better ask for some help. I thought about calling a psychoanalyst, but the prospect of hours of unilateral Freudian analysis was just too … well, depressing. One of Ann's friends, whom I was somewhat acquainted with, was being treated for her debilitating depression with a new form of psychotherapy, and she was apparently doing well. Her psychiatrist had given her a substance called lysergic acid diethylamide, or LSD-25, during their sessions. I made an appointment for a consultation. Dr. James Watt's office, on the ground floor of an upscale East Side brownstone, was plushly carpeted and dimly lit, and it held a big desk, the inevitable couch, and, I was interested to note, a serious record player. The toilet in the waiting room was filled with ornate furniture meant to coyly hide its function. I told myself it was silly to be annoyed with the decor.

An attractive man around my age, Dr. Watt explained that LSD therapy was quite experimental and, although it was having interesting results, people were affected in different ways; it may not be for everyone. I said I was willing to try, and we made a date for a trial session. It would take most of the day, he said, and he would be with me throughout, but I needed to arrange to be picked up at five by someone who could stay the night with me.

A week later, Jim Watt gave me two tiny white pills and put a record on the player. I lay on the couch feeling silly. Nothing was happening. But yes, there was music playing, and I saw it vividly—as long satin ribbons, pale lavender and yellow swirling skirts, and festoons of bright brass buttons on vivid red jackets. A nineteenth-century military dance? Then, ominous chords sounded and a huge, gray shadow swooped down, hovering over the celebration. "Oh," I thought. "It must be a fairy tale."

"What is this music?" I whispered.

"Sibelius," Jim answered.

The dark chords resonated once more, and again came the gray shadow.

"Duck!" I giggled. "Here it comes again!" Tears of laughter ran into my ears, while another part of my mind thought, "What a marvelous colorist Sibelius was—maybe a little obvious, but brilliant." Meanwhile, the music kept me sailing on "as with a fair wind on a limitless sea of sound." Where did I find that phrase? Did I read it somewhere?

The music plummeted, and then swept upward into a tower, throbbing at the very peak. I was awestruck! Oh, he was a genius!

"Sibelius was an unappreciated genius," I whispered, but then Jim told me that we were listening to a Brahms symphony!

The music took me to where clamor reigns—ambition, hunger for approval—but then humbleness flooded through me, and I was filled with a feeling of grace. "Can I begin to work from here, free from crippling self-criticism?" I wondered. It was a goal writ large. Writ? Where did that word come from? "A writ of *habeas corpus?*"

"What is '*habeas corpus*'?" I asked Jim.

"I don't know. What do you think?" he countered. I didn't respond.

Hell, I knew what *habeas corpus* was: "produce the body." There had to be a body. "Uh-oh," I thought. "I'm not ready to get into that subject with him."

I watched myself in a soft grey gown descending a circular staircase into the soft purple light of an underground cavern, a sepulcher. I was not afraid in there.

On a gray day, Jim and I set out for a walk as part of a session. An unpleasant sound rumbled in the street—a huge generator at a construction site for a new high-rise building. I was about to whine that we definitely should have walked toward Central Park instead, but then I looked up to see iron red girders against the dark gray sky, bright yellow shiny dots moving along them. It was like a construction work ballet on a giant Mondrian painting! My eye was drawn to a lone man in a yellow slicker on the highest girder. He was carefully settling a huge cauldron onto a lift in front of him. He watched it descend and then clasped victory hands over his head, swiveling his hips left, right, and around. What a trip! Doing the twist in the rain at the top of the world! I felt so happy for him. The generator roared on, a miracle of human ingenuity.

· · ·

Lisa, not yet ten years old, was curious about my going to the doctor for a few hours now and then. "I'm not sick, don't worry. It's a different kind of doctor," I reassured her.

"Doesn't he listen to your heart and bang your knees and take x-rays and all that?"

"No; he teaches me to remember how to have fun."

I once had our housekeeper, Amy Banks, pick me up after a session. I oohed and aahed over a sprinkling of tiny white flowers at the edge of a path. "They're weeds," she said, puzzled. I felt so grateful to Amy for her kindness and the safe, pleasant nest she maintained for my little girl and me. But I began to feel a bit anxious, wondering: Am I extra high today? Will it scare Lisa?

Something was troubling Lisa—schoolwork. She had a math assignment and had been quizzing herself with arithmetic cards.

"It's no use," she whispered. "I'm no good at math. I'll never get it. The test is tomorrow and I'm going to fail." Hopeless tears.

I pulled out a packet of the cinnamon Red Hots I sometimes carried in my purse. "Let's practice one more time. Here's the rule," I told her. "Right answer, you get a Red Hot. Wrong answer, you get two."

"Mommy, you're silly," she sniffled. So we had a dopey, comfortable hour together, and my wonderful little dame of a daughter, minus her heavy anxiety, did fine the next day, of course.

It was a little personal miracle, like the day Lisa and I, back from chasing around Central Park, were drawing trees with charcoal. Lisa had just pulverized her second stick of charcoal when we heard a crash from the kitchen, followed by Amy sobbing. I managed to calm and congratulate poor Amy for her accomplishment: breaking the little cast iron casserole pot! Lisa said, "I don't know what's happening around here, Mommy. I get chalk all over the rug, you laugh. Amy breaks something, you laugh. I think that course about fun is a good course."

FIVE

Moving On

Sam Brown, my new guitarist, had a head full of music, pot, and resentment. We all smoked too much in the sixties—both tobacco and marijuana—but Sam would start the day with inflamed eyes and manage to keep them that unmistakable shade of "grass red" all day. He was my first accompanist after the Weavers disbanded in December of 1963. I'd been audition-ing young acoustic guitarists who didn't know much more than folk material and folk styles. But there was no way I could carry the Weavers' folk banner alone. I had to explore new musical ground and build my own solo repertoire. Sam, who could play anything, came to me after working for Miriam Makeba, the great Xhosa singer from South Africa.

We had been working companionably for a couple of weeks when I asked during a break one day, "So, Sam, how come you left Miriam?" He stared at me silently for a moment and then began to adjust his tuning. "Traveling," he muttered finally, "too much traveling." It was clear my question upset him, and I regretted having brought up the subject, even though I wondered what the "traveling" problem would mean for us. "I'm sorry," I said. "Didn't mean to make you uncomfortable." He was frowning. "Hey, it's none of my business, right?" I added. He shrugged. Wrong! It was most definitely my business, and I should have called Ms. Makeba to ask her about it, but I didn't. Months later, I learned that Sam had failed to show up for a concert performance at least once. For a professional, once is far too many times. So why didn't I do the research? Why didn't I take full charge of my own interests? "Don't be pushy," I told myself. On the other hand, if I had been more cautious, I would probably have missed out on some fine music making.

Sam's personality matched his playing. He was sharp, thoughtful, and delicate one moment, turbulent the next. Although in his early thirties, he reminded me greatly of a boy I loved when I was a teenager. Jerry Meltzer, or "Whitey," as he was called, played piano at Camp Wo-Chi-Ca and violin in the high school orchestra. On our one wonderful New Year's Eve date, we went to see Judy Garland and Mickey Rooney in *Babes in Arms*. Wartime it was. Whitey went right from high school into the Air Force and died in a bombing raid over Germany. Sam's hair was darker than Whitey's, but he had the same cowlick flopping over one eye and the same quick energy. Still grim from my question about his history with Miriam, Sam ran a few riffs on his guitar. Then, to my great relief, his tight face cracked itself into a wide, boyish grin, and he asked brightly, "Hey, Ron, have you got some grass? I'm out." And we toked away the afternoon. Or maybe it was just an hour. Who knew?

We developed an attractive set of songs, and my manager Harold Leventhal cut a deal with Mercury Records for me to do an album and hired two other fine musicians, Lou Misciagna and Bill Lee. Bill, Spike Lee's dad, had played stand-up bass on most of the Weavers' Vanguard recording dates and on my Vanguard single. Lou, dignified and handsome, played rhythm guitar. Lou was a fine player, but the memory I keep most fondly is his response to some know-it-all who confided a secret about a fellow musician: "He's Mafia, you know." "Wow," said Lou, deadpan. "You see that in the Yellow Pages?"

The living room of my eighth floor apartment in an old high rise on West Ninety-Sixth Street was our rehearsal hall. Ninety-Sixth Street, a pleasantly wide thoroughfare coming off of Central Park, was irresistible to double-parkers, who daily made sociopaths out of law-abiding citizens. Unable to move their vehicles, victims used their car horns like Uzis, spraying the street with murderous blasts that destroyed every vestige of peace and quiet in the neighborhood. It was not an optimal condition for rehearsals, but the location was convenient, and the price was right.

On the morning of the day of our first rehearsal together, I was in a stew. How should I—Ronnie Gilbert, solo recording artist, in charge of my own professional life—act, when for fifteen years I'd been "the girl" in the Weavers? This was the mid-sixties in New York City. Women were burning their bras, demanding equality, and learning to take themselves seriously. How would I lead the group? Would I lead? Wasn't Sam the musical director?

"Anyone for coffee?" I bubbled when all were present. Three hands went up, and I, choosing the good homemaker role, dashed out, leaving the guys to get acquainted on their own. Bouncing back into the room with the already-prepared tray of coffee and accouterments, I plugged in the coffee pot. "Help yourselves when you're ready," I said, hoping for a casual, offhand effect. I was a woman with thirty-eight years of worldly experience, and it was like I was playing a nervous bride hosting her first guests on some stupid sitcom. Except for tuning, no one was talking to anyone else. Bill was clearly bored, playing scales on the bass. "The men are doing their musician thing," I thought. "Just shut up and wait." So I followed the tuning with an air of alert, intelligent attention.

SAM: "Uh-uh, that one … "
LOU: "This one?"
SAM: "No, the other one. Yeah, that one. No, down."
LOU: "Down?"
SAM: "Yeah, down. Better."

Suddenly, just as I was about to ask Sam what he wanted to do first, an agonized shriek from the street split the air, followed by three quick blasts from a car horn. Lou and Bill quickly laid down their instruments and ran to the window, wondering if there had been an accident. Sam and I stayed put. We knew what was going on. Three more blasts, deliberate and menacing. Then the driver leaned on his horn and didn't let up. The noise was horrendous, sucking the air from the room. When he had seen that it was just an incensed driver trapped by a double-parked car, Lou cupped his hands to his lips and yelled, "B-flat, I think." Bill cracked a grin. "Nah," Sam screamed back, "B-natural."

Everyone broke up. Bill played at improvising around the pitch of the car horn. We could barely hear the strings, but it was hilarious. We choked with laughter; tears rolled down my face. When it seemed there would never be an end to it, I began to experiment with vocal tones, holding the major second against the ongoing blast, then the fifth and the sixth. I made a little tune and played around with it. By the time the horn stopped, the musicians had fallen in behind me. We were jamming. The group worked well together.

Sam and I became friends. We would linger after rehearsals, smoke a joint, and talk about music and our families: his wife, who was "a terrific singer"; his musician father, who criticized his playing; my daughter, age ten, who was visiting her father in California. Having a work partner who was also a pal was a new thing for me, and it felt really good. The Weavers hadn't buddied with each other. Pete would go home to his life up in Beacon, to Toshi and their kids and their cabin; Lee had his friends at home in Brooklyn Heights, his typewriter, and his beer; Fred was usually busy being some sort of "man about town"; and I had been Marty Weg's faithful wife. It had been a "work only" pattern, at least for me.

When Sam would leave, we'd typically wind up our conversation standing in the open doorway waiting for the elevator, Sam resting his hand lightly on my shoulder. One evening, that hand slid up and down my arm and around to my back, which he stroked with his fingers. I looked at him, surprised, and wondered if it was "brotherly" affection or seduction? I decided it was brotherly and kissed him lightly on the cheek, "sister" fashion, when the elevator arrived. But he returned the kiss on my lips.

Smiling sweetly, he pressed the lobby button—reluctantly, it seemed—and whispered goodbye in the argot of the time, "Later, man." At the next rehearsal, Sam didn't linger when work ended and followed the others into the elevator. "Okay, it was definitely brotherly," I thought. A little disappointed and quite relieved, I began dumping ashtrays and replacing chairs. Suddenly the doorbell rang. It was Sam, leaning on the doorframe with one hand and propping up his guitar case with the other. "Look, can't I stay awhile?" he asked, as if I'd told him to leave. "I've got the new Beatles. I want you to hear it. There's really something great going on there." "Sure, of course," I said. "Come in." He unlatched his guitar case in the foyer, pulled out an LP, and walked to the turntable and set it up. "I thought the Beatles were a lot of hype," he said. "Didn't you? But I don't know. You have to listen to this." I was still straightening, plumping couch pillows, aware of him walking toward me, behind me, but I jumped when I felt his hand touch the small of my back. The strains of "Michelle" oozed out of the speakers. I wanted to straighten up and turn around, but with the couch behind me, we'd be face to face: kiss or dance! I sat down quickly, my body rigid, my brain sloshing in confusion. Sam stood for a moment looking down at me, then sighed deeply and sat down next to me. He picked up my hand and looked into my eyes. Did I really want to do this? "Relax, go for it," I said to myself, and leaned toward him. But then he was whispering something, stuttering: " ... I've never ... older woman ... I'm sorry." My cheeks flamed. I stood up, fighting for balance, walked to the record player, and switched it off. Silent seconds passed.

"You'd better go," I said.

"Really?"

"Yes, really."

"Don't you want to hear the rest of the album?"

"Leave it, Sam. I'll play it later. Just go."

I followed him to the foyer. He picked up his guitar and went out the door. The elevator did its clunk and slide as it headed down from the eight floor. Slowly, I walked back to the living room and stood by the window. It was evening, and the street had settled down for the night. Cool air fanned my face, and I sat down in a chair trying Sam's comment on: "older woman," eight years his senior. It was funny, but it also hurt. The gold haze of afternoon light faded from the room. I got up, switched on the record player, and listened to the rest of the album in the dark.

There was something eerie about the Beatles' sound. It wasn't like groups whose blend was homogenized and soothing. You could hear individual voices—rough, nasal, hard—yet the blend was perfect, disturbing. And their weird, silly, oddly beautiful songs, their wry takes on love and romance and honesty, the brilliant instrumental choices—yes, it was a terrific record. I listened to *Rubber Soul* through the night until I fell asleep, knowing that I would do my part the next day and pretend nothing of consequence had happened that afternoon. That's what you did if you wanted to play with the boys.

Harold Leventhal managed my solo singing career for three years. He found exciting new instrumentalists to work with me and booked performances at venues from the familiar Bottom Line and Bitter End in Greenwich Village to Chicago's Mother Blues. Audiences appreciated my revised and new material, and I very much appreciated traveling on my own and getting to know myself as an independent performer.

Big-bellied, big-hearted Sam Hood, owner of New York's Gaslight, had opened a Coconut Grove extension of the club in Florida, the Gaslight South. His wife and partner Alix Dobkin (yes, girls, *our* Alix Dobkin of *Lavender Jane Loves Women!*) was a singer, but she wasn't your usual airy-voiced female folk singer of the sixties with long blonde ironed hair. Her flip was dark brunette, and she had a big, luscious, deep, emphatic voice. I performed at the Gaslight South along with two wonderful Western yodelers. I was thrilled when they offered to teach me their craft. I am a closet yodeler, but I have an extremely limited yodeling vocabulary despite having practiced for years alone in the car or with anyone who would put up with it. Thus, I renewed my attachment to the much-loved Westerns of my childhood in which Bob Steele made us kids gasp at his trick riding while Bob Wills, Gene Autry, Roy Rogers, and the other Sons of the Pioneers crooned and yodeled their heads off around the Universal Studios campfires: "Odl-lehi, odl-lehi-hoo!"

Spanky (McFarland) and her Gang, whom I'd met in Chicago while playing at Mother Blues, were in town, and we hung out together, getting stoned. Another time, I went sailing with Fred Neal, singer and composer of the hit song "And a Little Rain." We sailed out on the bluest water under the clearest sky, and then a small cloud came along and misted our faces and hair. Much later, when we were on a TV show together, the director spotted me tearing up a bit when Fred sang that song in his pleasantly raspy voice. The director dragged a camera over. "Can you do that again, please?" he asked. I love TV.

VISITING MY FATHER

Coconut Grove is a fairly short drive from Fort Lauderdale, where my father had been living for some time in a house I'd never seen, with a wife I'd never met. Clearly, a visit was in order. My relationship with my father had been distant—not unfriendly, but lacking in emotional content. We didn't seem to have much interest in one another; our contact seemed like a duty to civilized life. We kept in touch on the phone intermittently, telling each other briefly what was happening and responding appropriately—"that's nice" or "that's too bad"—and we saw each other once in a blue moon when he was in New York.

For many years, "home" for my father had been a neat but impersonal studio apartment in the old Carteret, a residential hotel on West Twenty-Third Street in Manhattan, across the road from the McBurney YMCA, where he took his exercise. I spent many hours myself in that landmark gym, plodding away on the treadmill and doing stretches while staring at the windows across the street, trying to remember which one was his. It was a pretty good bachelor setup he had, and he seemed quite comfortable with it, but when I visited him there a faint guilt would creep over my heart for his single state. I never imagined my father would remarry. Maybe, in spite of our flat relationship, or possibly because if it, I still carried that childhood egocentricity that doesn't let one imagine that a parent has serious life interests apart from oneself. Nor did it occur to me, since my mother had been his second wife, that Charles Gilbert was optimist enough to try a third time.

At any rate, he certainly got my attention when he announced one day, quite casually, as if it were just another "what's happening," that he was getting married and moving to Florida. I waited for the punch line. There wasn't one.

"Who's the woman, Dad?"

"A nice person."

"I'm sure she is. How long have you known her?"

"A while."

"What's her name?"

"Paula."

"Paula."

Dad wished to drop the subject; that seemed clear. Stunned, I said the requisite "that's nice," wished him luck, and that was that. Briefly, I felt some mixture of annoyance and amusement at the mystery. Then I went about my life, and he went about his, as usual.

Sometime later, maybe as much as a year, I dreamt that my father was a passenger on a train speeding along the rails, while outside the window the landscape flew by in a blur. That was it. That was the dream. The content was obvious, the tone matter-of-fact, flat. The surprise came when I woke up. My pillowcase was saturated with tears. On the phone, my father's lack of enthusiasm about his life as a Florida retiree gave me the impression that it was a punishment forced upon him by the District Attorney of Dade County. But when I finally saw him in person, he admitted that upgrading his home, building a rental unit in his backyard, and bordering his lawn with flowerbeds was actually quite enjoyable. "That's how I stay in shape," he said, flexing his muscles and positively twinkling. Certainly he looked fit, trim, and tanned, especially next to us pale New Yorkers. He spoke of visits with his friends, especially with his old boyhood pal Jack Ducoff, who lived somewhere not far off.

Jack Ducoff, or John, as my father sometimes called him, had been a police official. My father was proud that his friend was "the first Jewish captain of detectives in Hackensack, New Jersey." My mother regarded this accomplishment with much distaste. "Yes, sure," she'd scoff. "He got there by being even more vicious than the others. Ducoff likes to break 'the heads of niggers.' That's what he says. He brags about it." I'd like to think that John Ducoff only invented stuff like that to bait my serious Communist mother. But it's easy to believe that her outrage may have been justified. When I saw him in my childhood, Mr. Ducoff was a large, beefy man with thinning blonde hair, light blue rather bloodshot eyes, and a pair of full curved lips that seemed to be arranged in a perpetual sneer. The Left press couldn't have had a better physical model for their cartoons of the murderous "bull" cop. Still, he was an old man by the time of my visit, and he had been my apolitical father's good buddy when they were boys. For my father's sake, I was glad he lived close by and was prepared to be my most friendly and charming.

I had reserved a table for my father and his friends on my opening night at the Gaslight and arranged with management that I would pick up the check and so forth. But my father showed up alone. He brought no one, not even his wife. Maybe he needed to check out the scene before inviting anyone. I don't know what he thought of the show; he didn't say.

I arranged to visit him and Paula at their home on my first day off. On that day, I rented a car, bought a map, and went visiting. Fort Lauderdale, at least the part my father lived in, was a sea of small stucco bungalows, side by side for blocks and blocks, each with a postage stamp of green front yard. My father's house had a small front porch and a striped green canopy. His neatly clipped pocket-handkerchief of a lawn was bordered with small gaily colored posies. Not a blade of grass was out of place. I parked the car, walked up the path, knocked, and waited. And waited. And waited. I thought to my self, "He's very deaf. Ring the doorbell. Do you expect him to be standing there just behind the door? How silly. Ring the bell." So I rang the bell, and waited. And waited. "Do I have the wrong day?" I wondered. "Did he mean next week?" But then I heard quick footsteps inside, and the door opened.

"Paula! It is Paula, isn't it? How nice to meet you at last, Paula!"

She seemed, well, flustered.

"Oh, Irene—I mean Ronnie. Charles! Come in, come in. Please sit down. Charles! Would you like some lemonade? I have lemonade, fresh made. Charlie! Come into the parlor, Irene— *tsk*—I mean Ronnie."

She turned from me, leading the way a few steps into a tiny pleasantly dark and cool living room. I was still a bit blind from the harsh light outside, but I could see my father in silhouette, slowly get up from an armchair with a newspaper in his hand. A memory of one of his reprimands lashed out at me: "Why can't you fold up the newspaper in order when you finish with it!" followed by the slap of the newspaper against the table. That day, as in the past, he took care of his paper, slowly folding and refolding it. At last, he moved toward me, meeting me in the middle of the room, his greeting calm and dignified. Apparently, it was the right day; Paula's bustling confirmed it. She was as mercurial as he was deliberate. My mind cranked out captions: Decades his junior! Not Jewish! Heavy German accent! Mystery solved! Meanwhile, I dialed up my smile to the max, trying to say with my face: I'm happy for my father that you are taking care of him, and don't worry, I accept it all. "Well," I thought to myself, "maybe not the German part—Hitler Youth? Stop. Get used to it."

"Make yourself comfortable, Ronnie. Lunch will be ready in a few minutes. Here, take this chair. It's the best. You sure you don't want any lemonade? I just fixed it. Fresh. What about you, Charles?"

"What are you talking so loud for? She's not deaf!" he barked.

I oohed and aahed about the food. It was meticulously prepared and served, every leaf of lettuce carefully positioned. But my father complained about everything, and Paula kept hopping. I felt the scampering of little rat feet behind my eyes; a headache was gathering.

"So, Dad, how is John Ducoff? Don't you want to bring him to see my show?"

"He's not very well."

"Oh, I'm sorry. How about you, Paula? Wouldn't you like to come to the club? It's a nice place. Do you like folk music?"

"Well, we don't go out so much at night. Your father likes to watch the TV."

Yes. It was going to be a big one, that headache. We sunned ourselves in the backyard, pretending to be drowsy from the sun and therefore speaking little. The quiet was pierced now and then by an order or a complaint barked at Paula by my father, until finally, my head pounding, I leaned over and said to him, "If you scream at her one more time, I'm leaving." He cupped his ear, "What? What did you say, Ronnie?" I gave it another hour then took my leave.

"Must you go? You only just got here," Paula said.

"Yes, I really want to beat the traffic. It was lovely to meet you, Paula. Your house is so pleasant."

"Why don't you stay overnight with us? We have room."

"Don't nag her," my father snapped. "She said she has to leave." And I did.

SIX

Theater

THE OPEN THEATRE

I was still making a living as a singer, but my interest in theater had been kindled by my summer with Ann Shepherd in Indiana. At her urging, I registered for study with two respected New York theater teachers: scene work with Uta Hagen and acting classes with Ann's mentor, Stella Adler, doyen of the Group Theatre. Miss Adler's version of the celebrated "Method" was an effective approach to actor training. She had been taught by its inventor, the Russian actor and director Constantin Stanislavski. As for Miss Hagen, I'd seen her play Desdemona to Paul Robeson's Othello when I was eighteen. She was earthy, witty, and no Stanislavskian, and she taught by her own masterful training system. I was eager to meet her and work with her.

I might have guessed that the two drama divas would be complete opposites in temperament and style. One day, regal Miss Adler interrupted a classroom lecture to shoot at me, "You are studying with Uta Hagen, Miss Gilbert? Do you find my

studio does not provide you with all you need?" Without waiting for a reply, she went on with her lecture. I wondered what
ambitious little snitch found it useful to reveal my business
to her.

Theater critic Gordon Rogoff and playwright Peter Shaffer
were our downstairs neighbors on Ninety-Sixth Street. Gordon
knew both women. I laughed ruefully when he asked how my
classes were going. "Miss Adler no longer acknowledges me in
class," I admitted. "Maybe she's right. Maybe I shouldn't be trying to dance to two different theatrical beats." "You know, there's
a third," Gordon said. "Come downtown with me some time and
have a look." He was involved with an experimental workshop
called the Open Theatre. Some weeks later, we climbed two
flights of stairs on West Twenty-Fourth Street to a dingy loft to
watch a demonstration. Fifteen people in workout clothes were
chatting quietly or doing stretches. A man and a woman standing
to the side waved to Gordon. He stopped to exchange a few words
and introduce me to them—Megan Terry and Peter Feldman.
"This work might not interest you," Gordon whispered as we settled ourselves on a rickety riser. "We won't be here for their
whole rehearsal, only some of their exercises, maybe an hour."
That was fine with me. I could tolerate anything for an hour.

The group came together in a silent circle. Seconds passed.
We waited. Faint noises floated up from the street. I saw that the
people in the circle had their eyes closed. Nothing was happening. "If this is about 'experiencing the occult,'" I thought, "it definitely is not my cup of tea." I was about to tease Gordon, who
was a rational type. I glanced at him. His eyes were closed, too.

I hadn't noticed, but the people in the circle were actually
making a sound, so quietly and with such control that I'd missed
the start. Slowly, the hum was gathering intensity to become a

vocalized unison. From there, it moved up and down in pitch and volume, gradually becoming a diatonic chord, rose to a crescendo, filled the high-ceilinged space, then descended gradually into consensus, and finally into a communal exhale of breath. The staggered breathing had been perfect; there had been no break in sound. There had been no evident conductor. Another exercise consisted of sculpting imaginary shapes from air and then tossing, catching, and transforming them and passing them around the circle. It seemed like fun, although I wasn't sure to what end. Improvisations were next. Characters and situations kept changing. They weren't easy to follow, but I was moved by the focus of the actors as they picked up each other's ideas and jammed on them, or changed them, tossing them back and forth, like a good jazz band at work. The exercise was called Transformations.

"I liked watching them, Gordon," I said when we had coffee later. "But what's it for? Is there a play in it somewhere?" "Sure. But not plays like the scene work you've been doing. Megan has written a one-act based entirely on Transformations, and the workshop is helping her develop a musical play about the war." Actually, Open Theatre pieces were already being shown in off-beat locations for Village cognoscenti. Stirred by the ensemble playing and curious to watch how it developed, I returned several times at the invitation of Peter and a quietly charismatic man, Joe Chaikin, who turned out to be the philosophical spur to the workshop. Joe would suggest an inquiry and an exercise through which the actors could improvise. Once he had outlined the idea to be explored and the set up, there wasn't much discussion. The improvisations were physical, with only as much language as was necessary to the invention. I began to audit the workshops, looking forward to them between my singing rehearsals and tours.

The actors' intensity, sensitivity to each other's ideas, and the serious playfulness of the improvisations kept bringing me back. And I was also enthralled by the subject matter: identifying what was camouflaged in life and making it physically, theatrically visible. I was reminded of Lee Hays's stories.

Ann Shepherd came with me once to watch an Open Theatre workshop. She found it both fascinating and disturbing, and she asked the same questions I had put to Gordon: How do these explorations result in theater sharable with an audience? And how does "truthful acting"—which was the goal, after all, of the Method—figure into it? Eventually, I came to the conclusion that the Open Theatre and the Method were at cross-purposes. The Method was concerned with "me," while the work of the Open Theatre explored "we." This is how Joe described the Open Theatre's improvisational work: "The goal is empathy with others, support for others' initiated action, sharing of attention, not competition for it. There comes a point where you no longer know exactly which actor is in support and which actor initiated the action; they are simply together."

At this point, in 1965, I was singing on my own, accompanied by brilliant guitarist Stuart Scharf. Joe Chaikin asked if we would perform for a benefit at a West Village theater. We agreed. Stuart preceded me to his seat as we walked onstage. When I reached the microphone, a huge, ornate chair suddenly appeared behind me, shoved onstage by someone in the wing. Stuart had already begun the song's introduction. There seemed to be nothing to do but sit down on the "throne" and sing. As I did, several people slowly crawled onstage from the wings and sat quietly at my feet, an amusing, if somewhat embarrassing, tribute. A week later, Joe Chaikin invited me to join the group, and I happily accepted. My first participation was a scene from

Megan Terry's antiwar musical, *Viet Rock,* performed outdoors on a walkway in Central Park. I participated in Open Theatre workshops whenever I was in town. I gave up on the Stella Adler Studio after the first year, but continued Uta Hagen's energizing scene work classes.

One day, Harold Leventhal told me, quietly but seriously, "Ronnie, you need to stop playing around with the theater stuff and pay attention to your music." As my manager, Harold had been doing his best to help me build my solo singing career—and lately he was doing it without much help from myself. My creative energy had been completely diverted. Of course he was right. Where was my personal drive to succeed as a singer? I would have to shape up. There was no money in Open Theatre. On the contrary, everyone chipped in to rent the workspace and lived on intermittent unemployment insurance. But it felt like the most important thing I'd lent my brain to since the start of the Weavers.

By 1966, the club scene was changing. The big news was rock shows and go-go clubs featuring topless dancers in cages. Coffee houses and clubs like San Francisco's Hungry-I and Purple Onion, Chicago's Gate of Horn and Mother Blues, and New York's Gaslight and Bitter End, which had made the reputations of artists like Odetta, Joan Baez, Phil Ochs, and Bob Dylan, were folding, trying new policies, or just barely hanging on, their audiences reduced to true believers. Harold could not find me work.

AMERICA HURRAH, 1966

Meanwhile, Joe Chaikin's friend Jean-Claude van Itallie had written a trilogy constructed on Open Theatre work, *America*

Hurrah. It was to be given an independent commercial production, a first for the Open Theatre. I was offered a part. It meant tiny wages for rehearsal time and probably a few performances. It was an obscure play by an unknown playwright at the tiny Pocket Theatre on Second Avenue (which had formerly been a male burlesque house), way off even the off-off Broadway track.

Joe directed the first part, "Interview," which began as a caricature on applying for unemployment insurance. Without set pieces or narrative, we actors transformed the stage space (and ourselves) into other, painfully absurd slices of life in America. "TV" was the second piece—a comedy with an undercurrent of farcical horror. The third, "Motel," was a surreal affair played by three actors hidden in grotesque dolls. We opened on November 6, 1966, and the producer Stephanie Sills posted the notice of closing within a week, since there had been no ticket sales to speak of. Walter Kerr, however, the super-influential drama critic of the *New York Times,* had been present at the opening, and wrote a long, thoughtful review advising readers not to miss "the whisper in the wind" at the Pocket Theatre. The next morning, Stephanie took down the closing notice. Within days, the major magazines weighed in with kudos. *Time Magazine* called the play an "off-Broadway trip through an air-conditioned blightmare towards an icy emptiness at the core of American life, the land of the Deepfreeze and the home of the rave, of the neon smile and the plastic heart." *Newsweek* agreed, declaring it "a compelling image of American violence all right, but on a much deeper level—it is an extension of our powers of envisaging ourselves."

America Hurrah galvanized the theater of the sixties just as Group Theatre's *Waiting for Lefty* had in the thirties. It ran in New York for two years, and a concurrent performance with the original cast played for a month at the Royal Court Theatre in London. It was a hit, and I quit singing.

LONDON, 1967

In the United Kingdom, Jean-Claude's play did not find favor with the Lord High Censor, who threatened the Royal Court Theatre with a ban. It bypassed the ruling by registering itself as a private club, and we played for four weeks to packed houses. *The Times* opined that *America Hurrah* was "the finest product of the American theatre since *West Side Story*." A larger West End theater offered to extend the run, but the Censor promised to close the theater. Outraged luminaries of the London stage failed to change his mind.

In London, I was delegated to find accommodations for the cast plus Lisa, now thirteen, who would join us when school was over. I found a generous Pembridge Square flat that was perfect for our needs. The moment I entered it I had a powerful sensation of familiarity. The bookshelves were filled with beautifully bound collections of English folk songs. It was odd that in all of London I should have stumbled on this place. The owner, Mary Ashbee Ames-Lewis, was a daughter of C. R. Ashbee, founder of the English Arts and Crafts Movement and devotee of the socialist designer William Morris. Mary's sister Felicity Ashbee, an artist and theater buff, and I became longtime friends and correspondents.

Just before we finished out the month at the Court, I was handed an invitation: "Please meet Harold Pinter and Robert Shaw at the American Bar at the Ritz." Until then, I had thought "meet me at the Ritz" was a joke from an old movie. Pinter and Shaw were considering me for a role in the Broadway run of

Shaw's hit London play, *The Man in the Glass Booth.* I would play an Israeli secret service agent, who arrests and prosecutes a character inspired by Adolph Eichmann, to be played by the marvelous Donald Pleasence. Pinter would direct the production. Would I be available? I was almost too breathless to say, "yes, thank you, I would be available."

I should have headed home to New York at the end of the month and rejoined the Open Theatre Workshop, but the offer of a small part in *The Loves of Isadora,* a Karel Reisz film about the life of the American dancer Isadora Duncan, starring Vanessa Redgrave, deterred me. I was sent to the giant costume warehouse Angels of London to be fitted with gorgeous beaded silks and a sable-lined cloak for my role as a wealthy, gushing fan. I remembered my mother raving to me about seeing Duncan dance. Not a knowing critic of dance, my mother might have been a trifle influenced by the dancer's outspoken support of the Bolshevik Russian Revolution.

The movie was filmed in Opatija, Croatia, which stood in for Nice of the 1920s, the locale of Isadora's final years and her death. Opatija was everything magnificent a coastal town on the Adriatic could be. I had an immense room in a gorgeous hotel with a huge swimming pool overlooking the sea. I had five days to wander around the rocky fishing villages and wonder at the silent, black-gowned peasant women in the town square, endlessly crocheting tablecloths for tourists. I made a trip to Trieste, and I became friends with the friendly, lively women working costumes, Ruth Meyer and Jane Cowood.

One day, while another cast member and I were sunning and chatting, we watched Vanessa, on the opposite side of the vast pool, being interviewed by a small, thin-haired man in a black suit and tie, doubtless a journalist. They sat side by side on a canopied couch partially shielded from the sun. Vanessa posed in upright elegance in a silk blouse, short suede skirt, and leather boots that reached almost to the knee. Now and then, she would glance across at us. We watched awhile and then went back to our conversation. After a time, they were still there, only now the man, from his gestures and the tilt of his head, was impressing something truly urgent upon her. A polite little nod of her head toward the man told us clearly, "I cannot endure this for another minute," but she did, for several more. At last, tall Vanessa and the small man stood and formally shook hands. Vanessa watched him walk into the hotel. Then she walked straight into the pool, boots, leather skirt, and all.

To celebrate her birthday and that of the actor playing her lover (who was actually a Serbian rock star), Vanessa gave the company a taste of twenty-four-carat decadence one night in a palatial villa of the Hapsburg era. There was food and alcohol to the max. Three eviscerated little piglets hugging telephone-pole length spits were hand-turned over a gigantic barbecue pit. Two different bands played dance music all night, and there was also an ensemble of gypsies for the occasional interval. I danced so hard I could hardly walk the next morning. A few days later, director Karel Reisz was ready to film my two little scenes. It had been an utterly magical week. The shooting took less than an hour.

When I returned to New York, I went back to acting in *America Hurrah* at the Pocket, but—blow to the heart—I had lost my place in the ongoing Open Theatre Workshop! Open Theatre's internal workings had been unsettled since the start of business around the commercial production of *America Hurrah.* Joe would soon take over and move the organization to its true creative heights with an extraordinary piece of theater called *The Serpent,* developed from a script by Jean-Claude van Itallie that was inspired in part by the Book of Genesis. At that moment, however, the Open Theatre was operating under democratic collective rule, and the collective was collectively unhappy with me.

Over a sad lunch, Joe, apologetic, explained that the main issue was the potential disruption of the group by members who were likely to be tagged for outside work. Members had to commit to four days a week and no absence for more than two weeks. Angry and hurt at not even having been offered a choice, I kept my distance from the Open Theatre for some time. *The Serpent*, a kind of ceremony exploring biblical myth and the rituals of present-day life, had been to Europe and back before I went to watch it. It justifiably made Open Theatre's name. However, their next project, *Terminal*, Open Theatre's meditation on mortality, written with playwright Susan Yankowitz, truly grabbed at my soul.

Joe Chaikin had barely survived a severely damaged heart in childhood and had been living with a rotten prognosis ever since. In *Terminal*, he and the group translated his matter-of-fact familiarity with mortality into a haunting, humorous, shattering take on death and dying. "You're in love with Joe Chaikin," laughed Marcia Jean Kurtz, an ex-Open Theatre actor, watching me watch the play. I was annoyed, but on some level, I knew she was right. It was a decade, though, before Joe and I would work together again.

In March 1968, I left *America Hurrah*. I was offered the part of Miss Furnival in Peter Shaffer's *Black Comedy* and the part of the Countess in *The White Lies*, its companion piece, which would run at a New Jersey regional theater. *Black Comedy* is a hilarious play, built on a clever conceit: a fuse blows just as an important dinner is about to commence, and the whole action is played as if in the dark. I had a very good time playing Miss Furnival and earned praise from Peter Bull, the one real Englishman in the cast. "How did you come by the authenticity of your accent and phrasing?" he asked, after offering one small correction. "Mostly from TV," I confessed, citing my addiction to *Upstairs, Downstairs*. Alas, Peter Shaffer wasn't thrilled with my countess in *White Lies*. "I didn't realize she was so middle-class," he said politely. Ah well …

Then Joe Chaikin phoned. One of his friends, director Peter Brook of the Royal Shakespeare Company, had a grant to create what would be called the International Centre for Theatre Research in Paris. Brook was assembling an international company of actors to test the project for several weeks that summer, under the auspices of the French Ministry of Culture. Would I like to go as part of the American contingent? Why, yes Joe, I would, thank you very much. Peter Brook! I had seen three of his astonishing stagings, and each had set my heart hammering: the terrifying *Marat/Sade,* his breathlessly sensual and magical *A Midsummer Night's Dream,* and *US,* his courageous challenge to apathy over the Vietnam War. At that time, Lisa was a freshman at Performing Arts High School in New York, and she had two weeks until the semester ended and she would join her father for their summer visit. I arranged for a couple of women members of the Mormon Tabernacle Choir on tour in New York to sublet our apartment and co-parent along with Gordon and Peter, our willing friends downstairs. Lisa was game. So I headed for Paris.

I ascended the Metro stairs up to the Boulevard Saint-Michel and received my first vivid impression of Paris—tear gas! In May 1968, escalating battles between police and student activists against reactionary education and the Vietnam War were threatening to bring down the de Gaulle government. Universities were shutting down. The night before I arrived, riot police had attacked Sorbonne students with tear gas and truncheons. The demonstrators fought their way onto the streets, joined by students and faculty from surrounding schools and patrons from the cafes in the area. The battle had abated somewhat during the night, but in the morning, as I made my way to our group's meeting place, the taxi's radio broadcast a resumption of the conflict. At street-side cafes, customers conversed over drinks while at the not-so-distant end of the Boulevard a reporter shouted to make himself heard over the smashing of stones and the explosion of tear gas canisters. It is one of the more surreal memories I have of my time in Paris.

French, English, and American actors and one Japanese gathered on the vast second floor of the Mobilier National, a government building lent to Brook's project by the Ministry of Culture. After explaining to us the virtue of the open, centerless space, Brook wasted little time on formalities. By way of introduction, he put us to rolling on the floor together as "aspects of fire, air, or water," startling one or two of the more formally trained French actors. For a text, we began to explore Shakespeare's *The Tempest,* digging for the significance of the fierce storm that opens the play, while outside on the street another gale howled.

That night, groups of militant anarchist students climbed over the roof of the state-run Odéon theater and turned it into strike headquarters. With several other actors, I went there to watch one of the strike committee's open meetings, an exercise in frustration for me since I had long forgotten my college French. The occupation of the Odéon upped the political ante considerably, and demonstrations proliferated throughout the area. The French actors convinced the strike committee of the "revolutionary" nature of the International Centre for Theatre Research, and we were assured that the project would not be interfered with. I so wish I had been present and articulate at that conversation.

Research continued at the Mobilier, the French and English actors working to surrender their intellects to the wisdom of their bodies, and we Americans trying to sharpen our intellects. Peter, ever gentle, suggested that American actors tend to "choke themselves off with insistence on total emotional involvement, as if that were the end in itself." Joe Chaikin said something similar in his book *The Presence of the Actor:* "An actor who is fully emotionally prepared is overwhelming his internal life.... This functions against discovery."

Brook had fifteen-foot rolling pipe scaffolding built in the Mobilier, and startling theatrical images were developing around it. I remember especially Glenda Jackson's huge, hovering bird of prey and Yoshi Oida inducing in us the gasp of "suddenly falling in love" by walking a treacherous height on a plank above our heads. Peter spoke to me about the witch, Sycorax, Caliban's mother: What if she were a live element in the play? I went to work on her, birthing Caliban and creating an amazing growl.

Outside, the ferocity of the battle in the Latin Quarter increased. On TV, the attacks against the student demonstrators played badly for the cops. Parents watching their children herded and pushed by increasingly violent police seethed with fury at the silent, intransigent de Gaulle government. After initially criticizing the students' actions, the CGT (the French General Confederation of Labor, a powerful confederation of trade unions), decided to back them, calling for a one-day general strike. The public response was massive. On Monday, May 13, 1968, a million people marched through the streets of Paris, our company among them. Prime Minister Pompidou gave a speech agreeing to the release of incarcerated students and to a discussion of their demands for educational reform. But it was too late. Spontaneous strikes were breaking out all over industrial France. Workers occupied their work places, and revolution was in the air.

Meanwhile, France waited to hear from silent President Charles de Gaulle about the political crisis. At last, he spoke on television, but by that time the burgeoning militancy among factory workers had momentum, and there were work stoppages and occupied factories throughout the country. The rumor, the French actors told us, was that de Gaulle was not actually in France but in Germany, meeting with the head of the French Army. What would that mean? The keystone topic of my life had been people's rights, and here I was, sitting smack in the eye of the hurricane, caught up in a revolution in a language I couldn't understand. I was thrilled, daunted, proud, and scared shitless all at the same time.

At 2:00 am, the police attacked the demonstrators in the Latin Quarter with a vengeance. In the morning, set designer Jean Nonot appeared at the Mobilier with his head bandaged. Observing the demonstration, he had been clubbed by a cop. He was carried to a first aid station, where he was treated by medical school students and released. He said people were throwing cloth out of their windows to help protect the demonstrators from tear gas. Hundreds of people were injured and dozens were arrested. The entire country went on strike.

Sympathetic student councils notwithstanding, the all-powerful French actors union insisted that our French actors stop work. Instead of rehearsal that morning, Brook called a meeting: "After the violence of the police attack on last night's

demonstration," he said, "the students and the government cannot simply sit down for an exchange of pleasantries about the
education system. The situation is far more widespread. The
government may fall. No one knows what is ahead, and we are in
a vulnerable position as guests of the state. We have to end the
project." What I had missed due to my insufficient French was
that, on top of everything else, Jean-Louis Barrault, our sponsor
from within the Ministry, and the Minister of Cultural Affairs,
André Malraux, were at loggerheads over Barrault's support for
the student takeover of the Odéon.

Shaken, we made preparations for departure. Eight of us were
flying Skyways to London. Peter was talking with the Royal
Shakespeare Company to see if it would pick up some of the
project's financial damage. Natasha, Peter's wife, planned to take
their children to the French countryside, but first she drove Bill,
Marsha, and me through the Saint-Germain district to the airline office to purchase our tickets. It was terrifying. Barricades
filled the streets like wild and malevolent jungle plants. Half-
round cast iron gratings had been dug out from around trees and
piled on top of upended and burned-out cars. Railings had been
removed from around the Metro station, leaving the entrance a
gaping black hole. Trucks, telephone poles, trees—anything
that could serve for protection had been pulled up or cut down.
Store windows, cracked from the police's concussion bombs,
were otherwise strangely intact—there hadn't been any looting.
The streets were quiet, except for small groups of stunned people staring at the wreckage. A large crowd had gathered on the
Boulevard Saint-Michel. There was trouble in the air, along
with lingering *gaz lacrymogène*.

We bought our Skyways tickets and took lunch in a cafe, our
eyes smarting. Finally, our friends arrived to pick us up—in a

military transport! People stared and several shook their fists at the government vehicle, the only wheels moving in Paris. We were taken to a little-used airport, an Air Force emplacement, where an unpleasantly officious woman warned us not to wander around or take pictures. But after what we'd seen, who cared about an airport?

The Japanese actor Yoshi and I were waiting together, attempting communication in English, when an Asian gentleman approached and asked us something complicated in French. I said *désolé*, letting him know that neither of us spoke adequate French. He took out an envelope from Japan Air Lines. Yoshi immediately addressed him in Japanese, but the man apparently didn't understand. He bowed and excused himself. Feeling sorry for the fellow, I asked some French speakers for help. A serious, pretty young woman and I approached the gentleman; she had trouble understanding his French. Soon, another woman and a man came over, all five of us trying to work out what this poor soul needed. Finally, someone put it together: the man expected to be lonely in London and wanted the name of my hotel! Blushing, I told him that, *désolé*, I was staying with friends. Everyone said *désolé*, and we withdrew to our seats. Just a small scene in the theater of the absurd before my Parisian adventure came to a close.

LONDON, 1968

Felicity Ashbee graciously offered to put me up until affairs were settled with the Royal Shakespeare Company. I loved her small three-story house in Notting Hill Gate, but she insisted on sleeping on a pullout couch downstairs and giving me her bed. Ruth Meyers, my costumer friend from the *Isadora* film, and her new husband, John Heilpern, offered me accommodation if I stayed on in London. It turned out that I would. The Royal Shakespeare Company would support the project if we agreed to remain for six weeks and work specifically on *The Tempest*. I would send for Lisa to come over. She had loved London when I was doing *America Hurrah*. Now, at fifteen, she could really sink her teeth into the city. Fun-loving Ruth and John played "royal guest" with me, pretending I was queen of something or other. They served me tea and toast in bed in the morning, and funny John got down on his knee in the street in front of Harrod's.

I'd been there a few days, and one morning, while I was having my lovely tea and toast in bed, Ruth went downstairs to collect the post and have a glance at the TV. Suddenly, I heard her shout: "Ronnie! Robert Kennedy has been shot!" We met at the top of the stairs and stared at each other in shock. But that wasn't all. Ruth had an envelope for me in her hand. After a moment, I glanced at it. It was from my sister. We never corresponded. I opened it. "Dear Ronnie, the terms of Daddy's will … " My father was dead! I knew that he'd suffered a heart attack while I was in Paris; Lisa had phoned me. But when I called his wife in Florida, he had recovered and was going home from the hospital. The news of my father's death and Robert Kennedy's assassination ricocheted around my mind like bullets around a room. Death and assassination! I felt faint and deranged. How could I have left my little girl alone in this terrible, perilous world? I called the Royal Shakespeare Company to reach Brook and asked if they would contact the travel agency that brought us here. Ruth and John calmed me down. They advised me not to quit the project, suggesting that I bring Lisa to London instead. Ruth, who was between jobs, would love to show her around

London. And there was my cousin Bella, who'd known Lisa at five and at thirteen, plus the rest of my mother's side of the family. I let myself be persuaded. I wrote to Lisa, telling her that my work had been extended and proposing that we bum around London together after I was finished and even go to Paris.

The company's London home was the Round House in Camden Town, an old railway system barn that had newly been converted to a theater space. Scaffolding was raised, and bleachers were built for visitors. The final weeks with Brook were exciting as he pulled together and shaped the work we'd been doing on *The Tempest.* Stage and film personalities attended rehearsals. I was thrilled when Dame Peggy Ashcroft called me over to her. She had played Desdemona in the London production of *Othello* with Paul Robeson a year or so before I saw the play in New York with Uta Hagen. Dame Peggy seemed confused at our odd *Tempest,* as did several other visitors. With a worried expression, she whispered, "My dear, aren't you afraid for your voice?" There's a film of that work, I think, in some dusty Royal Shakespeare Company archive. I have never seen it. The experience was a mixed bag for me. I couldn't wait to see my daughter, who had decided not to come to London.

When Brook bade us all goodbye at the end of the production and spoke of his hope for a permanent International Centre for Theatre Research in Paris, I asked if the present company of actors would be part of it. "Some, no doubt," he answered. I wondered boldly about myself. He assured me, "I can't imagine doing it without you." Alas, I didn't recognize that this was simply subtle English courtesy.

Imagining that Paris would possibly be in our future, I joined a French conversation class when I got home to New York, and I persuaded Lisa to take French as her language in high school.

With bourgeois bias, I assured her that it was "the language of preference for cultured people." To my shock, when Brook's permanent company was formed a year later, I discovered it could be done quite well without me. I was deeply disappointed not to continue my international cultural adventure and not to be able to afford Lisa the enrichment of the great city of Paris. "Live and learn," I told myself. Looking back on it now, I wonder if the life of a teenage émigré without a thorough knowledge of French would have been such a gift to my daughter. Tractable as she was, a quick study and open to discovery, Lisa was no longer a complaisant child.

In fact, when Lisa had turned down my plan to bring her to London, she had asked if, instead of staying in Europe, I would consider coming home to meet Jill and Becky, the new friends she'd made at Performing Arts High School, and their parents. My little girl was growing into womanhood; she had a life of her own, and she was standing up for it. I didn't end up leaving London early, but when I did get back to New York, I met Jill and Becky and their parents. Jill's Mom, Elaine, and I became friends. Unfortunately, Becky's parents were difficult. According to them, Becky was a disobedient and willful child because she insisted on wearing miniskirts, although her PhD father ("Call me Doctor, please") forbade it. "You don't know what those skirts do to men," he chastened her.

In September, work started on the Broadway production of *The Man in the Glass Booth*. I would be playing the role of Mrs. Rosen. Brook had warned me it was a one-man showcase, but I was excited to be on Broadway and directed by Harold Pinter. From day one of rehearsal, the experience was a disappointment, however, partly because of my lack of craft in conventional production and the hurry to "get it on its feet." The interesting nuances in the play had previously been explored during its run in London. Rehearsal for me was mostly a matter of Mr. Pinter blocking my onstage moves. Watching a marvelous actor at work, though, was a pleasure; Donald Pleasence in the lead role was eccentric with the dialogue, tossing meaning around like a juggler. Just as Brook had said, the play was a one-man vehicle. When Donald left and was replaced by a conventionally competent actor, Jack Warden, the Broadway experience was just a job to me.

Playing at being a Broadway actor had its smaller pleasures. Often, after curtain, I'd run around the corner to catch the last scenes of the much longer *Fiddler on the Roof,* in which my friend Rae Allen played Golde. A hamburger at Joe Allen's with colleagues sometimes capped the night, and occasionally we would have something more elegant at the Russian Tea Room, where we might share a booth with director Lindsay Anderson, whom I greatly admired for his film *If . . .,* or Harold Clurman, who often held court there. *The Man in the Glass Booth* played Broadway for nine months, and then it began a national summer tour, although it only got as far as Philadelphia, apparently for lack of money. Casting season in New York was over.

Then, of course, I did what most working actors do: I auditioned for commercials. Joe Chaikin had said, "When you take a job in the business theater, you must become the size and shape of that job." To earn the income that the business of commercials might bring, I would try to do just that. I took a class in auditioning for commercials. A note from my memory book at the time reads: "Relax, don't think. Present yourself as a winner. Sound and FEEL what they're looking for! Must get attention in first three or four lines (i.e., must touch or make laugh)."

What a joke. Ten years of marriage hadn't succeeded in making me the size and shape of a TV-style happy housewife, except perhaps for the shape of my eyebrows. Moreover, my TV dial was almost permanently set to the public TV channel due to my revulsion at being exhorted to buy, buy, buy, so how did I expect to sell floor polish? But I told myself that a good actor should be able to do anything, and I had a set of glossy photos made of myself feigning funny poses for pretend TV ads. They were good photos, and they brought me several auditions. But I was hopeless at them; I couldn't work up the appropriate seriousness. Obviously, I wasn't that good an actress.

By then, royalties from published or recorded Weavers' material were insufficient to run my household. With no other income in sight, I looked up an old friend who owned an art gallery and enquired about possible employment. She put me in touch with an ad salesman at glitzy *Connoisseur Magazine* who needed someone to take charge of his "one-girl office." It was the first nine-to-five job I had had since I was eighteen. The work was a cinch: a bit of correspondence, filing, mailing out copies of the magazine, answering the phone, and fielding my boss's unwanted calls. I also made sure he didn't burn himself up when he would fall asleep behind his desk with a lit cigarette after a liquid lunch. That was familiar, a little like good old Boro Hall Academy. My employer, who I'll call Ed Wilson, sometimes took me with him to the swank Madison Avenue and Fifty-Seventh Street art galleries to see the fine paintings, sculptures, and objects on display. Greenhorn that I was, it shocked me to see all that astronomically priced art stacked up in the gallery back rooms like so much Macy's merchandise.

Mr. Wilson—I called him Ed by then—generously let me work a short day once a week so that I could take over Joe Chaikin's spring semester acting class at the New School for Social Research (now known simply as the New School) to free Joe for other work. I approached the small class with an idea about *A Midsummer Night's Dream,* drawn from Jan Kott's provocative book *Shakespeare, Our Contemporary.* According to Kott, Peaseblossom, Cobweb, Moth, and Mustardseed (Queen Titania's "fairy train"), were known to sixteenth-century audiences as ingredients in the brews of malevolent witches and wizards. When we considered the characters in that light, the way they were generally portrayed, as conventional, pretty little winged elves, was boring. So I asked them to recreate the fairy train. The students liked the idea. Intelligent and creative, they threw themselves into explorations, and we moved happily along. I mused on the possibility of proposing a class of my own for the summer session.

And then the National Guard opened fire on a crowd of non-violent but persistent antiwar demonstrators at Kent State University, shooting four students dead and wounding several others. All over the country, students and faculty in fury and mourning called a halt to classes. I walked uptown to Carnegie Hall and listened in tears to members of the New York Symphony give a spontaneous performance of Faure's *Requiem.* Some schools stayed closed for several days, perhaps waiting for the anger to dissipate. It didn't. On the contrary, the lethal attack on those "normal, middle class" (meaning not hippie) Ohio students woke up our somnolent citizenry, and people started to pay attention to all the campuses seething over the ghastly war in Vietnam that youth were expected to fight, and to President Johnson's lies and President Nixon's "secret" bombing of Cambodia. The New School, with its large left and liberal population, did not close down. Instead, teachers and students could choose whether to continue with their classes. The spring semester was practically over. My small class was split on what to do. I gave them their grades, and we called a halt.

LISA

Lisa, who could have chosen to focus on either dance or theater at Performing Arts High School had chosen theater. Unfortunately, the brilliant professionals who had designed the program, including Sidney Lumet and Vinnie Carroll, were no longer on the faculty. A woman with scant interest or background in theater was put in charge of the department. For all the hours those young students spent in school, they should have been introduced to riches—or at least learned about *commedia dell'arte,* swordplay, and the basics of stage design. Instead, they "acted" scenes from plays, stumbling through them with little instruction in craft. Lisa had grown up witnessing far more absorbing theater.

Still, I was shocked when she announced that she wanted to drop out of school. It was the beginning of her junior year, and her friend Jill called Lisa the star of her acting class. But some of Lisa's friends were forming a student-organized "free school" that would be headed by a PhD, who would "teach the kids to teach themselves." Lisa wanted to be part of it. At first, I would not hear of it. Another sixties dropout scam, I thought, and put my foot down. But gradually, persuaded by the apparent seriousness of the teacher, the parents who had approved, and the enthusiasm of the students, I relented. Maybe it would be an improvement. In fact, it was.

Among the many area teachers and professionals that offered their services to the new "school," there was an artist and fabric designer with a weaving studio in Little Italy. Lisa and several other students learned to card and spin raw wool, dye with natural substances, and warp and weave on small handlooms that they built themselves. After a few weeks, the other students dropped out, but Lisa was hooked. A family friend, Joan Abelson, had moved to San Francisco and left her floor loom stored in New York. Lisa borrowed it and began her first full-size project. Sometimes I read to her while she wove. I'll never forget tearing up together over Thomas Hardy's description of the land at the beginning of *The Return of the Native.*

As I feared might happen, the PhD dropped out of the project several months later, leaving the young people to fend for themselves. I worried that Lisa wouldn't be able to return to a conventional high school class at that point. And how would she get into college? But my persistent daughter had grasped the teach-yourself principle. It took several years, but she eventually took the high school equivalency exam. She went on to earn a bachelor's degree in fiber arts, made her living for several years in arts administration and exhibit design, and later completed a program in landscape architecture. Maybe there were life lessons Lisa missed by not following the conventional route through school, but self-reliance and resourcefulness were not among them.

It was 1970, and for the first time in a long time I had no prospect of music or theater to engage me. I had been working at *Connoisseur* for nearly a year. My friendly boss had been hinting lately at getting friendlier, and I wasn't interested. Lisa was sixteen and wasn't in school, although she was teaching herself fiber crafts. We seemed just at the edge of the deep cultural changes going on around us but not part of them—perhaps I was too old and Lisa a bit too young. A letter came from Joan Abelson, whose loom Lisa had borrowed. She was going to Mexico for the summer. Would we be interested in subletting her San Francisco apartment? She could give Lisa some weaving lessons if we got there before she left. Far-off San Francisco was intriguing, and we needed a change. We packed up and headed west.

SEVEN

Heading West

BREAKDOWN

Joan's apartment in San Francisco was on the second floor of an old wooden house in the Haight, the same neighborhood that the anarchist theater collective the Diggers lived out their anti-ownership credo. Of their famed community free projects, a free health care clinic survives. The Haight was home base to thousands of idealistic youth who believed in the efficacy of flowers over guns, dressed themselves in romantic gypsy rags, and had flocked to the Summer of Love.

Lisa and I arrived two years too late for all that. Bad pharmaceuticals and other toxins such as the Vietnam War, the election of Nixon, the bombing of Cambodia, and, just recently, the Kent State massacre (all courtesy of the Mafia and the Government— the spoilers of innocent dreams) had wilted the children's flowers. I mourned the loss of their sweet naive vision, and cringed at seeing so many young victims in filthy finery strung out in the streets. Still, the city charmed us with its steep streets lined with architecturally amusing small houses, the blue bay below. Lisa was off and running, finding her way around town on the bus lines, exploring, and making friends. I spent the first week of the western adventure flat on my back on Joan's splintery floor, coaxing my distressed lumbar region to calm down. Eventually, I was able to tramp around and get familiar with the city, and I even went up Mount Tamalpais with a sleeping bag to camp out for a night.

Lisa was discovering her craft, although she was disappointed that Joan had reneged on the promised weaving lessons. Northern California, and certainly the San Francisco Bay Area, was a craft person's heaven in the late 1960s and early '70s. It seemed like everyone had a project: weaving, knotting elaborate macramé, carving boxes, or making furniture. A neighbor handprinted her poems on sheets of homemade paper and sewed them into chapbooks. One of my new friends, Joan Rosen, studied the art of elegant bookbinding.

We finished out the summer house-sitting in nearby Mill Valley, while Joan and Marty Rosen vacationed in Europe with their children, Derek and Marika. The Rosens left us in charge of Max, their sleepy Weimaraner, and a clutch of Derek's pet chickens. I hadn't been close to live poultry since toddlerhood, when I'd watched my mother choose a chicken from two or three squawkers in a cage at the butcher shop. The winner was quickly dispatched by the butcher, plucked clean by Mother, and ended up as our Saturday night dinner.

The rooster began to keep crowing long after dawn, and, taking my responsibility for Derek's pets seriously, I anxiously visited the library to see what information they had about roosters. All I could find said that the crow of a rooster is seldom heard in the modern chicken farm. Pat Goyan, the next-door neighbor, told me he was probably all right. I had read something about bizarre chicken behavior while I was at the library, so I took notice one afternoon that the flock was abusing one of its number. I shooed them away from her, but sure enough, the pecked hen looked sick. I took her to the vet.

"This is a very sick chicken," he said.

"Can you save her?"

"I can try."

Happily, all the animals were in good health when the Rosens returned. Derek was relieved. But after viewing the veterinarian's bill, Marty commented breathlessly, "You know, Ronnie, you can buy chicken for a dollar fifty a pound in the supermarket." I think he was joking, and in any case we remained good friends. Lisa and Pam, the teenage daughter of the Goyan family next door, struck up a good friendship. Pat and Jere Goyan went away for a week with their younger children, and they left me in charge of Pam. Neither Lisa nor Pam drove yet, and the seashore called, so one promising morning I took us to quiet, slightly out-of-the-way Muir Beach. It wasn't until we got there that it struck me that, while I prized peace and quiet, the sixteen-year-old girls might have preferred crowded Stinson Beach. However, the accident of finding ourselves on a beach that nudists also prized may have made up a little for the lack of other excitement.

With fall coming on, a return to New York was imminent. Neither of us was keen to go. We both liked San Francisco, but could I set up a home there for us? Doing what? I dreaded searching for a job in a city I knew nothing about, where I had no personal contacts. Fortuitously, my old friends the Cowans wrote to me. Ruth and artist Alec were living in Southern California's Laguna Beach and owned a small print gallery. They were planning their first trip to Europe and wondered if it would interest me to oversee their establishment while they were away?

Yes to both, I thought, but what would another temporary move mean for Lisa?

But she had her own ideas. She wanted to stay in Mill Valley and try to finish high school. Pat and Jere invited her to stay with them for the fall semester, at least until I figured out what we would do next. Maybe attending Tamalpais High with Pam would help Lisa re-adjust to conventional classes.

So I took the Cowans up on their offer. Selling art for three weeks? It might be lovely, and the experience could be something on which to start a job search. Also, a new adventure might knock out the depression that was closing in. I planned to spend a week in Los Angeles first, visiting with my mother, but I didn't stay long. I burst into tears as soon as I walked into her apartment. Mom, puzzled and worried, didn't know what to do, so she baked cookies for me. I ate them and kept crying. She baked her version of a 1–2–3–4 cake. I ate that and kept crying, so she baked more cookies. "I'd better get out of here," I told myself, and cut my visit short. I drove down to Laguna Beach in a fog.

I could see why Ruth and Alec loved the charming town of small houses and gardens tumbling rakishly along the seaside. Laguna Beach was a haven for artists and nonconformists. You could hear the Pacific from the entrance of their tiny Talisman Print Gallery, which was framed by Ruth's plantings of bougainvillea and other bright flowers. Alec's delightful prints hung on the walls and filled trays, along with a few prints from other artists. I sat waiting for customers. "If only the store weren't so far from the foot traffic along the main street," I thought. At first, a few people, having heard about Alec and Ruth's friend, the Weaver, came into the store to say hello to me. I couldn't sell them anything, thus confirming the impression I had had from my teens: I had no talent for retail sales.

The fog of depression continued to close in around me. I bought crossword puzzles and private-eye thrillers from a friend of Ruth's who owned a bookstore until she came to my rescue and introduced me to Doris Lessing's new novel, *The Golden Notebook*. From there, I read backward through the Children of Violence series. Martha Quest, the protagonist, could have been living the political, social, and sexual life hidden inside my periodic depressions. Then Jane showed me *The Primal Scream* by Arthur Janov, PhD, the inventor of a radical type of psychotherapy called primal therapy. The book discusses the cases of the first patients he treated after developing the method. I saw myself on every page and wrote to Dr. Janov.

"We all wept at your letter," came the reply. That upset me. My very personal letter to Dr. Janov was read by a "we"? He said that the Primal Institute would see me, but it wouldn't be for a year. I decided being upset over the sharing of my letter was probably neurotic egotism, and I called to say that I would come. I went back to New York to look for temporary work and wait.

When I opened the door to our apartment, unused for nearly three months, the silence felt like heavy quilts draped over the furniture. Would that feeling lift for me, alone in the house without Lisa? I couldn't see how. She would be living in Southern California with her father and stepmother once the semester in Mill Valley was over. It was going to be a long, lonely wait. I opened the windows, unpacked, and left "I'm home" messages with a couple of answering services.

My neighborhood looked odd—completely familiar but curiously one-dimensional, as if it were a painting. I felt lightheaded and ridiculously disoriented. Walking home with my groceries, I thought, "Why did I come back to New York? Why didn't I stay in California near my daughter and my mother?" I wanted to cry, but no tears came. Riding upstairs in the elevator and shifting my bag of groceries to unlock the apartment door, I felt I was repeating actions I'd already done an hour ago. When I got inside, I saw that my answering service had one message. I called it.

"Ron, you're home!" said Joe Chaikin's affectionate, cheerful voice. "Listen, Ron, I've just started developing a new piece. And what do you say; want to work on it? Then I'm shutting Open Theatre down. No more after this."

I joined the team already exploring *Mutations*. Tina Shepherd, Paul Zimet, and Joe's sister Shami welcomed me warmly. Big Ray Barry's powerful presence gentled into a marvelous sweetness as he taught me the Tai Chi moves the group had been practicing. Ellen Maddow played a tune on a pennywhistle that she was developing for an improv. Joe laid out impressions of the first week's improvisations, which he thought we should work on.

This was the theater I most deeply cared about, with people I respected and admired. It would be a good year, after all, I thought. But two weeks later, I still hadn't connected with the work. I felt separated from it by a fog resembling the thick silence of my apartment. Nothing kicked my slumbering imagination awake. A letter came from the Primal Institute; they had an opening for me at the end of the month if I wanted it. Should I leave *Mutations* and go? "Take it, Ron," Joe said.

PRIMAL THERAPY

The vast red plush lobby of the Primal Institute in Hollywood, a short walk from my motel room, reminded me of a dance hall. There was even a glass-enclosed booth. An attractive young woman came out to welcome me for my first session. Her eyes were red and her hair disheveled; obviously, she'd been crying.

"Hi, Ronnie. I'm Julie," she said.

"Are you alright?" I asked hesitantly.

"Oh yes, oh yes, I'm fine. Thanks," she answered, wiping her nose.

She led me to a door that opened onto a smaller red-carpeted room, where a stout young fellow with a high shiny forehead and thinning hair sat waiting. I noticed that the walls were padded.

"Ronnie, this is Dick. He will be your therapist," said Julie, and she left, closing the door behind her. I felt a wave of claustrophobia. With a tight little smile, Dick gestured for me to sit, or, since he was occupying the only chair in the room, to lie down on the carpet, I assumed. Dick's chubbiness was somehow reassuring, aware as I was that, from above, I probably resembled a whale beached in a red tide. The instructions had suggested we bring something that reminded us of our childhood— a picture, or a beloved stuffed animal. Never having owned a stuffed toy, I had bought a small teddy bear at the LA airport.

The first three weeks, the "intensive period," was meant to "break down into feelings." I had a head start. Saying goodbye to Joe and the Open Theatre had been a big wrench. Bidding goodbye to my daughter had been worse. And living in a crappy motel (which was all I could afford) made me feel very sorry for myself, as if I had already achieved perfect misery.

The therapy was designed to break through neurotic survival and resistance strategies that repress feelings of real pain. Twenty-four or forty-eight hours before your first session, you are told not to drink, smoke, watch TV, take mood-altering meds, masturbate, read, or talk to anyone. Primal theory hypothesizes that adult emotional misery (depression, addictions, phobias, chronic anxiety, etc.) results from repressing memories of intolerable traumatic experience in infancy and early childhood and that the path to curing neurotic pain lies in uncovering and reliving the original primal pain of those experiences. During the three-week intensive period you continue to avoid mood-pacifying behavior and see a therapist every day for an open-ended session (which usually lasts two to two and a half hours). The therapist's job is to aid you in breaking down into an undefended, infantile state. Some time in your second or third week, when the therapist thinks you are ready to primal on your own, you will join a group.

For me, it happened in the second week. During a session, after crying for days about my mother and many dumb mistakes that littered my life, I lay fingering the nap of the carpet when, suddenly, I was cradled in someone's arms, my small cheek against the rough worsted fabric of a brown suit coat, looking up into bright eyes crinkled with pleasure and a smile full of love. "Where did you go, Daddy?" I heard myself cry out, and then I sobbed like a baby, the full-throated, stomach-deep, unstoppable sobs of a tiny child. I thought I would never stop, and I didn't want to stop. But, finally, I heard Dick say gently, "How do you feel? Do you think you can get up?" To stand and answer seemed impossible, but I did, a well-behaved little girl coming shakily back into semi-adulthood. "You're ready to join the Primal Group, now," he said. I followed him to a door across the lobby.

I imagined we would sit around in a circle taking turns sharing "intensive" experiences. But as he dragged open the heavy door to a huge red-carpeted room (which had been a dance hall!) a wave of sound poured out that all but knocked me over. Bodies scattered about in fetal or early childhood positions lay howling, wailing. Upright among them, someone (I recognized Julie of the teary welcome), apparently responding to a timidly raised hand, put an ear to a patient's mouth to hear words through the cacophony. Hesitantly, I joined the bizarre picture and sobbed away with the rest. At some point, the din abating, a facilitator nearby prompted, "You can sit up now; this is the wrap up." I opened my eyes to see Dr. Janov—paterfamilias—in a chair across the room, patiently fielding comments and complaints from his weepy brood.

When the session was over, I walked back to my motel, extra careful at the huge intersection to stop at the red light and walk at the green. A cop in a yellow patrol car stared at me, so I waited for a second and then a third round of light changes before crossing. Only at the other side did it occur to me that his alert attention to a large, gray-haired, teary-eyed woman in a muu-muu hugging a teddy bear might not have been about catching a jaywalker in action.

A few months into my stay at the Los Angeles Primal Institute, several therapists left to establish therapy centers of their own. Dick, the therapist I worked with, and his colleague John went to Berkeley. They offered me the position of office manager and trainee group facilitator. I was anxious to get out of LA, and Lisa was in Berkeley. Their partnership was promising—Janov-trained therapists, each with his own quite different personal interests: Dick was a gay collector of antiques, and John was a collector of adoring young women. But it turned out that as business partners they were not such a good match. I enjoyed my work, and I enjoyed Berkeley, but after some months of evaluating applications and facilitating therapy groups, my ignorance worried me. Other than a brief experience with Freudian analysis in the early 1950s and LSD therapy in 1962, I knew little about psychotherapy. I heard that there was a professional program at Lone Mountain College in San Francisco. The instructors were all practicing psychologists in their fields. I called the director, Joel Latner.

At our first meeting, Joel assured me that I was a good candidate for the masters program in Clinical Psychology, but my only undergraduate credits were from three decades earlier: two on-and-off years of night classes in theater at New York University and a few music classes at a junior college in Los Angeles. Joel suggested I query the director of the Music Department. Maybe my life experience as a "renowned folk singer" was worth undergraduate credit. It wasn't. Lone Mountain was a religious institution. Bachelor of Arts graduates in Music would be conversant with Buxtehude, Bach, and the pipe organ, not old-time fiddle tunes. Disappointed and feeling quite chastened, I remembered my theater resume, which was laced with the names of the distinguished stage directors I'd worked with. In the Drama Department, I hit the jackpot. Although he frowned at my total lack of experience in "stagecraft," the dean qualified me as intellectually fit to enter graduate study in psychology.

I delved into the program hungrily. It called for us to become familiar with at least two major therapy theories. Jung's concept of archetypes resonated perfectly with my theatrical fascination, and Joel's *The Gestalt Therapy Book*, along with writings by Paul Goodman and others, drew me to present-centered Gestalt theory. I joined Joel's therapy workshop. I was already familiar with Freudian theory, or so I thought. In the early 1950s, legions of wise young analysands like me often littered our conversations with "As Freud said ... " How poorly we understood Freud's words became evident as I dug into the details.

Meanwhile, as the seventies moved onward, Arthur Janov's idea of breaking through neurosis by re-experiencing buried infantile and juvenile pain had been gaining huge momentum.

Primal therapy was au courant. "Feeling and scream" centers were popping up all over. At Dick and John's Berkeley center, the applications rolled in, yet tension between the two men worsened. I felt trapped between their complaints, and the increasingly toxic atmosphere was an embarrassment.

I was offered an escape by Sylvia, a Berkeley therapist, who wanted help setting up her own facility for primal practice. Working with a woman was an attractive proposition, and I accepted. A friend from New York, social worker Lois Schwartz, joined us. It turned out to be a big mistake. Sylvia was unstable and a little scary, and I quickly realized I shouldn't be there.

Among our clients was a group of friends from rural British Columbia. They had only five months available for their therapy because they needed to be home to plant their gardens in the spring. An attractive, diverse bunch, their common denominator was surprise that tangled emotions can also thrive where there's pure air and chainsaws. Lois and I decided to visit their community to conduct follow-up treatment with them. I wrote to an acquaintance, who was interested in participating in therapy, to tell her about our plans.

Dear Barbara,

I have left the Center; so has Lois. Sylvia is planning to undergo electroshock therapy and has put her boyfriend, an untrained therapist, in charge at the center.

Primal Therapy can be a wonder … but it's no miracle. If it were, Sylvia would be ditching her boyfriend instead of scrambling her brains; Janov would be arranging seminars and lecturing at primal centers instead of threatening to sue them; I would weigh 120 lbs. instead of 210; and probably all us "primal therapists" would stop digging these hell holes of sorrow and get useful jobs cleaning the streets.

That said, B, I offer you the following possible alternative to a nervous breakdown: late in May, Lois and I are going up to Canada to a rural settlement in British Columbia to work with some of our clients who were at the Center for several months until they needed to go home. We will continue to work with them there for three months, doing primal groups.

There will be time to start some new people primaling, too, if we start them as soon as we get up there, so that they'll have a full 3 months with us before we have to leave. At that point, one could decide either to stay up there to work with the support of the older group (some of whom will be able to give direct help), or come back down here to Lois and me when we've found a suitable place to practice together in the Bay Area.

If you can see yourself in that Canadian picture, we'll be glad to work with you there. I don't have much more to tell you about it, as I've never been there. It's a rather loose arrangement, to be sure, and all I know about it is that the place is beautiful, remote, sparsely settled, cheap to live in, and that the people there will know what you'll be going through. Let me know.

Love,
Ronnie

It turned out to be a wonderful summer. The Canadians prepared a perfect, old freestanding building on a pleasant site for us. There were even rooms for out-of-towners like Barbara. A new client worked out his therapy fee by preparing good, simple meals for us. It was a huge relief to be able to care for our clients and ourselves in that simple, tension-free, beautiful setting. I returned to Berkeley in the fall, but my British Columbia adventure was just beginning.

MOTHER MOVES TO MARIPOSA

My mother had been a restless renter of dwelling places on both coasts, but she finally seemed to have settled down in a second-floor apartment on a typical, quiet Los Angeles street off

Western Avenue. She enjoyed the tree in front of her house that brought leafiness and birdsong to her living room window, the convenience of the neighborhood markets and stores, and, most of all, the short walk to the communist-newspaper office, where she had a part-time job. One day, she phoned to tell me that her best friend and neighbor's arm had been broken by a mugger in daylight, right in front of her building, which was just down the street. There had been other incidents, she admitted. The thugs and junkies from nearby Western Avenue were moving into the quiet streets and preying on the old people who lived there.

"Mom," I shrieked, "you've got to move!"

"I know, I know," she said impatiently. "I've been thinking about it."

"Shall I come down and help you look around for a place and help you move?"

"No, no," she said. "You're busy, and I have plenty of friends."

I was busy, working in a therapy center in Berkeley and taking classes in San Francisco for my master's degree in psychology; papers were due. It was a truly inconvenient time for me to take off. I wondered about the "plenty of friends" who would help her. Were they the other gray heads from her Communist Party club? "Oh no," she chastised me. "There are very fine young people in the Party now." I counted on my mother's gregariousness and her stubborn self-reliance. She'd be okay.

Within a few weeks, she had found a new apartment. It was in the same general neighborhood, but far enough away from commercial Western Avenue to be out of prowling range. I phoned when she'd been there two or three days.

"You like it, Mom, your new place?"

"Yes and no ... it's nice."

"Uh-oh. What's wrong with it, darling?" My conscience went into overdrive. Why on earth hadn't I gone down and helped her find a suitable apartment?

"Wrong? Nothing in the world! You should see how bright it is, and it has a view right to the sunset. And do you know what I'm paying? Sixty-five dollars a month! Did you ever hear something like this?"

"Well, that's terrific!" I agreed. "So what's wrong?" Something surely was. I could hear it.

"Oh, come on, what do you mean wrong?" she said. "Clean and airy, three nice rooms, and a good walk to work every day. Of course there's nothing wrong. Everything's right, in fact! Nicer furniture even than mine."

"You mean you don't have your own furniture? Why is that?"

"Well, it's already furnished, and nicely enough. That's nothing," she said, an edge of defiance in her voice.

"Nothing?" Just before I had gone back to school, she had adamantly refused my offer to replace her couch, whose cushions held the shape of her afternoon naps, and her bed, with its sinking mattress.

"Okay, so you're feeling pretty good about the move?" I prompted.

"Yes … yes … " Again the rising inflection, the hesitation. I knew that I had better get down there and take a look.

"Right, darling. I'll see you next Friday," I told her.

My mother's new building stood tall, a brick Masai warrior in a line of pastel pygmies. Along the curb in front of the entrance, the bare trunks of two palm trees rose skyward to their plumed crowns from a strip of grass. To the left of the door, a plaque with blue lettering on white enamel read: "City of Los Angeles, Senior Citizens Housing Facility." Clearly, this was what was behind some of the "no" in the "yes-and-no" of my mother's assessment. She had always despised the "demeaning" term "senior citizen." I wondered what other personal adjustments she'd accepted with her new low-rent apartment.

As a security measure, there was no buzzer—but they didn't have a phone, either. I lugged my suitcase to a phone booth some yards away, rang her number, and heard her shout in the middle of the first ring, "Coming down, coming down!" The second security provision was the automatically locking, steel-framed front door, massive enough to protect the US mint. Between the two of us, we managed to force the thing open far enough for me and my suitcase to squeeze through, and we embraced happily. Glued above the inside door handle, a five-by-seven file card hand printed in red pencil indicated how some of the frailer residents dealt with the problem: "Tenents [*sic*]! This door is not to be propped open. It has to be kept locked at all times. This is for your own good. The Manager."

A few residents, in various degrees of senior, sat on chairs inside the lobby, staring silently at our progress. I nodded at them and smiled. My mother ignored them, pointing out art-deco motifs left from the days when Charlie Chaplin owned the building, including the old reception alcove with its cubby holes for mail and a fine beveled mirror overhead. Nothing reflected the building's fall from grace so much as the single low-wattage bulb hanging over the row of regulation US Postal boxes beyond the elevator.

Finally, Mother broke the silence by introducing me ceremoniously to each of the people in the seated group. The first was a woman in flamboyant caftans with blazing red hair and unfortunate makeup: her eyebrows were McDonald's double arches and her lips were smeared with scarlet to twice their actual fullness—like Bette Davis dying at the mirror in *Of Human Bondage*. "Hello," cooed Mother. "This is my daughter Ronnie, the singer." I would always be "my daughter, the singer" to my mother, who didn't register my later career as an actor or my present one as a therapist.

"Oh, you're a singer?" was the woman's response. Whatever the ritual meant to my mother, I decided I would play my part. "Yes, I used to be," I said cheerfully. Then came the inevitable question from the wrinkled old fellow next to the lady with the makeup: "You're a singer? How come I haven't seen you on the TV?" "You probably don't watch that program," I answered, with a grin that I hoped wasn't as frosty as my voice sounded to me.

My mother's apartment was on the fourth floor, but the button she pushed said twelve. As she had said, the apartment was light and airy. You could see west across the flat rooftop of an adjacent building to another flat rooftop and some distant trees, so that in the late afternoon light one could imagine the sun setting somewhere out there. The furnishings—genus cheap motel—were functional, the old carpeting was clean, and the place was freshly painted. I imagined that putting pictures on the walls might relieve the institutional feel. She had a large oil painting she liked very much of fishermen at the shore mending nets, a gift to me from Lorraine Gordon, Max's widow, which I'd passed along to her when I gave up my New York apartment.

"Mom, where are your pictures? I'll help you put them up."

"Irene has them," she said.

She gave my painting to my sister? I felt the heat of wrath climb up my throat and struggled to keep my voice neutral.

"How come?"

"They don't let you put holes in the wall here."

"Come on, surely you could get permission to put a picture up!" She summoned her and-that's-all-there-is-to-it tone and said, "They're very strict. And I'm not going to beg."

"Swallow it, Ronnie," I told myself. "It's too late." Mother settled into Mariposa Avenue as she'd always done elsewhere, making the best of things and devoting herself to the meetings, lectures, and social actions of her Communist Party club. I visited her three or four times a year while I was living in Berkeley.

NEW MUSIC

Since childhood, music and theater had been my passions. I always followed my curiosity and then fell in love with the work. I wasn't ever making "career choices." Music interested me, so I sang; theater interested me, so I acted; therapy interested me, so I practiced therapy. Doing these things woke up stuff in my imagination, and when I pushed it a little they became vocations. Much of it was good luck and the collaboration of extraordinary people. In 1975, living in Berkeley, I wasn't looking for yet another career, but life is full of surprises.

Lisa, on her spring break from San Francisco State University, was visiting an old high school friend in New York. She phoned.

"Mom, do you know a singer named Holly Near?"

"Uh-uh, never heard of her. Should I have?"

"Well, Jill has her new record, *Holly Near: A Live Album,* and it's dedicated to you. Your name is right across the back of the jacket: 'To Ronnie Gilbert: a woman who knew how to sing and what to sing about.'"

I had been out of the music loop for almost a decade, and I didn't miss it. I had mostly stopped listening to music altogether. The lovely, acid-inspired ballads of the '60s had been supplanted by various "rocks"—punk, acid, glam, etc.—none of which I could fathom because I couldn't hear the lyrics through the sheer noise. The folk-pop scene, cheerfully or moodily without content, rather bored me now that even Peter, Paul and Mary had gone their separate ways. The Beatles, whom I much admired, had disbanded as well. Dory Previn's sly "Twenty-Mile Zone," in which she rides in her car "screaming at the night," was the one recording that perked my ears, perhaps because I was a primal scream facilitator. Now, some undoubtedly long-haired, wispy girl-with-a-guitar had advertised me as a mentor, with nary a "may I," and dragged me back into the music world of the sixties without even bothering to send me the recording. Typical of today's youth, I thought crankily.

Lisa sent me the album after the phone call, and it arrived a day or so later. Hoping to get in a lick of housecleaning that morning, I put the record on the turntable, prepared to hate it and to skip through the songs quickly. But the first cut, "Started Out Fine," stopped me cold. A little girl and her truck driving single mom are on the road together, and ... I put down the dust cloth. For the rest of the afternoon, a clarion-clear voice filled the room with tough and tender lyrics bright with the personal and political issues of the day, brilliantly supported on piano by Jeff Langley, Holly's cowriter. There was no guitar.

I called Holly, who lived in Ukiah, and we met a few days later. She was a tall, serious young woman with hair the color of her golden-warm voice. She apologized for assuming, when she dedicated her album to me, that I was no longer living. "It's okay, Holly," I told her. "I'm glad you were mistaken, and I'm honored." Revealing my Gothamite biases, I asked her how a kid growing up on a Potter Valley ranch near someplace called Ukiah, California, came to have such an incisive societal view?

Holly had grown up a generation later than I, but in a similar political tradition—both of us with unionist parents who believed in progressive politics. Her parents had met in an auto assembly plant during World War II. Her father, Russell, was a union organizer and her mother, Ann, was from a patrician East Coast family. On their family ranch outside Ukiah, Holly and her siblings had listened to an eclectic collection of recordings, including those of Paul Robeson and the Weavers, and they had even seen us perform live. Still, they were children of their time. Holly loved Broadway show tunes and Janis Joplin, Judy Garland, Joan Baez, and Sarah Vaughn. I loved that her writing and her politics weren't rigid and that she could express herself in different musical idioms. Everything seemed to be home to her. Holly's progressivism was more than casual. She had abandoned a promising career as a film and TV actress to work for the Indochina Peace Campaign, and she and Jeff Langley had accompanied Jane Fonda and Donald Sutherland on their Vietnam tour. *Hang in There,* her first album, released in 1973, was inspired by that trip.

That Holly and I would become friends was fated, but, at that moment, our paths seemed to lead in different directions. Holly was reorganizing her young company, Redwood Records, to be the strong left arm of the burgeoning women's music movement, and she was becoming a star in the movement's lesbian pantheon, alongside Cris Williamson, Meg Christian, Teresa Trull, and Margie Adam. I, on the other hand, would soon be moving to rural British Columbia to practice therapy. As a progressive, straight (as far as I knew) woman, I completely empathized with lesbians as an oppressed minority struggling for their civil rights, but I didn't know exactly what "women's music" was. Phil Spitalny's 1940s radio program *The Hour of Charm,* featuring his novel *All-Girl Orchestra,* was all that came to mind.

At Holly's suggestion, I visited a women's music festival in Portland, Oregon, on the way to British Columbia. I was curious, mostly to see Laurel, Holly's younger sister, perform with her dance group. If I had been unprepared for Holly, the Northwest Women's Music and Culture Festival shocked me. Singers, musicians, poets, dancers, the ecstatic audience! Where was all this female talent coming from, and how could I be so out of touch with it all?

Laurel Near danced with a six-woman company called the Wallflower Order—gorgeously, powerfully feminine, technically exacting, and choreographically exciting—who stirred me to tears and cheers with a piece about Vietnam, the most moving antiwar statement I'd ever witnessed. At a poetry workshop, a woman about my age, fifty or so, read a haunting poem, "The Jewel in the Cave." About halfway, it hit me: "Omygosh, this is about her … It's an ode to her clitoris!" I threw a quick glance over my shoulder—were there any men there? "This is an all-woman audience," I assured myself. "And even if there were men present, so what?" I scolded myself. "You need to take a look at this embarrassment."

By late afternoon, my brain on overload, I decided to skip the second day of the festival. I had hours of driving ahead to mull over the high points of the day, the blanks in my feminism, and my mixed feelings of loneliness and comfort in the all-women crowd, and to muse on the creative female community growing up without me. What was I missing? Would I have chosen a life in remote British Columbia if I'd known? I purposefully ignored the questions and drove on. With me was an armload of reading material from a Portland women's bookstore. I took Adrienne Rich, Robin Morgan, Alta, and several other poets and essayists with me to my new home in New Denver, British Columbia.

Two years earlier, when my friend and co-therapist Lois Schwartz and I had led a lively summer workshop for a group of clients in their hometown of New Denver, British Columbia, I'd fallen in love with the place. It may have had something to do with the two Japanese ladies strolling the main street under bamboo and waxed-paper parasols with the Kokanee Glacier behind them—looking like a perfect Hiroshige print. It certainly had a lot to do with the mixed population: young back-to-the-landers in nineteenth-century rancher clothing, ex-urban Canadians, American Vietnam War refusers, Ukrainian-Canadian Dukhobors, Anglos (adamantly straight local Canadians), and Japanese. I'd always had a romantic thing about the countryside—the rural life, trees, and campfires. Pete and Toshi Seeger building their log cabin and raising their kids on the banks of the Hudson was, for me, a fundamental image of optimism in the face of government corruption. Moreover, living as a therapist in a city full of therapists was suffocating. I needed … *something;* and it wasn't the shrink-glutted, middle-class Bay Area.

Lois laughed when I told her that I wanted to move. "Bury yourself in a place like this? You're surely crazy." But, by the time I returned to Berkeley that fall to complete my master's in clinical psychology, I knew I'd be coming back. Lois married a Norwegian and established a flourishing primal therapy practice in Norway. I obtained status as a landed Canadian immigrant to practice psychotherapy and counseling in that intriguing corner of British Columbia, and, two years later, in my red Toyota mini-wagon, pulling a four-by-six-foot trailer crammed with puffy foam-rubber chairs, cartons of books, some pots and pans, and my typewriter, I arrived in New Denver with the goblins on Halloween night, 1975.

EIGHT

British Columbia

Housing was a challenge. Participants from the earlier primal workshop that Lois and I had hosted in New Denver helped me get started. Judy Maltz and her guy, Gerry, shared their large early-grunge style house with me, in which seventy-five years of retail marketing history were visible under peeling layers of wallpaper and linoleum. Still, the plumbing worked, with the help of a large canning pot that was more or less permanently installed under the sink. The rent was thirty-five dollars a month for each of us, including utilities (heat from the ancient, curly cast-iron woodstove). There was a piano in the parlor, and Judith was a fine pianist. I had brought a small collection of choral music with me—madrigals, Pete Seeger's Bantu choral collection, a fancy glee-club arrangement of "She's Like the Swallow"—and we soon had regular Sunday-night sings going.

I watched the snow line moving slowly down a nearby peak, its brow furrowed like a neighborly admonition. Then, as if I hadn't been warned, winter burst upon the valley: stillness, white, all the hard lines gentled. In the Slocan Valley, nature and the land let you know who's the boss. Deer came down from the hills for better forage, and, after them, the cougars. Bears visited for the last fruit hanging from the trees. Occasionally, they left some behind. On our front lawn one morning, I found two bright-red apples hanging from a branch, etched white by the frost. I bought a puffy anorak and mukluks to keep my toes warm. My brave little Toyota seemed happy enough during the snowy months. In fact, she took me and two friends all the way to Vancouver to see Peter Shaffer's *Equus* at the Vancouver Playhouse and got us home safely after only one small altercation with a snow bank.

Very soon, I was longing for my own living space. Another former primal participant, Leah Main, went south for the winter months, and she sublet me her place in the Orchard, a settlement of tiny houses near the lake. With my rent tripled, it was time to get to work. The Department of Human Resources hired me to help a few families who were fostering young people from the cities. I also got involved in the start of a publicly funded alternative high school. The pay was minimal, but my living costs were low. I offered a Gestalt weekend and began private therapy sessions with new and former clients.

New Denver meant driving to Ainsworth Hot Springs for baths in the snow; small Japanese ladies with strong wills recruiting people to be followers of Tenrikyo, a kind of Japanese Holy Rollers; driving across the mountains in the snow to Kaslo for a classical concert in the school gym, given by two Rumanian musicians working the provinces in a cultural-exchange program. It also meant any new settler (hippie) excuse for a dance—pretty young mommas dressed up in their best rags, hair flying and hips rolling; daddies dancing with babies in their arms; little kids racing, whooping and hollering, and then falling asleep right in the middle of the action on secondhand fur coats, everyone careful not to step on them. With all that fun, it was easy to forget that New Denver also meant alcoholism and unemployment.

HILLS OF HOME, 1976

Michael Hartley, a friend of a friend, offered to build a simple home for me on the property that he and his wife, Margaret, had in Hills, about ten miles north of New Denver. They shared a cleared hillside with three neighbors, their homes all far enough apart that they couldn't see or hear each other. John and Bay Herrmann, primal therapy friends, lived on a parcel back behind the trees. The financial arrangement Michael and I agreed on struck me as fair. What made me nervous, though, was someone's reminder to Michael that the spot he planned for my new abode was "on the bear trail."

Bears are a large presence in the West Kootenays. So, if the bear trail had served the local *ursa* population for perhaps millennia, was it such a good idea to put a house there? Dire warnings from Yellowstone Park rangers came to mind. "About the bears, Michael," I said, "one thing city life has taught me: if you want peace, you respect boundaries." He chuckled, thinking I was joking. I wasn't. He answered cheerfully that he and Margaret had bought and paid for the land, so the bears would have to move. I thought he was joking. He wasn't. It was a small miscommunication; there would be others. I deferred to his superior rural-Canadian know-how.

Until the house was built, I tested my resourcefulness at keeping clean and warm without electricity or indoor plumbing in a handsomely built log cabin that sat up on the hill in a grove of birch and aspen. Pretty fancy camping, I thought, smiling at memories of roughing it years ago on tent trips. A 1926 photo of my parents standing in front of a big canvas tent came to mind. In it, my mother was smiling, modestly hiding her pregnant belly (which was full of me) behind the tent flap and my father looked strong and handsome, the sleeves of his work shirt rolled up. The tent had been their private quarters when they lived on his parents' farm near Plainfield, New Jersey. He reminisced over that tiny piece of land all his life. Dead now for six years, my father would have loved the life I had in Hills, lugging water, hoeing and digging with Margaret in her garden, and helping the Herrmanns on the other side of the hill with theirs.

One gorgeous, sparkling day, with the sun high in the sky and the leaves dancing on the trees, I thought of my mother's pleasant face in the photo. I called her in Los Angeles. "Come for a visit, Mom," I said. "You simply must see this place." Two weeks later, I met her at the Spokane airport. She was as excited as a child. For the first time, it occurred to me that flying was still an adventure for her. We buckled up in the Toyota and set off for the five-hour drive due north to Hills. It was mountain highway through dense forest most of the way. She kept up an eager chatter about the flight for about an hour, telling me all about the man in the seat next to her, "a very fine person," the kindness of the flight attendant, and the skimpiness of the meal. Then she nodded off and slept the rest of the way.

Glancing at her face as we traveled, I saw a far different Sarah Gilbert from the emphatic picture of her I carried in my thoughts. With her cheek muscles slack in sleep, her mouth relaxed, and the tender skin of her eyelids closed over eyes deep-set in their sockets, I recognized the vulnerable old person my mother was becoming, and I was nearly overcome by the wish to hold her in my arms, as if to protect her—and perhaps myself—from her mortality. What was I doing bringing my aging and very fastidious mother into that primitive scene in Hills? How had I managed to forget that she never spoke of the Gilbert farm in Plainfield without a shudder? I tried to reassure myself: "The beauty of landscape was never lost on her. She will surely share my pleasure in the hillside with its dramatic vistas. And she's always been interested in new people. She'll be fine with my fascinating back-to-the-land friends, and especially their lively, charming children." But misgivings answered: "How in the hell is she going to deal with the lack of personal amenities?"

We arrived in Hills in late afternoon, tired after the long drive. That is, I was tired; Mother was chipper. I hurried us up the road to the log house, anxious to introduce her to the routine of water, fire, Coleman stove, oil lamp, and non-bathroom while there was still some daylight coming through the window. In the past three hours, we'd eaten nothing but a small bag of potato chips, so our supper of crackers and cheese and canned tomato soup, eaten by lamplight, actually tasted delicious. We climbed into our sleeping bags (hers borrowed from Bay Herrmann) and, after only a little more chatter, fell fast asleep. If Mother had been thinking of the farm in New Jersey, she didn't say. And even nature didn't call until full daylight the next day.

In fact, my mother turned out to be an amazingly good sport about it all, even about the board between two trees that served as my "bathroom." She was such an appreciative and delighted guest at friends' homes that I marveled at my narrow idea of her. Always a determined walker, she took the hill up to the Hartley's without breaking her stride. She listened to the banter at dinner at a friend's table and joined in as if she'd had a long acquaintance with chainsaws and pickup trucks. She took her shower outdoors from a sun-warmed garden hose with a gasp and a laugh as the hot water turned cold while the shampoo was still in her hair. Only on the day of her departure, after emerging from the woods for the last time, did my mother look me straight in the face and say calmly and with dead certainty, "You're crazy."

.   .   .

The house that Michael and I planned would have a porch and be large enough to divide into rooms at some later date. It was a basic rectangle that he could build by himself, with only me as a helper. With his pickup truck, we crossed the border into Washington to scrounge for cheap materials and shop for home furnishings. My familiarity with make-believe rooms at Bloomingdale's in New York was a completely different world from the salvage yards of Nelson and Spokane, where treasures were to be had! Windows and doors of every description beckoned, and we found mismatched but serviceable toilet fixtures. My financial resources were tiny, but I was thrilled with our loot, and I breathed a sigh of relief when our loaded truck passed the border with no trouble.

The summer weeks passed but nothing happened with my cabin. Michael had work he had to finish elsewhere. By September, I began to wonder what I would do with all that salvage. Finally, Michael announced that he had engaged a backhoe operator to dig the holes for the foundation and level a small area for the septic tank. It would happen! I was up half the night with excitement. Zipped into my sleeping bag, I could keep cozy enough with my own body heat, but trying to read by a kerosene lamp and keep warm at the same time makes for a tortured and endless night. At 5:00 am, I rushed through my ablutions, made tea on the Coleman, grabbed my new pair of heavy work gloves, and ran up the hill to the building site—literally ran, which was a new accomplishment, my happy reward for giving up smoking. The first time I'd tried that hill, it had been all too clear that I would have to choose between cigarettes or cabin; I couldn't have both. I had chosen the cabin, and I felt strong and healthy and powerful!

Michael was already there, sitting on a pile of lumber in the pale pre-sunrise light. I hooted and waved, and he jumped up, swinging his large drawing pad in front of his head in a figure eight, like a semaphore flag. Michael was thin and sinewy, and although he was fairly tall, his excited movements suggested the antics of a little monkey. "Wait until you see this, Ronnie, I've rethought the whole thing!" I heard him yelling. "Believe me, this is a much better house. You're going to love living in it," he insisted as I closed the distance between us. I examined his drawing pad. "But, but, but, but Michael!" I wailed. Gone was the simple four-walled, one-story cabin, the details of which we'd planned so carefully. Michael's new vision extended from behind the tree line way out onto the hillside and included an upstairs and three complete rooms. The new roof was a hip-and-valley type, very attractive, but would I be able to climb onto it in winter to shovel off the accumulating snow? Would it even carry the weight of a heavy snowfall? Michael was perfectly sure it would. "And look!" he said happily. "Here's the backhoe operator with his machine, right on time." I turned my palms skyward, and the work commenced.

Through the remaining days of summer and well into the fall, the sun warming our backs, I helped carry lumber, pour cement, pull old nails from boards, and hammer in new ones. Michael cheerfully showed me how to use the plane, sander, and rotary saw. Wonderful terms like "plumb bob" and "counter-sink" became part of my vocabulary as I came to know the ever-helpful hardware store family in nearby Silverton. I didn't "saw wood" anymore; I "ripped boards," my shoulders straightening when I pronounced the words.

Meanwhile, I carried on with my work as the local therapist. It was early December and very cold indeed when I at last moved out of the log cabin and into the house. The downstairs would eventually be the kitchen, but now, because of cold and the oncoming snow, it served as the indoor wood shop. I was more than thankful for the shelter, even though it was still a construction zone, and began to make myself at home. I hammered together crude shelves for my books and belongings and barricaded the open stairwell to prevent dropping downstairs into black oblivion during the night. I quickly learned how to split firewood—you don't hammer on it directly with an axe as I imagined; instead, you insert a wedge and hammer on that. And I figured out how to stoke the old, battered, leaky, and inefficient wood-burner—mis-leadingly named the Airtight—so it required only one trip down-stairs during the night to keep myself and the house from freezing. I learned to respect the unaesthetic plastic film that covered glass-less open spaces, to set mousetraps, and, when they were full, to grit my teeth, overcome anguish, control disgust, and empty them so they could be used again. And again, and again, and again. I was, in other words, learning to live "simply."

After many weeks of cheerful hard labor, numerous clever innovations in construction (some that actually worked), and frequent unannounced comings and goings, Michael decided that he'd done enough. By then, the toilet upstairs and the bath-tub downstairs both worked as long as I remembered to leave the water running so the pipes wouldn't freeze. "Turn off the

faucet!"—one of those motherly admonitions from childhood—
had to be banished from my memory. Tucking a small propane
cook stove between the woodstove and the sink turned the now
emptied woodshop into a cheery kitchen, even though I didn't
yet have fuel to run it. Meanwhile, I cooked on a camp stove and
on the lid of the Airtight when it was going, which, in winter,
was most of the time. There was plenty of wood around the
house to burn. Eventually, John Herrmann helped me coax a
stovepipe up two stories, through the floor and ceiling and out
the roof, to heat the upper regions of the house and carry off
smoke. My electricity came overland via a heavy-duty extension cord from Michael and Margaret's house. I traded the
lovely soft glow of an oil lamp for the clear sharp illumination of
electric light. I had enough juice for light bulbs on both floors
and even a very small heater, if I was frugal with it. John and Bay
Herrmann gifted me with a beautiful ladder made from axe-
hewn poles, which turned an otherwise unreachable loft into a
snug, warm sleeping space. The floor of the loft became the ceiling for my "writing room," a tiny windowed space big enough
for a table and chair and my typewriter. I could even stand up
without hitting my head on anything. There are occasional
advantages for us vertically challenged people.

"Listen, Ronnie," said John Herrmann one blustery day, when
he found me mopping up the rain that was sloshing down from the
floor of the unfinished front room onto the kitchen floor below,
"we can at least roof it. We'll collect some poles. I have a couple.
And we'll get more. Ed and Matthew and I could put them up in
half a day and roof the damned thing in another." "But John," I
said, "how could I pay you guys for all that work?" He grinned and
scratched at his beard. "Well, let's see—you could bake us a big
pan of your carrot cake to keep us going." My carrot cake, a sinful

variation on the recipe in *The Tassajara Bread Book,* was stupendous. "You've got it, buddy," I told him, sniffing back tears and letting my mind wander over what I could make with the ingredients I had available to satisfy three or four large working appetites for two days: bean and cheese casserole; broccoli and cheese casserole; chard and cheese casserole; rice and beans; tofu, cheese and onion pie; and lots and lots of carrot cake, coffee, and beer.

With the help of my friends, I survived the winter of 1976 quite well in my unfinished house in Hills. They were hardworking young women and men, whom the locals (not always without hostility) termed "the hippies." I was grateful to them for accepting me as a therapist and family counselor, rather than as the famous Weaver, and for helping me to explore changes in my life as they explored changes in theirs.

Occasionally, I remembered that my relative isolation could be risky. I had no phone and wouldn't get one for quite a long time. One night, some kind of flu grabbed hold of me, and by morning I couldn't get up off my mattress, much less get down the stairs and down the hill for help. Feverish, and aching from my ankles to my neck, I drifted in and out of sleep, wondering how long it would take for the first whiff of my decaying body to reach someone, announcing my death. Some time later, I think it was the following afternoon, I felt the gentle touch of an angel's cool hand on my forehead, and I opened my eyes to see lovely Leslie Peterson from the knit shop kneeling next to me, her face concerned but calm. "I'd never seen your place, and I've been thinking it was high time to look at it," she said. "Something called me to it today." Cynic though I usually am when it comes to mystical phenomena, I believed her, and I was humble and grateful. She helped me up, made tea downstairs, and stayed with me until I felt able to fend for myself.

Author and local historian John Norris, who was then a high school teacher, lived just above the village of New Denver. I had house-sat his splendid place briefly, tending the chickens and gorgeous white turkeys he raised each year as if they were pampered pets, even though their futures were tied to Thanksgiving dinner. On a still-warmish December day, elegant John drove up to Hills, looked briefly at the house, and proclaimed it "lethal." He spent the afternoon stuffing the visible chinks with newspaper, telling me the story of the Japanese presence in New Denver.

I hadn't known that the Canadian government, in a fit of racist panic similar to the reaction of the US government after Pearl Harbor, had rounded up all the ethnic Japanese—citizens and aliens, Canadian-born and immigrants alike—that were living on the West Coast and sent them to isolated camps in the harsh interior of the country. New Denver had been one of these relocation centers. What for me was a willing adventure in a picturesque setting had been the last stop of a grim journey forced on hundreds of women, children and men who had been dragged suddenly from their fishing boats, farms, and homes on the temperate coast and banished to live in crude shacks without indoor plumbing or electricity—three families to each shack, often complete strangers—to survive the climate, and each other, as best they could. They succumbed to flu, tuberculosis, and pneumonia in droves. In the case of the New Denver encampment, the able-bodied men and boys were even further isolated, sent to live in Sandon, an abandoned mining town far up the mountain, leaving the women, children, and the very old to shift for themselves. Leah's house in The Orchard, winterized and improved over the years, had been one of the barracks. The tract of land by the lakeside was a pleasant place, with its upgraded cottages and pretty gardens, a few still occupied by some of the Japanese families that survived. Only the colorful Shinto shrine at the end of the farthest street hinted at the town's history.

A BEAR

One day, when it was nearly spring, I walked out onto my "deck," otherwise known as the "front room," into a morning as sweet as the end of winter can be, the sun warm on my cheeks, the alders and sycamores greening before my eyes, and the meadow grass gone verdant as if overnight. The hillside was quiet except for the faint, far-off tapping of a couple of hammers. Soon, I would get to see my favorite fine-weather view: the children of the families who lived on the hill and their friends traipsing follow-the-leader along the meadow's crests and dips, like a troop of tow-headed traveling players from Lilliput, costumed in finery from the village free box, where grownups recycled their used clothing. But—oh my gosh! What was that sitting in a hollow between two rises? Not a child, but ... yes, a bear!

I remembered John's retort when I first came to Hills and was waxing poetical about red apples left by serene bears: "They're so damned serene they'll tear the whole limb off the tree to get at the apples." He showed me an ugly amputation on one of his trees. And now there was one of the fierce creatures right in my backyard! "Oh my God," I thought. "What should I do? The kids will surely come out today, and they won't see that animal until they're almost on top of it! Make noise," I said to myself, coming to life. "Chase it away." The wilderness books tell you bears will run away, that they are more frightened of us than we of them. So I ran into the kitchen, grabbed a saucepan and a spoon, and ran back out to the porch, clanging on the pan. The animal heard. He turned his massive head toward the sound, slowly rolling himself up from his teddy bear sitting position and getting up on all fours. He stood there, looking, and then started walking right up the hill, straight toward me! It seemed I'd called him to lunch.

I found my voice. "Bear! Bear! Bear up here! John, Michael, Ed! Please, somebody! Bear!" I had never tried to reach anyone on the hill by screaming, and I had no idea if I could be heard, but I kept yelling, and the bear kept coming. Then I saw John and his helper Larry running up over the lowest rise. They'd heard me. The creature was now bounding fast toward my house. "Go inside!" John yelled at me, flinging stones at the bear. "Get inside!" I jumped down the steps into the kitchen and slammed the "door" behind me. Then I remembered it was just a plastic film. I ran upstairs. But there were no closets, no doors, no place to hide. I ran back downstairs, looking for a weapon, a stick, anything. And there he was, right outside my one glass window, standing straight up, his huge, clawed front paws against the glass, his snout between them, staring straight at me. I screamed, and the creature dropped below the sill out of my sight. I heard the crash of the brush as he fled up into the bushes behind the house, both men in pursuit, while I leaned against the cook-stove, trembling.

Bay came up from her place—laughing! "You all right?" she asked. I nodded with as much dignity as I could muster. I tried to answer, but there wouldn't be much talk from me anytime soon. I'd ripped my vocal chords to shreds yelling.

"Young bear," John said, returning from the bush. "Probably a yearling." Larry nodded sagely.

"How big does a bear have to be to rip a tree limb off a tree?" I croaked.

"At least a foot or two bigger than that one," John teased me. Larry nodded again, solemnly. I considered finding another rock, to throw at him. "Come up for supper later," Bay said. "We've got biscuits and a big pot of bean soup."

We ate in our parkas and mufflers, and John told bear tales all evening, Bay gently chiding him for his creative exaggerations, their daughter Skye giggling and me trying (unsuccessfully) not to laugh out loud in my painful frog voice. When it was time to go, I got a reassuring hug from Bay. "You'll get used to it," she said. I wondered if I would.

I damped down the Airtight, brushed my teeth, and climbed the ladder into my loft bed. Although I couldn't see up to the sky through the small window at my feet, I knew it was a sparkling night. Bay's good soup and all the friendly laughter had warmed my belly and my soul; I fell asleep over the first page of a book. It must have been about midnight when I heard the first primitive snuffling sound. Instantly, I awoke, listening in the dark. Nothing. "Don't be a dope," I told myself. "You're giving yourself a nightmare." I closed my eyes and was soon asleep again—but not for long. Two short snuffles soon shocked me awake. I went rigid, staring blindly into the dark. It had to be coming from the deck. Would a frustrated bear come back to see why he was driven off? "Oh, God," I thought. "That damned door of plastic film." I didn't dare go downstairs to check. I reached for my flashlight and switched on the light. Immediately, there was a quick shuffling noise on the deck, but the sound was definitely receding. "Not a bear," I reassured myself aloud in a whisper. "The footsteps were too fast. More like a cat's, or even a bird's. Birds? Right! Since when do birds snort?" But plenty of nights I had heard and ignored small animal sounds. I would ignore them now. In any case, whatever was there had run off. I had heard it, hadn't I? I switched off the flashlight, shifted on my mattress, and listened again. There was silence now. I closed my eyes and fell deep asleep.

The short, sharp, single snuffle that startled me awake next was close to my head. Terrified, I struggled to free myself from my sleeping bag, yelling, "Who's here? Who's here?" And then it dawned on me: that was no bear, it was me! I had been snuffling and snorting on my pillow all night! My croaking laugh sounded completely mad, but relief slowed my heartbeat. While I slid back into sleep, I imagined John telling his version of "The Revenge of Ronnie's Bear" to his Slocan Valley cronies over beer at Frank Foe's tavern, while Larry nodded superfluous agreement. "No," I thought. "I'm going to keep this little post-script all to myself, at least for a while."

FIRE

That year, Joe Chaikin sent me a letter. "Enough of the remote," he wrote. "I have funding for a new theater project in the winter. Come back from calm, safe British Columbia to smelly, noisy, old New York." "Safe?" I thought to myself, remembering my run-in with the bear. The day before, the wind had walloped the hill, shaking the house like it was a squirrel in a dog's teeth. I could swear the building shuddered and shifted inches back and forth. Throat-searing smoke from a fire forty miles down the valley boiled up the road past Cape Horn and backed up against our hills. I was sure there would be rain in the afternoon. Wind scratched at clouds, but only light poured through the rips, turning patches of the field a sulfurous yellow.

In the afternoon, Ed and Linda trudged up to visit me from their place down the hill, their faces clenched. Building a new room onto their cabin was proving complicated. "We've been fighting," Linda said. "Who wouldn't on a day like this?" I answered. But they were in no mood for cajolery and asked for a session, apologizing for it being Saturday. I thought I should probably stick to my guns and tell them to come back Monday. One lesson I had learned during my four years as therapist-on-the-hill was to guard my private time like a dragon or be prepared to never have any. But how could I say no to neighbors in trouble, especially Linda and Ed, whose commitment ceremony I had led? Also, I thought it might be a relief to focus on something heavily human as a counterweight to the day's spooky atmospheric malevolence. So we sat down together.

> LINDA: I've been working so hard for weeks on the cabin and the garden and where is he in it?
> ED: She knows, I have told her a dozen times. I can only concentrate on one thing at a time.

"Talk to each other, please," I suggested. "Not to me."

> LINDA: At this rate, Ed, it won't get done before the snow flies.
> ED: It's a matter of trust, just lack of trust.
> LINDA: No, it's lack of commitment.

And so it continued, for half an hour, disappointment feeding resentment. I let them go on shaking out what was worst between them. When they slowed down, I asked them quietly how long it had been since either had told the other "I'm so glad you're here with me," and watched their tired expressions dissolve slowly into tears. I teared up a bit too when they finally fell into each other's arms, sobbing with relief. Sometimes, two people stuck in a righteous war with each other just need permission to remember how good it was when it was good. It doesn't solve anything, but it's a place to stop for a while until a workable strategy can be developed. I watched them walk home hand in hand via the garden, so they could pick salad before it got too dark, and then onward to their kitchen.

My skin still prickled with the fine hairs of anger they had shed, or maybe it was only the electricity in the air, caused by the fire. The smoke from below had thinned some; I went outside and aimed the sprinkler at the propane tank, just in case, before turning in. For hours, I lay in bed trying to read myself to sleep, noticing how the sound of water pinging and crackling against metal resembles the sound of wood burning in a fireplace. If I were asleep, would I be able to tell the difference if the brush started burning around the house? Would I wake up in time to save myself? Should I get up and put a backpack together in case I had to run? What should I take? Pre-dawn light was threatening when imagination finally gave way to exhaustion. I conked out and dreamt of my high school Spanish teacher, severe Mrs. Greenberg with her black bun, circling the classroom, slapping her ruler against her palm. "Conjugate!" she ordered in her crow's voice. "Flee, fly, flu!" I struggled, trying to say, "'Flu' isn't right, it's 'flue,'" but I couldn't get my voice out. Then I recognized I was spelling and punning in my sleep, and I woke up to thin morning light squeezing through the loft window. And to rain. I dozed and woke until eleven o'clock, when I dragged myself out of bed. I snailed my way through the day— making some notes for my client files, writing a few letters, reading, scrubbing the bathtub, taking a bath. Damned narrow bathtub—I never did feel clean from it. "Ah, the joys of the antique!" I thought. "Thank you Michael, dear landlord, for choosing this darling old piece of junk. Thank you for building the simple little cabin you promised me, three stories high, so that it shudders and sways in the wind. Thanks for the leaky old wood burner that eats up fuel as if the stuff runs free from a faucet. Thanks for the gaps in the walls, home to the squirrels who nest there, calling to each other at three in the morning for a fuck."

"What am I doing here?" I wondered. "Could this land, this house, ever feel like home?" The daylight was going; it would be black soon if I didn't turn on a light. "Maybe I'll just go to bed and read," I thought. "And what will I do with the fears and furies that lurk in these walls?" I was afraid of wind that could come back in the night and shake me awake, and of fire. I was still afraid of fire, even though it had rained all day long—rained and rained and rained.

"Dear Joe," I wrote back. "Tell me more."

NINE

The Winter Project

In 1977, I took a break from my British Columbia life of therapy and theater to join Joe Chaikin's newly funded experimental theater company, The Winter Project, in New York City. The grant he had received provided for several weeks of alternative theater exploration yearly; public performance was not the object.

My Slocan Valley theater cohorts were none too happy. Over the past two years, Theater Energy had produced two engaging plays about our valley life, with the support of the Canada Arts Council, and a still-shaky third production was in preview. Although my uneasy conscience nibbled at my sleep, my generous friends sent me off with sweet reassurances and a lovely silk kimono with the Kootenay hills hand-painted on the back.

Rosemary Quinn of Joe's management group, Arts Services, arranged for my flight to Manhattan and for pleasant temporary housing in Little Italy, a neighborhood near the rehearsal space of the La MaMa Experimental Theatre Club, my old Manhattan stomping grounds. Two years driving around the boonies in my little red Toyota had blurred my memory of the fun of traipsing through the lively Greenwich Village and Lower East Side streets on foot.

"So-o, where are you from?" inquired the grocer on the corner.

"Right here," I grinned.

"Naah, you smile too much for a New Yorker."

My theater life had been fairly active since the sixties, when I'd worked with Joe in the Open Theatre and *America Hurrah*. I had enjoyed challenging roles like Medea's Nurse, Beckett's Winnie, and so on, but making theater with Joe challenged the soul; I hoped I still had the stamina for it.

The participants assembled for year one of The Winter Project were six actors, two musicians, and dramaturg Mira Rafalo-wicz. Each of us had worked with Joe Chaikin in the past, and we shared the vocabulary and sensibility for the developmental theater we built with him. This time will be different, Joe told us: "We can't rely on what we already know. The funding is for creating new approaches, new forms for exploring theatrical potential. We have to uncover possibilities we aren't yet aware of. For instance: the profound nature of tellings and listenings and the collaboration of actor and audience. The study is about telling, so for a start let's begin by telling a story—personal, invented, borrowed from plays, even poems." I thought, oh God, not a lot of personal stories. As a therapist "on vacation," I was leery of the unhelpful amateur "psy-cho analysis" that personal stories tend to elicit. But it was soon clear our research would be about the "how" of telling—the transmission, not the personal content. I was relieved.

After a vocal and physical warm up, we "told" our material for hours, either solo, or with improvised piano music by Peter Golub, or with a collection of old jars and cutlery arranged by

Steve LaPlante, the "Paderewsky of Garbage Pails." We explored
the music of the "telling voice," particularized sounds for their
musical effects on words, played with making music into speaking and speaking into music, and practiced "jamming," a group
storytelling exercise modeled on jazz improvisation. We interviewed each other about everything. At some point, we began
taking "listenings" apart. I wrote in my notebook: "The content
is in the rhythms rather than in the information." Happily over-
stimulated and exhausted at the end of the day, I went back to
my small apartment, hungry for the next day's experiments with
wattage, gender, snips from overheard conversation, and so much more.
The weeks flew by. It turned out that although I could take
myself out of the theater, I couldn't take the theater out of me.
So back and forth I went, from "home" in British Columbia to
The Winter Project in New York, where I lived in borrowed
housing for several weeks at a time.

Over the next two years, we worked on diverse material
brought in by the participants of the group. Mira Rafalowicz told
an interviewer, "Without the pressure of public performance we
have the luxury of just playing. What I like to call creative waste.
You get to play around a lot and you have the luxury to throw
away a lot. And then, you learn by what you don't want." Joe
summed up the project in a letter to Sam Shepard:

> During the winter a bunch of people got together to tell words or
> sing words and to listen to each other. To see what could be heard
> in words spoken or sung. We tried also to examine qualities of lis-
> tening. There was a big emphasis on the music in speaking—
> rhythm, melody and a lot of discussion about the degradation of
> language—that it's empty to use words like "love," "truth," etc. and
> yet one can't live without them. So, are there other words, code
> words or ironies in language, or is it better to use them anyway

accepting the pollution of language, etc. The idea was to investigate questions of telling and kinds of listening and maybe to find other ways to speak or sing thoughts and feeling.

This exploration was never performed outside the group of actors and composers and musicians and writers who came around and were part of it. No one told anyone what to do. We used each other as audience and said what we got ... No conclusions or formulas about approach, but a few very elementary things were revealed about the relationship between the listener and the teller. It's hard to go into by letter and the significant things you can probably guess.

Toward the end of the second year, Joe revealed that an important funder wanted the sessions to be open to observers: "If it's about theater, where's the play?" Joe was greatly concerned about showing fragmented experimental work to an audience unfamiliar with the project's process. "Give them credit for some brains," I argued, proud of our work and thinking of friends whose curiosity I trusted. But Joe was right. Brilliant poet Allen Ginsberg's completely uncomprehending (and unnecessarily disagreeable) response to a brief showing earned *me* due credit for my rash insistence.

In its third year, the work of The Winter Project changed in deference to presentation to an audience, and the directing team of Joe, Mira, and secretary Steve Reiser played a more traditional critical role. We focused our research on specific modes of human behavior and chose the theme "love and relationships" (the comings and goings of romance). Actually, I wasn't thrilled at that choice, but I had gotten delayed in Canada and missed the first meetings of the season.

Interviewing remained the core of our work process. Mira Rafolowicz prepared a list of potential interviewees—an Ecstatic Person, a Dreamer, a Reserved Person, a Laugher, a

World Leader—and suggested questions for them: Do you believe in God? What are your sexual fantasies? What thoughts are a refuge for you? What happens when you die? What if you had only one minute to live?

These were not to be character studies. Rather, they were meant to be personal representatives of specific human conditions recognizable in everyday life, only heightened—clownlike, but without the funny noses. The interviewing techniques we had developed over the past two years provided the content and structure for many of the scenes.

For an actor, improvising "non-characters" was like pulling teeth. The study was about conditions and behavior modes, not interesting people. There were no answers to the interview questions, no playing types, nothing that hinted at personal history or a reason for the condition. "Who am I to give the audience my history?" I thought. "Who am I to be a 'Who Am I' at all?" We struggled to improvise "pure" responses. Joe was merciless. Responding to my request for more of a backstory to my character, he said bluntly: "Who cares—it's not interesting. Too historical. Too didactic. Too psychological. Too therapeutic—like TV." My frustration is evident in this passage from one of my notebooks: "Is this it? No. Is this it? No. Is this it? No. This is it, yes? No. Yield, damn it, yield. Quietly—no answers—Keep trying."

Dangerously close to a real snit one day, I refused to answer any of the questions, instead laughing at every one. Somehow, that made its way into the play as its opening scene! It was even praised by critics:

> Miss Gilbert's laugh, like the appetizers in a peasant restaurant, is a meal in itself. Years of living have gone into that laugh; it possesses her, rocks her, squeezes her, and all but lifts her from the tiny chair on which she is precariously balanced. It is not a

gargantuan laugh, nor a sardonic laugh, nor an aggressive laugh. It is a helplessly infectious laugh.

Sometimes, I felt that really good stuff was getting sacrificed in the trimming-away process. Yet what remained suggested an enviable level of truth. The play was called *Re-Arrangements,* and a section in the middle, titled "Love Moments," became the core of it. The *New York Times* described it with reasonable accuracy:

> It is a silent pantomime of three sets of lovers. Two are rigid at a breakfast table that revolves slowly; two are trying to make love on the floor but never quite match, with elbows and noses and chins constantly getting in the way, and the third couple adopt various bereft and [consolating] postures. The characters and the scenes shift continuously; it is a lovely and subtle series of variations on love and what resists it.

In conventional theater, rehearsals usually take place in a fixed playing space designed for the ultimate production. The Winter Project did things differently. Designer and builder Jun Maeda, a Japanese man who spoke only a few words of English, improvised and built his designs along with our ongoing explorations, almost as if he were a member of the acting company. He would bring in a variety of materials and build, saying his favorite English word, "Imagination, imagination." It sounded like both an explanation and a command.

Our increasingly important interviewing technique always presented a basic problem: the audience expected a circumstance, a "how come?" This was, for us, an unwanted component. So we sought a neutral questioner who didn't imply "relationship," a presence that would not get in the way of the behavior of being questioned—cop, preacher, lawyer, torturer—but nothing was quite right. One day, Maeda brought in with his collection of playthings a long tube of jersey material. "Entrance! Imagination!" he shouted. Tina Shepard, small and athletic, crawled into it to test his idea for a possible entrance. Her struggle amused us until we became captivated by the numinous impression of her face inside the soft cloth. At Joe's request, this "Bag" interviewed the Reserved Person, and we had the perfect solution: the pure act of being questioned. For both *Re-Arrangements* and the following year's play, *Tourists and Refugees,* Maeda supplied ephemeral set pieces in the mode of our transformation-based productions: a window that came and went, a door that unfolded into something else, a movable backdrop of huge silken flags that follow the action.

The Winter Project theme of 1978 was "home and homelessness." Joe and I had talked with each other on the phone a lot about traveling, moving, changing addresses, and the phenomenon of so much movement around the unsettled earth—was it choice or compulsion? These ideas became *Tourists and Refugees.* It played for several weeks at the La MaMa Experimental Theatre Club to audience and critical approval and won an Obie award. Brilliant work on the "tourists" part of the play evolved from "Questions to Tourists Stopped by a Pineapple Field," a poem by W. S. Merwin.

I wanted especially to work on the "refugees" part. I queried the United Nations Refugee Agency for some concrete information, and the response was a current list of many pages. It thoroughly shook me up: 15.6 million internally displaced people, 10.4 million refugees, 2.5 million returnees, 6.5 million stateless people, and more than 980,000 asylum seekers. These people left their country and went there and then there, and those people went there, and so on and on ...

Could anything theatrical be made from these tragic columns of numbers? I didn't think so, but Joe had challenged us to find "the breathing" and the "vocal emblems." Reading the statistics aloud over and over, I found an emblem: the boring announcements of schedules in train and bus stations. On stage, gray-clothed "refugees" with their gray bundles moved along a track to the sound of colorless, insistent announcements of their travel details.

We wanted to include some of the compelling stories of refugees fleeing for survival, but on stage the stories lost their quality of immediacy, no matter how well they were performed. Our solution was for the refugee/actor to find an urgent, non-verbal "vocalese" for the story, with the help of a musical instrument. In production, the refugee stood spotlighted, telling their story in his or her (vocalese) language. An actor on a stool slightly downstage "translated" the story into English for the audience. The translation of my refugee story was: "She says: When you have to leave, take with you a warm sweater, a few small valuables for bribes, a few photographs. She says: Keep busy. Don't pity yourself. Laugh whenever possible. Don't wait for God to change things."

A year later, The Winter Project met in the spring and created an expanded and deepened treatment of *Tourists and Refugees,* which included some aspects of *Re-Arrangements.* The following summer, we toured Venezuela and performed the new production at the Fifth International Theatre Festival in Caracas. We were the only representatives from the United States.

MOTHER TAPES HER STORY

Since my teens, I'd pressed my mother for her history but had only been given bits and pieces of a life full of drama. I decided I wanted to preserve her memories, so when I had an opportunity for a three-day visit to Mariposa Avenue, I took my tape recorder with me. We'd have lots of time for conversation and "culcha." We would go to the art museum to see an exhibit of paintings by women through the centuries and watch a film of *La Traviata* with the wonderful Frederica von Stade, and when we got to casually talking about the past I figured I could record some of the conversation before she clammed up and got confused.

I needn't have worried. Mother instantly took over the recording session, improvising a formal introduction in honor of the presence of the microphone! "Ronnie, I think it's time for us to sit awhile and for me to tell you a little bit of your mother's background." She talked through several tapes, her memory unrolling the troubles and joys of her early life like her own personal Torah. She had told pieces of stories randomly in the past, but now she was painstakingly putting them in order and recalling particulars—like the address of the house in Warsaw where she lived with her parents when she was six or seven years old and the names of distant relatives.

She retold the story of her father being taken to the hospital when she was eleven years old, recalling how she'd gone there in the morning with kosher food and how, at the hospital gate, "one of those 'sisters' with a big white hat with wings and a long cross" turned and walked away, saying, "Your father died last night." As it had the first time I'd heard it, the story gave me the shivers and brought tears to my eyes, and to hers. She had never told me the details of her mother's illness, which was followed by her death just a year later, and I asked her if she would now. She went silent, curling a paper napkin around her thumb, then around her forefinger, and then smoothing out the curl with the edge of her hand. I asked if we should stop.

"No," she said. "I want to tell it, but it's hard." After a moment, she continued. "You know we were poor before my father died. When he went, we were complete paupers. The family who took us in was only slightly less poor than we were. We were given a mattress on the floor of a terrible room with rats, and my mother took very sick, fever and coughing. I slept with her, you know. And one night she ... " She broke off, pointing to the microphone, and whispered, "I don't want to tell this part to the ... " I switched it off immediately. She continued in a whisper, just in case. "One night, she—you know, I was sleeping next to her—and I felt that she ... " Tears spilled from her eyes as she forced out the unspeakable words: "She ... she wet the bed ... you know, she urinated! I screamed and screamed. They took me away into another room, and I never saw my mother again."

I held her while she cried, thinking it had been stupid of me to resurrect this sorrow, but then she took a deep breath, blew her nose, and impatiently waved the tape recorder back on. She continued, but it seemed like she had lost the thread. The effort to keep the details straight wrinkled her forehead, while her fingers, never still, made little pleats in the napkin next to her coffee cup until it was in shreds. In her struggle to find her place in the narrative, she began to tap the microphone with each thought. I moved it gently out of her way, but, like a cat tracking a mouse, her hand followed it. "Mom," I said softly, "you know, when you touch the microphone while it's on, it records noise on the tape." With a sharp intake of breath, she pulled her hand back as if she had touched fire and giggled. "Oh, for goodness sake," she said. "Grabbing, always grabbing. It must be the Jew in me."

I could feel the hair on my head uncurl with shock at that ripe piece of anti-Semitism. All her life an activist against bigotry, the mother I knew would rather have washed her mouth with Clorox than allow a racist slur to cross her lips. All I could manage was a breathless, "Mom, really!" But she went on, cheerfully voluble, as if nothing was amiss. I shook my head in disbelief and confusion but let it drop. By the end of that day, I had much of my mother's life on tape, and some of my father's, too, as she knew it. I intended to pin her down about the anti-Semitic remark, but we had been talking for hours, and I let it go. Something about letting sleeping dogs lie.

SOVIET ART

At the museum the next day, I gasped with pleasure at all the marvelous art. What a fraud that great painters had always been men! One painting in particular, with clean simple shapes in brilliant hues, drew my mother. She stood glued to it.

"Yes, wonderful, isn't it, that Georgia O'Keeffe?"

"I don't get it," she said.

I wasn't too surprised. Knowing that O'Keeffe painted the desert, I could see a blazing sun in a blue sky as seen through a bleached skeletal pelvic arch. My explanation was useless, though. To my mother, a devotee of socialist realism, it made no sense at all, as a painting or as a concept. That was okay. What did it matter? But what did bother me was that she couldn't seem to make sense of the traditional paintings in the show, although she stared and stared at them. There was nothing to really "understand" in those realist paintings, but she just couldn't seem to put what she was looking at together. I heard a faint alarm ping in my head. But it was easy to pass the confusion off as fatigue; we were both tired.

Mother was like Olga in Chekhov's great comedic drama of pre-revolutionary Russia, *Three Sisters*. "Oh, if only we could live in Moscow," cries Olga in an early scene, "how much happier our lives would be." Moscow was a mythical place to Sarah Gilbert, as it had been to Olga, although for different reasons. Olga, stuck in a provincial town, imagined that her longing for refined bourgeois intellect would be satisfied in cosmopolitan Moscow. My mother, on the other hand, saw Moscow as the center of a great human experiment, socialism, an economic system designed not to meet the longings of the bourgeoisie, but to provide security for the working class: steady employment, a room or two to call home, warm boots and clothing, three meals a day, medical attention whenever needed, and college for the kids—a virtual Paradise. How could that not be Eden to a Polish Jewish immigrant whose bones held the memory of a childhood of dire poverty, dislocation, and despair?

I never lived without the basic necessities of daily life, and I had other priorities. I challenged her continued absolute faith in the Soviet Union. Why, I needled, must there be cultural commissars telling writers, painters, and composers how and what to write, paint, and compose? There must be daring and surprise in art, I insisted. What is art if it doesn't convey astonishing shapes, sounds, textures, and concepts that most of us don't hear or see? Did imagination have a place in Soviet Russia? She said proudly that there was beauty and daring in Soviet art and pointed to photos in *Soviet Russia Today*, the official magazine of the Friends of the Soviet Union, showing factory workers and collective farmers marching together with banners flying, eyes raised toward a red-star-tomorrow. It was stuff that had thrilled me at age twelve, but not anymore. "Yech!" I scoffed. "Boring beyond bearing." How pointless to argue the merits of this art over that. I should have said, "A government that regulates its artists is afraid of its artists, and that's a government with plenty to hide." But I couldn't go that far. I thought it would break her heart to hear that from me.

How could she accept that Soviet citizens were being imprisoned for their poetry, or simply because they were Jewish? In truth, for a long time, even I didn't take such anti-Soviet accusations as fact. At age twelve, I believed the imperialist press had invented Siberia. "Why not?" I thought. "They invent so many lies to dampen our hopes for change and the healing of the oppressed peoples of the world." Nevertheless, as an adult, my life was music and theater, and I knew that at least on that score something was definitely wrong in Paradise. So my mother and I would fight. Round and round we'd go until she tired of the argument, at which point she would inevitably say, voice flat with disappointment and closure, "Ronnie, you don't read enough." By that of course she meant that I was not studying the principles of Marxism and Leninism and the analysis of this or that issue by Party theoreticians, always in line with the official Soviet point of view. She was right about my lack of intellectual preparation in that respect. I lacked the stamina to get at the jewels of theory in her books, which she insisted half the world found precious. I, on the other hand, found them wrapped so carefully in excess verbiage that, struggling to disentangle one idea, I would lose track of the previous one in the link. Maybe the translations were lousy. Or maybe I was just lazy. Whatever the reason, I simply couldn't keep my eyelids open through a dozen paragraphs.

Mom sent me back to Canada loaded up with sandwiches and cookies, of course. I promised that the next time I came I would bring a video camera. Down in the lobby, the social staring group was gathered. As usual, the lady of the caftan was there with her bright orange hair. I smiled at them as they silently watched me struggle with my packages, my suitcase, and the door. Just as I was finally getting the thing open, the caftan lady heaved herself up from her chair and came toward me. I thought she was going to offer, albeit a bit late, to hold a package. But no, she'd come over to whisper something. "Miss," she hissed, "your mother is not what she was." With that, she turned around, walked back to her seat, plunked herself down, and resumed her staring. "Poor thing, you should talk," I thought, and went on my way, passing off her remark as a swipe at my mother in payment for some slight. Mother could be quite superior at times.

In the months that followed, I was in a peculiar state myself, trying to balance the spartan life I'd chosen in British Columbia with the newly revived call to theater. Now and then, I managed trips to Los Angeles, where Mother's life appeared to be moving along normally. She gave up driving, but she wouldn't say why, other than that an old person she knew had caused a death. I thought she sounded depressed, but I figured, who isn't? All in all, she seemed to be functioning well enough.

TEN

The Weavers' Last Concert

NEW YORK, 1980

Filmmaker Jim Brown approached Lee Hays with the idea of making a documentary about the Weavers, and the project grew to include a reunion concert at Carnegie Hall. So, how does a quartet that hasn't sung together for almost twenty years plan and prepare a concert for a film that will outlive them? With difficulty. Old favorites we'd sung as the Weavers in the 1950s and '60s leaped back into our minds at rehearsals—words, musical arrangements and all—and we had our old recordings to set us right if memory failed. But trying to learn and arrange a new song was nearly our undoing. In the old days, we had found the parts for new songs in a matter of minutes—backstage in nightclub kitchens, in cars on the way to performances, by hotel swimming pools on the road. For this concert, Pete had put a tune to a lyric of Lee's and was eager for us to sing it, but even after two weeks of rehearsal, we simply couldn't get the song to catch fire. But we needed material that would relieve the nostalgia and show that we still had a lively interest in the world. I thought I had the solution in two songs by my friend Holly Near, "Hay Una Mujer Desaparecida" (A Woman Has Disappeared) and "Something About the Women." By the tenth day of rehearsals, I still hadn't found an opportunity to present my suggestions, although I'd mentioned them every day. Finally, at the end of yet another day of struggling with Lee's song, I pleaded, "Please just listen to these songs, they'd be so right for this concert, and they're relatively simple." I whipped out my tapes and played them. "Hay Una Mujer Desaparecida" lists the names of eight women among the hundreds of students, unionists, and artists "disappeared" by the murderous CIA-backed Pinochet dictatorship in Chile. The chorus simply repeats the title of the song. "Something About the Women" is a love song to the spirit of sisterhood and personal liberation, which were reshaping society's perception of women:

> One woman weaves a message,
> Singing the sounds of silence.
> Another wheels her chair to the center of the stage,
> Changing minds and attitudes
> With hearts that see and hands that speak.
> These women living, working, independently.
> I look to you, I look to you for courage in my life.

The chorus rocks cheerfully, repeating the title of the song over and over: "Oh there's something about the women, something about the women in my life." Surely the two songs were a contemporary expression of the heritage the Weavers were leaving—sing for sorrow, sing for hope.

I watched my partners' faces, expecting some hint of emotional connection. Nothing. Silence. "Well, what do you think?"

I prodded. Lee shook his head slowly. "I don't know. It would take us forever to learn the Spanish—at least it would take me forever. No, there isn't time." I felt the heat rise. I had been asking for this time from the start of rehearsals, but apparently I had been talking to deaf ears. "Lee, there is no Spanish to learn. Sing the title of the song, add 'in Chile, in Chile,' and you have the whole chorus. The verse is just a list of names, and I'll sing those. Pete, what do you say?" "M-m-m, I don't think so," he answered. "Those chords for 'Something About the Women' are very tricky. I don't think we have enough time to learn them." What? Pete had discovered something he couldn't play on the banjo? Fred had been silent. "What about you?" I asked him hopefully. "I say no." Tears threatened. "For god's sake, don't cry," I told my angry, disappointed self. "Okay," I said. "Everyone's tired. Will you take the tapes home and listen carefully to them? Tomorrow, if you still say they're too difficult, I can't fight with that and I'll forget it." We agreed.

The next day, honest Pete came back with the chords all worked out on his banjo, and Fred, not to be outdone, had them on the guitar. I hugged them both. But Fred's jaw was rigid. "You really don't like these songs, do you pal?" I asked, attempting empathy. I could afford it. After all, not being an instrumentalist, I didn't have to play them.

"The song about Chile is very nice," he said.

"And the other one?"

"I hate it, absolutely hate it!" he spit out.

"Because of the music or what it says?"

Fred shook the question off. "I just hate it."

This was 1980, post the women's liberation movement and post primal therapy; my Barbie Doll days when I deferred to the boys were long past. But I was still struggling with old patterns.

I still needed to convince myself, that my opinions counted. Should I compromise? Settle for the acceptable song like a good girl? No. I would not pack away my disappointment in tissues of resentment. The Weavers sang militant battle songs of labor and the Spanish Civil War. Here was a song that wasn't combative, but that celebrated strength, the kind that Lee Hays himself represented on that stage. In the end, we sang them both, and both moved the audience to cheers, as I knew they would. I hated that we had insufficient time to work out really smooth arrangements, and especially that I flubbed the names in "Hay Una Mujer," having trusted my memory instead of using a cue card. But it didn't matter. The audience cheered long and loud. But, oh, the reverberations . . .

The *New York Times'* music critic took a potshot at "Something About the Women" in his review of the concert, which he otherwise admired. The song rambled, he said, and suggested that it was beneath us. He liked the Spanish song. A music magazine also reviewed the concert, and the writer singled out the same two songs, with accolades for "Hay Una Mujer" and intense dislike for "Something About the Women," which he termed a "jingo-istic song." Warlike? He'd heard a battle cry, not a celebration! I wrote the reviewer: "Is it possible that you can find sympathy for martyred women but can't tolerate women raising themselves up from pain to power successfully?" He didn't respond. It seemed unanimous, at least as far as men were concerned: the song was just no good. On *The Today Show,* we sang the chorus over the show's closing credits—seemingly endlessly (short chorus, long credits). A burly crewman growled, "It's unnatural for a woman to talk that way about another woman." I found this letter in my files, and I can't honestly remember if I mailed it or not, but it sums up how I felt.

Vancouver, BC, Canada

Hi, Pete, Toshi, Fred, Lee, Harold,

While I take a break from studying Beckett's 64-page memory crusher *Happy Days,* some thoughts on Nov 28–29: Toshi, thanks for convincing Pete to try Holly's songs. And thank you Fred for overcoming your resistance and coming up with the strong accompaniment and lending your voice to the vocal work. Still affected by your opinions, my old partners, I was not as sure as I may have sounded about the workability of the songs. I only knew we had to break through the euphoric sentiment, and do something that tied us to today. Judging from the audience response, we accomplished that. Afterward, two or three people surprised me asking if I was making a public statement with Holly's songs, i.e., coming out as a lesbian. I wouldn't have used (y)our concert to do that, though it's nobody's business who loves whom or how. I want you to know how I do relate to those songs, particularly "Something About the Women," the one which caused Fred so much consternation. Some day, it would be good to discuss the politics with you. But for now, this is what I want to share with you—

It's spring or summer 1974 in Berkeley. I'm walking down crowded Telegraph Avenue, the squatting place of so many burnt out young junkies, wondering at my being there, wondering how much I personally, as a member of their parental generation and a citizen of this country, have to do with the disillusion and fury that leads them to litter the streets with themselves. I am thinking: God, we have produced a generation of monsters and cripples. Even given what we understand about this poisonous capitalist system, how could this happen? Is this the way it will topple, through the decay of our children? I had just passed by two filthy, sneering young guys offering a totally strung-out young girl a drink out of a bottle in a paper bag. I felt literally sick watching them move off together. At that moment, a young woman in a motorized wheelchair separated herself from the slow, sauntering crowd on the sidewalk, veered out into the road, and came scooting along past me, tiny hands twelve inches from her shoulders, rag doll legs. I caught my breath, the word "thalidomide" flashing in my brain. Pale blond hair streaming out behind her, she smiled as she passed me and tore on. I smiled, too, but her smile was not for me. Its business was down the street, where a dark-haired girl in a wheelchair waited under a sign: "Center for Independent Living." I watched them come together, laughing, babbling, lean to kiss each other, and roll away side by side. It scrambled my perceptions, a changeful moment for me. I had to laugh at myself. This is precisely what Holly's song is about for me.

I was completely unprepared for so much resistance to it from the three of you. I had not been an activist "women's libber," hadn't personally experienced male wrath over the movement—yet. I hadn't even recognized the song's deep political significance. It was the tenderness of the lyrics that got to me. When I chose the song, I was thinking of Lee Hays's courage in deciding, like the woman in Holly's song, to "wheel his chair to the center of the stage," and I imagined him in his wheelchair singing about her in hers, a picture of cross-generational comradeship.

I thought about Betty Sanders—you remember Betty, People's Songs Board stalwart, almost the only female soloist in those days. Betty had been living for years in Sonoma, teaching at a local college. She sent me a message when she heard I was in Berkeley, and we became close. But we only had a year; she was dying of a nasty cancer. Betty talked about the future with great excitement—not hers, she knew she didn't have one, but her protégé Kate Wolf's, a talented young singer. Have you heard of her? So yes, there's something about the women in my life. And from their applause, the audience at Carnegie was delighted to hear that statement sung by all four of us. I hope that will show up in Jim Brown's film. But whether or not it does—it was a good moment in our history, I think. Thanks.

Ronnie

DESCENT INTO ALZHEIMER'S

Two years after her visit to my cabin in the Slocan Valley, I brought Mother to British Columbia again, this time to the city of Vancouver, where I was living in a proper apartment for a few weeks while I collaborated on the creation of a new play with a Vancouver theater company. "She'll enjoy a vacation from Mariposa Avenue," I thought, "and she'll like Vancouver." She did. She arrived on Friday, and for two days we drove all over the beautiful city, surrounded by water and mountains, walked around Stanley Park, spent a morning at the famous Granville Island Public Market, and saw a play.

On Monday afternoon, I went to rehearsal. The apartment was within walking distance of the rehearsal hall, and my mother and I had walked there and back several times. She said she felt sure that she could find me easily if she got lonely or just wanted a walk. I had left the refrigerator stocked, and a good shopping street was nearby. That evening, I came back to discover she had not moved from the apartment. It looked as though she hadn't moved from the chair she had been in when I'd left. She was sitting in the dark, and she couldn't say for how long.

"Have you had any food?" I asked, concerned.

"No," she said.

"Did you make yourself a cup of tea at least?"

"No."

"How come?"

"I was afraid to light the stove. I might make a mistake and it would explode."

It was an electric range. Something was clearly wrong. I had expected her to stay with me for a week or so, but obviously that wasn't advisable, since I couldn't be available to help her. Very uneasy, I called a mutual friend in Los Angeles, arranged to have her meet my mother at the gate, and sent her home on the plane. As soon as the Vancouver project was finished, I would drive down to LA and check things out, I told myself. Although we talked on the phone frequently, it was several weeks before I saw her again.

When I arrived, nothing in my mother's behavior seemed unusual. Her conversation was perfectly intelligible. She seemed to go about her life competently. After all, I assured myself, in Vancouver she had been coping with a totally new environment. She was a little eccentric. So what? That night, I went into her kitchen for a drink of water and found it overrun with roaches. This was not a visit from a few overnight guests, but the night revelry of a happily ensconced colony. My mother hated roaches even more than social democrats, and she had never before flagged in her battle against them. The next day, I cleaned her kitchen from top to bottom and did what I could to make life less hospitable for the creatures, but I left really worried. Something was decidedly off.

Several weeks later, my mother phoned me. "Ronnie dear," she said, "please get me out. I'm dying here." I had no notion of what had triggered that dramatic statement, and she couldn't or wouldn't tell me. I called my sister, who lived with her husband and two children in the same city as our mother.

"Irene, what is going on with Mother?" I told her what she had said to me.

"Oh, she's crazy," my sister said. "I told her she should come and live with us, but no. Alright, let her stew."

"But wait a minute, what do you mean stew? Why is she so upset?"

"How do I know? She's crazy."

My sister Irene and I had squabbled through our childhood and ignored each other as adults. Now all the old resentments came to roost over caring for our mother. Mother was the battleground and there would be no détente.

MENORAH VILLAGE

Within days, I was in Los Angeles, talking with Mother about the possibility for a radical change in her living situation. When I suggested that she take Irene up on her offer, she replied, "No. I'd have to be crazy!" It wasn't hard to imagine why; their relationship had always been troubled. And to be fair, my sister had sometimes born the brunt of Mother's more difficult moments, since she lived in the same city. In any case, living with Irene and her family was out of the question, and I had no real home to offer her. The solution was some kind of retirement home. To my surprise, Mother actually seemed delighted by that prospect. I thought she would be happiest at Sunset Hall, where intellectual stimulation for lifetime political activists like herself held priority. But, for some reason, she adamantly refused to go there. Instead, she spoke of Menorah Village, in Reseda, where some old comrades she knew were residents. She had helped organize their fundraisers for years. After several months, and with much difficulty, I secured a place for her there. Our friend and cousin, Naomi Engel Seratoff, whose mother had been my mother's beloved friend, pitched in as her local guardian angel. With Naomi's help, the move was accomplished, and I breathed a sigh of relief.

I took Mother to the woman who had been her doctor for years. Who would be better able to evaluate changes in her? After talking with my mother privately for half an hour, the doctor concluded that she did not have Alzheimer's, as far as she could ascertain. She spoke of small strokes in the brain that can cause confusion and memory loss but said that tends to clear up. She also mentioned depression. She may have been right about the depression, but she was wrong about the Alzheimer's, which my mother was diagnosed with some months later.

"I'm stupid, just stupid," my mother admonished herself angrily. "I can't keep two things together in my head." When my sister and I were young, she would lash out at us with "You! Stupid!" when we misbehaved—furious at our misdemeanors, her ever so slightly accented English softening the vowels, aspirating the final consonant so that it came out sounding like "stoopit," a word that was a lot like spitting. Now I argued with her cruel assessment of herself. "You're not stupid, Mom. What's happening is a physical problem in the brain, which happens to the most learned professors, the most brilliant people. It's not about being smart or not smart." Eyes narrowed, head tilted attentively, she'd listen and nod and then begin her litany of complaints about herself again. My explanations never made a dent in her compassionless view of herself. For ten years, I mourned the terrible slow death of my mother's brain with her, trying to bring her courage and comfort, even when I felt none.

I brought her Meredith Tax's *Rivington Street,* a novel about Jewish immigrants on the Lower East Side, the building of the Garment Workers' Union, and the Triangle Shirtwaist Factory Fire—a life she knew well, having come to it only a generation after that disaster. She seemed to cherish that book, and she read it over and over. Then I brought her more books. These disappeared from her room. When I asked where they were, she said she didn't know what had happened to them. I enquired of the staff, but they said they knew nothing about it. Maybe they were never delivered to her. It was always hard to know what was her confusion and what was the confusion of Menorah Village.

I saw that her closet contained clothing she'd had for years. "How about we go shopping for some new clothes, Mom?" I asked her. "We haven't done that for a long time." "Oh, yes," she said, crinkling her eyes in delight. The outing was not successful.

Tense and uneasy in the dress shop, she seemed unable to summon interest in anything. At first, I thought she was judging the clothes by the long-gone retail standards of her youth, when seam allowances were inches wide and buttonholes were still finished by hand. We tried another store.

"Too expensive," she declared as soon as we walked in.

"Don't worry, darling, I'm treating today," I joked.

We looked at garment after garment, but nothing seemed to appeal to her. Finally, fed up, I said, "Okay, Mom, these clothes are expensive, and I don't want to waste my money, so, please, help me choose something you'll really like." Somehow, we settled on a casual, simple linen jacket of good quality. I say "we" settled, but she protested to the last about the cost, even though she smiled and preened a little in the mirror. We were tired and quiet driving home.

I came the following day to take her to Sizzler, her restaurant of choice. She was cheerful and talkative, and when I mentioned our shopping trip the day before, she said, "Oh, yes, wasn't that fun?" For the hundredth time, I thought to myself, "What is wrong with these doctors? At seventy-nine, she's entitled to a few peculiarities. So what that she doesn't remember people's names?" After lunch, we went for a walk, and then returned to her room. As we kissed to say goodbye, she suddenly said, "Oh, by the way, you know, I keep forgetting to tell you, a long time ago when you were here, you left something," and she pulled her new jacket out of the closet. I laughed. "Mom, did you forget? That's the jacket we bought yesterday. It's yours, it belongs to you." "Oh, yes, of course," she said. But she looked confused and uneasy. I was leaving to catch my plane back to New York, so it was too late to return the thing to the store then. It had been expensive, and I wasn't happy about losing the money. Give it a

week, I thought, and if she still didn't want it, I would ask someone to return it. But a few days later, she gave the jacket to a visitor, an almost complete stranger, telling her that she had found
it. The woman was delighted to get it.

DAVID AND BRURYA

Mother had often spoken fondly of her friend Anna's son David
and his wife, Brurya. I knew them a little and liked them very
much. They were gracious when I suggested a visit and invited
us to brunch at their home in Santa Monica. The ride from the
San Fernando Valley to the Pacific Ocean on the San Diego
Freeway was pleasant enough for scenery, if you could stand the
traffic, but we'd no sooner hit Interstate 580 than the skies
opened up, and we were driving through an incredible down-
pour. My mother was gazing out the window. "Oh, Mom, what a
shame. Look at this weather! Why did it have to rain just today?"
"Rain? Why, it's sunshine to me," she answered. And, truly, her
face, framed by her old silk headscarf, shone as if in sunshine at
that moment. I touched the thin, incredibly soft skin of her hand
with my fingers, feeling her old, ropey, fragile-boned hand ...
Bittersweet memory, never fade!

David and Brurya welcomed us warmly. At the door, Mother
immediately recognized David as someone from her past that
none of us knew. It was a great disappointment to me, so sure
was I that this little scrap of memory had survived. But my
mother wasn't disappointed. She chattered away, ate heartily of
the sumptuous bagels and lox and the other goodies that Brurya
had prepared for brunch, and convinced our hosts that, in fact,
she was not in bad shape. As much as I wanted to think so myself,
the day finally taught me to accept the inevitable.

For a little money, I rented a now-and-then room in Venice to give Mother a few hours at the beach on my trips west. On one of these visits, we sat together in "our bedroom" and tried to practice writing. "Let's write a note to Aunt Pauline, Mom," I said. "You write it, and I'll address the envelope and send it." Pauline was my mother's oldest friend in America, the sister-in-law who had welcomed Sarah as a sixteen-year-old Polish immigrant and steered her through the mysteries of becoming an American teenager and then a wife and mother. My mother struggled with the pencil and note pad. After several attempts, this is what she wrote: "Dear Pauline, I am lost. Can you help me?"

ELEVEN

Women's Music

SOMETHING ABOUT THE WOMEN

In the mid 1970s, living in the hills of British Columbia without the benefit of television or the *New York Times*, I followed the women's movement via its poets and essayists, and it seemed to me to be a wonderful development, the necessary key to the liberation of not just bourgeois women and men, but all oppressed peoples. I saw that the labor and servitude of women and their children, forced or compliant, was (and is) the rock and cement upon which all exploitive systems depend. How can any people expect to achieve freedom without liberating women? Yet I found no signs of agreement among the men I knew, but rather an ugly defensiveness. This eventually had a liberating effect on me because I realized we women were choosing to explore our oppression outside the sphere of white progressive thought and its power. Years earlier, in the Civil Rights Movement, I saw, and now better understood, how many African Americans had made this same shift in consciousness.

As a straight woman of the left, I wasn't in favor of exclusion of any kind. I was thrilled to stand up and say, with Bernice Johnson Reagon, "I love women." But the discomfort of the men in the Weavers over "Something About the Women" started me thinking: hey, if mixed company can't tolerate hearing "I love women" from women, perhaps it would be best not to mix the company? We women certainly weren't going to give up our newfound joy in each other. Women's music became a major aspect of the women's movement, and it was created and developed by lesbian women.

The documentary *The Weavers: Wasn't That a Time!* filmed our last concert at Carnegie Hall and was released in 1981. The director, Jim Brown, and his mentor, George Stoney, who was also one of the producers, wished to include musicians considered "children of the Weavers." They heard my insistent plea to include Holly along with the bigger names. In our brief segment together in the documentary, Holly and I spontaneously sang her "Hay Una Mujer Desaparecida" together, and it became one of the film's most poignant and powerful moments. The documentary was shown on PBS channels across the country. Our duet created an audience for the two of us, and Holly invited me to join her for a concert tour.

ON THE LIFELINE TOUR WITH HOLLY, 1983

Although a second singing career had certainly not been in my life plan, I went on the road again, this time in the company of women. My first tour with Holly set me to cramming my musical head (and heart) with songs by women who spoke to women about women. In all my previous singing years, I had never seen women backstage do more than answer phones and bring coffee. This time, it wasn't Sol or Eddy or Max loading in sound equipment, patching cable, and testing amplifiers, it was Myrna and Sheila and Helen. A woman named Kim hung lights, balancing at the top of a twenty-foot ladder, and cheery, super-competent, ever-resourceful Jill shepherded our luggage and us from airport to interview to concert hall to hotel, coolly turning every emergency into a "no problem." Our road managers, stage crews, sound engineers, concert and record producers—they were all women! Women all over the country were training themselves and each other to bring music—especially women's music—to an audience that was hungry for it. I came to love the women-only events, when the audiences let it all hang out, their hair and their ferocious adoration.

Eventually, my tours with Holly took us from small churches to the same major concert halls where I had played as one of the Weavers. Only now, the folk music audience and women's music audience sat beside one another, spiky, technicolor hair next to smooth gray beards and chignons, lovers, hetero and same-sex, smiling and holding hands to "Perfect Night," Holly's wink at lesbian romance; tapping their feet to the rhythm of Walter Robinson's rocking "Harriet Tubman"; thrilling to Tom Paxton's "There Goes the Mountain" and Holly's "Kentucky Woman"; and at the end of every concert swaying to Lead Belly's "Goodnight Irene," completing a circle in time.

People thought Holly and I were lovers. What did it matter how they defined it? We *were* passionately in love with each other, in love with our cross-generational presence onstage— her hair golden-red, mine silver-white—with the music that we made, with the audience, and with the history that had brought us together.

That's what the women's movement was about for me: poetry, music, and passion. The message? The best message, the only message: Love yourself, your friend, and your lover. If possible, love your enemy. If not, walk away and love something else. Love all of Mother Earth's parts—animal, vegetable, and mineral—and not just some of her children, but all of them; and take care of them, and take care of one another, passionately.

CHANGING LIVES

I imagined that our road manager, Jill Davey, had been recruited from some high-paying job until I read a letter she had written years earlier, when she was simply a fan trailing Holly's performances. Jill's letter is a description not only of her personal experience and that of her friends and community but also of what was happening with many women across the country at this time.

> Holly,
> This is number six! Each one different ... each one superb. We thought at this ... our last stop before the gas runs out ... we'd like to explain the reasons behind our madness!! It is hard to call ourselves "groupies," because, even though some of that "adoration" is there, it is not the primary reason we have followed you across the countryside!
> Two years ago, La Crosse [Wisconsin] was a real sleeper (some preferred to call it a corpse!). What was then our "women's community" consisted mainly of beer and softball. Then, as if out of the night, came Women's Music ... and with it women's culture and feminist politics. It told us of people like us. *Everywhere!* It was all inclusive ... affirming ... healing!!
> With that newfound energy ... La Crosse has changed drastically within two years! A small but dedicated Women's community emerged, and grows daily: a women's bar/coffeehouse opened, a women's production company was formed to promote and produce feminist artists on a local, regional and now a national level, a com-

munity women's center was formed with real feminist therapy available, the La Cross Community Coalition Against Rape was organized, and the El Salvador Solidarity committee. Anti-nuke demonstrations are common; there's a people's food co-op. A chapter of the National Lesbian Feminist Organizations is active promoting support groups for lesbians, lesbian mothers and alcoholics. The Women's Studies Department has become an active sponsor of feminist speakers at the university and we have the beginnings of a feminist bookstore. There is burn out, but we seem to revitalize each other and keep going. That's where you come in!

It's hard sometimes … in a small, conservative mid-western town to believe it's all worth it … to keep on working … keep on trying. We get a lot from each other and we realize how important it is to continue, to realize our differences, respect them and work within them because "we've [we're] all we got!" You, your music and your politics help to make that happen. The energy we get from your concerts is directly transferred into our community. It continues to be a source of growth and support for us. You were a catalyst for us … and you continue to be.

So … if it seems … 'it's just foolish idolatry' that makes us gaze at you,—and Adrienne, Susan and Carrie—I hope this lets you know … *It's a hell of a lot more!* On this, our last excursion … we'd like to thank you, Adrienne, Susan, Carrie—etc.—for struggling, working … continuing.

Jill Davey

Women's music festivals sprang up all over the country. In the 1980s, I performed several times at the National Women's Music Festival, the Michigan Womyn's Festival, and others, but the one I loved best was Sisterfire, with its moving cross-cultural concerts in an urban setting near Washington, DC. Sisterfire was initiated in 1982 as a one-day, one-stage, eight-performer fundraiser. By 1987, it had evolved into two days of ongoing performances, featuring over eighty artists and over a hundred

craftswomen, with a special performance area for children. The
first time I sang at the festival was in 1982, and I remember thinking, "This is fabulous." I felt like I had found home.

Sisterfire was the manifestation of the production company
Roadwork, which was an idea brewed on the back porch of a
Washington, DC, row house in 1977. Bernice Johnson Reagon
and Amy Horowitz formed a coalition of women that shared
power and responsibility across racial, cultural, and class lines
to produce, discover, and promote women's culture on a global
level. In the beginning, Amy sat on the back porch talking on
the telephone from morning till evening booking Sweet Honey
in the Rock, Holly Near, and the Wallflower Order dance collective. By August of 1978, Roadwork was also booking tours for
the band Alive, the poet June Jordan, and the Varied Voices of
Black Women Tour (featuring Linda Tillery, Pat Parker, Mary
Watkins, and Gwen Avery). June Jordan used to say that Roadwork put women's culture on the road. Hundreds of thousands
of people-hours went into creating and sustaining that vision,
and the back porch operation turned into the viable political
organization that produced the Sisterfire Festival. Sisterfire was
a concentrated celebration of the work Roadwork carried out
year round. Sweet Honey in the Rock was and remained Roadwork's guiding inspiration.

I found this poem by Alicia Partnoy in an old Sisterfire program. Alicia survived imprisonment and torture during the bru-
tal junta regime in Argentina. Her poem "Song of the Exiled"
for Sisterfire bears witness to the spirit of the festival.

> They cut off my voice:
> So I grew two voices.
> In two different tongues
> my song I pour.

They took away my sun:
two brand new suns
like two resplendent drums
today I am playing.
Isolated I was
from all my people;
my twin songs are returning
like in an echo.
And despite the darkness
of this exile,
my poem sets fire
against a mirror.
They cut off my voice,
So I grew two voices.
In two different tongues,
My songs I pour.

THE 1984 DEFEAT REAGAN ELECTION-YEAR TOUR

Lisa and I had transitioned to an adult relationship without much bloodshed, and in 1984 she was living in Berkeley, busy with her life and attending college. I was involved in theater projects around the country and in Canada and performing with Holly. Lisa and I didn't see a lot of each other, and a quiet moment before a concert was a good opportunity to reconnect with a letter.

Dearest Lisa,

We're sitting in the cramped dressing room of the ballroom/auditorium of Gettysburg College waiting our turn at sound check. We're in Reagan Territory. In this small school (2,000 students) with its prosperous enrollees ($7,000 tuition alone) only a very small percent are Mondale supporters. This afternoon I spoke to about 30 students and a few faculty members on what it was like to be blacklisted. The sponsors hoped most of the freshman class would come. They didn't. The freshman colloquium was on Civil Liberties, but the largest enrollment here is for Business Administration. It mustn't seem urgent to them to hear about blacklisting in the '50s. Even so, it was an enjoyable gathering in its way.

The house in which we're billeted belongs to the college. It looks to be about fifty years old. It was just painted and furnished, albeit sparsely. It sits alone on the road with playing fields across and around, fields that were part of the Civil War battleground. I find it hard to look out there, knowing the earth to have been so blood-soaked. It was worse at Antietam, we were told at a faculty potluck. 18,500 men died in 15 minutes. That figure sounds impossible. I'll have to check it. Could that much damage be done with just cannon and bullets?

The producer of this concert is the college's Program Director. She's beautiful, black and progressive and has been fighting for change. She brought Sweet Honey and others here to this school, which has no Women's Studies, no Black History (or Black anything—14 black students among the 2,000). She's married to a South African playwright. She thinks maybe 400 people might show up to the concert. It's free for the students.

(After the show.) Well 1,000 people showed up. Aside from five to ten who left during the show after Holly's anti-Reagan rap, most stayed. There were some students and faculty, but mostly outsiders, mixed in age and interests: women, peace, etc. It was a good show. Terrific response.

The night before, we'd sung in Charleston, West Virginia. Two nuns produced the concert, in a coalition of women, peace and social justice groups. Also Reagan territory, although different in character. Here was a working class community—unemployed miners mostly and the small group of peaceniks, women's issues people, working so hard to register people. 500 people came, and they were delighted, as were the producers, who had never done this before.

It's especially gratifying to play for groups that work under such conditions, the small, brave, out-of-the-way grassroots people who don't get much high-powered entertainment/encouragement of our kind. I love the mix we get, the great big audiences that are so ego-gratifying, and the small ones where I feel so grateful to these folks for the courage and stamina.

Holly and I both seem to be improving in the physical problems department. It was pretty bad for me the first week. I was in heavy pain a lot of the time, and my insides were in turmoil. But suddenly I'm relatively pain-free, except when sitting. I walked the other day for the first time without resulting pain and that seems to be holding

Holly is regaining sensation in her foot. Jill and John have been handling all big luggage, Susan the smaller loads. H and I are the great ladies. I'm still not comfortable about it, but am finally doing it consistently—asking others to carry anything. We saw a male chiropractor in Detroit, and a woman in Ithaca. The guy put me through a lot of pain, which I thought was OK. The day afterward I felt pretty good. But the next day—oy! This may have been due to the lousy mattress I was sleeping on, I don't know. Even on the floor it was bad. I left Detroit really crippled.

In Ithaca the chiropractor was 9 months pregnant. She did some kind of maneuver no one has done before. Also she used a machine that utilizes ultra frequency sound—maybe like the one they used successfully on Grandma some years ago. Anyway, work it did, or the emotional release that Susan and Holly did with me one night—I suddenly have begun to improve. Keep your fingers crossed.

I thought dieting would be easy with such rigid proscriptions on what we can eat, but people outdo themselves cooking up gourmet delights with our boring sugarless, meatless, yeastless ingredients. Everyone is gaining weight, even long skinny John, who eats every hour and a half. And all we talk about is food.

So now we're on the plane coming down into Pittsburgh. Our American Airlines flight to Milwaukee got canceled. We may get bumped in Pittsburgh, but with luck we'll make it to Chicago, then rent a car and drive the rest of the way.

Generally, we're getting along quite well. Everyone who saw us last time out seems to feel it's even a better show. I'm better represented, for one thing. It's a relief to have songs to choose from, the result of having done the Madison solo concert. Everywhere we go people have been wonderful.

So, our standby US Air flight left quite late, as did all the others—everything backed up due to fog in Chicago. Then we took off. They had boxed "snacks"—ham sandwiches on burger rolls, wheat crackers, tiny box of raisins, a Mr. Goodbar treat. We took out our food bags: brown rice, lentil soup, tofu, tahini sauce, pita. We are now happy as clams, the attendants wondering what in the world we're eating. Amazing how interested flight attendants get at anything out of the ordinary, such as four of us with our little dropper bottles of Imu-Stim or adrenal stimulators. Funny scene: all the attendants getting a holistic health lecture from Holly on one of our flights.

The only trial right now is that we're in the smoking section. We were standbys, just lucky to get on. Well, we land soon. Then—can we get a car for the trip to Milwaukee? Fortunately, no concert tonight.

Liz Karlin (Dr. Lizard) is coming to Milwaukee from Madison. It was she who produced my concert in Madison. Did I write you about the concert? Seems the word is out that it was a great concert. The tapes do sound pretty good to me. Arrived in Milwaukee in a chauffeured white Cadillac limo, hoo-ha, no planes or buses available because of the fog. Cost us $115, less than the airfare, and we didn't have to drive.

The Milwaukee concert was great. Castleberry and Dupree, two black women who do a kind of reggae, opened. They were excellent. Susan Freundlich has been dancing her solo opener regularly, so she was second. Did I tell you she developed a sign/dance show based upon two prose poems about Jewish angst over the Mid-East situation? Very effective.

We're housed here in a mansion belonging to the brother of one
of the two female partners in Midwest Music, our distributors. He
and his woman friend, both with clouds of beautiful hair, bought it
for a song in a transition neighborhood. They are like two little sixties' kids playing house. What a trip: moving chair lift, laundry
chute from the 2nd floor to basement, endless rooms.

Flying to Indianapolis now, on a 20-seat airplane. You wouldn't
believe the miniature transport we've been on. Didn't I swear I
never would? But here I am! We're heading for a gig where the concert hall went on strike; they had to move the concert to the basement of an armory. That should be interesting.

Wish I could connect with you on the phone … Love you so much

Muddha

DONNA

Settling into my seat for the flight to Minneapolis, the first leg of
the 1984 H.A.R.P. (Holly, Arlo, Ronnie, Pete) Tour, I was not
happy. Holly should have had the adjoining seat, and I had
looked forward to this opportunity to be alone with her so we
could evaluate our collaboration with Pete Seeger and Arlo
Guthrie. Instead, I found myself sharing the armrest with Donna
Korones, a woman I barely knew anything about other than that
she and her family had hosted Holly during H.A.R.P. rehearsals
in New York City. I could see two hours of polite platitudes
ahead because I hadn't even brought a book to hide behind. Ms.
Korones had one on her lap though, Alice Walker's *In Search of
Our Mothers' Gardens,* which I'd been looking forward to reading.

"How do you like it?" I asked, brushing just a little frost off
my annoyance.

She pressed her palms together and squeezed her eyes shut.
"Omygawd!"

I laughed. "That bad, eh?"

By takeoff, we were exchanging tales about our own mothers and comparing our delight with Alice Walker's first novel, *The Color Purple*. Talking about the relationship of Celie and Shug took us past Chicago. Discussing feminism, lesbianism and women's music, along with more chat about our mothers, carried us over Michigan and Wisconsin. By the time we landed in St. Paul, I was seriously smitten with the intelligence, wit, and lively mouth of Ms. Donna Korones and wished I could close it sweetly with a kiss.

It turned out that Donna had been not only Holly's host during rehearsals but also her intensive caretaker and chauffeur, supporting her through the excruciating back pain she had been suffering every day of rehearsal, picking up her meds, and driving her to and from medical appointments and work. We were all concerned. Holly could barely walk; how would she perform? How would H.A.R.P.'s first performance fare? Determined to see for herself, Donna bought a ticket to Minneapolis, hence the seat change. I would learn that "determination" was Donna Korones's middle name.

When the tour ended (successfully) and Donna and I were back home in New York, intimacy sealed our excitement for each other. Serious involvement didn't take long, despite the potential bumps in the road: Donna's family—her husband and two teen-age daughters (the subject of Holly's gentle warning, "I wouldn't touch that subject with a ten-foot pole")—and our eighteen-year age difference—my fifty-eight to her thirty-nine. She told me that her marriage had already dissolved, so I should not concern myself over being a home breaker, but neither of us knew how her daughters would respond to their mother's lesbian affair.

Work that year had me hopping. There would be a national De-feat Reagan Election-Year Tour with Holly; my first solo concert in twenty years in Madison, Wisconsin; roles in *Medea,* Sam Shepard and Joe Chaikin's *Tongues/Savage Love* in St. Louis, and Meredith Monk's *Specimen Days* in New York; two folk festivals, one in Winnipeg, Canada, and the other the Hudson Clearwater Revival festival in Croton, New York; and Sisterfire in Washington, DC. Donna and I grabbed every moment of fun together that we could find, spending a weekend at the beach in Florida, watching twice-a-day movies in New York, and visiting with friends.

I was living on East Tenth Street in the East Village in a one-room, three-story walkup across from what in those days was known as "Needle Park." Today, the location is chic and expensive, gentrification having veiled the decay. But, in 1984, Donna sometimes had to step around some street person sleeping in the doorway to make her way upstairs to my tight little haven. Strolling together uptown one evening after a movie, we paused at the Rockefeller Center skating rink to watch the skaters, and we admitted for the first time that our relationship was problematic for Donna. It wasn't that I was away so much, but that I wasn't there for us completely even when I was home. With some trepidation, we agreed on a radical solution—we would live together. So I left scruffy Tenth Street and moved in with Donna and her daughters on upscale East Fifty-Eighth Street.

Donna's daughter Alicia was about to start her junior year at high school; she asked to live with her father, but he turned her down. Her other daughter, Harlene, would soon be heading to her freshman year at college. At first, they refused to take any notice of my presence in their home. Alicia would come back from school, ignore my "Hi," and shut herself in her room. After many days of Harlene's grim-faced silence, I took her out to breakfast, hoping she would vent her feelings when we were alone. She did so and then some, berating me for the destruction of her family, ignoring my reminder that her parents had already been splitting up by the time I came along. "I blame you," she said furiously, "for my mother drinking too much and for Alicia's unhappiness." Disregarding her exaggerations, I apologized for my part in her understandable anger. "But don't hope for me to disappear any time soon," I advised. "Your mother and I have a solid commitment for our relationship to succeed." We parted calmly, if not happily, when Harlene left for college a few days later. Curiously, Harlene, who is today a brilliant lawyer and educator for lesbian and other civil rights, has no memory of the conversation. As for Alicia, one day, when I was preparing dinner, she suddenly appeared, perched on the kitchen step stool, staring at the stove.

"What are you doing?" she asked.

"Cooking a pot roast."

"How do you do that?" she wondered, and I demonstrated browning the onions and the meat. It was the delicious start of our friendship.

I had no trouble exchanging the noise of dope deals taking place at 1:00 am under the window of my cozy den on East Tenth Street for the absolute silence of watching the traffic on the Fifty-Ninth Street Bridge through Donna's double-paned dining room window. We also had an interesting view of urban nature on the downstairs neighbor's terrace, where sparrows happily splashed dirty rain puddles onto pristine tiles and determined pigeons pecked at the AstroTurf. The most intriguing sight was the weekly appearance of the neighbor (we termed him "the Squire"), who would reel out an enormous garden hose to water three narrow wooden boxes of red, white, and pink impatiens and then use a huge industrial vacuum cleaner to suck up a plastic sandwich bag or two that had blown in from somewhere. I wondered if the equipment had been bought especially for the terrace or brought from some wide estate the Squire owned in Greece or Italy.

Eventually, Donna became my manager, and we were work partners. In 1989, we formed the production company Abbe Alice Music together, which produced my live solo album *Love Will Find a Way.* Let it be said that I was (and still am) a total nincompoop when it came to the business end of my work life. I have mercifully been relieved of the responsibility by such competent managers as Harold Leventhal, during the Weavers and post-Weavers years; Redwood Records Company partners Jo-Lynne Worley and Joanie Shumaker, who shepherded me into the women's music world; and finally Donna Korones. But the frustrations our business partnership generated often took their toll on our personal relationship.

We were together as a couple for twenty-two years. The last four were filled with foolish unhappiness before we decided to quit. It's a miracle that we are close friends today. I attribute our enduring friendship to Donna's persistent visits and calls and also to a transformational experience I had in February 2011, when I was in the hospital and under morphine for a few days. During one of Donna's visits, I was woozy but conscious. I was watching her face as she talked, and I had the strange physical sensation of something like smoke floating out of my body. It contained old resentments and confusions and I was left overwhelmed with fondness and love.

LEAVING NEW YORK, 1988

Donna and I decided to move to Berkeley. It seemed like the obvious choice. Lisa lived there; Alicia was in college; I was working more and more with Holly, who lived in California;

Redwood Records, also based in California, was managing me at that time; and Donna was interested in the production aspects of women's music, which she could pursue there.

I remember the afternoon we left New York City behind. The big apartment, so brightly sumptuous a couple of days ago, was cavernous and gloomy, emptied of all the light and shadow of Donna's ten years with her family and our four years together. We sat together side by side before the dining room window on two worn plastic chairs, each holding her thoughts close to herself. On the windowsill, a begonia, the last of the houseplants, presented its scraggly behind. It too would be abandoned. We watched the trucks and cars, the heavy engines of mercantile and personal life, cross the bridge in the September light as we had during so many seasons of breakfasts and dinners. Silence. All that action, but not a sound.

I called my friend Dottie Gottlieb for one last so-long. Her voice on the phone was even deeper than usual. "You're all done babe?" She growled. "How'd it go? My God, that huge apartment, all that stuff, all the way to California?" Dottie had lived on East Tenth Street for thirty years.

"Yep. Finished. Out. Piece of cake. Moving across the country is no harder than moving across town; you just wait longer for your furniture at the other end."

"Have you called Schenectady, said goodbye to Jackie?"

"Yeah, sure."

I could hear sadness in both our voices. Jackie, Greta, and Dottie had been my friends since the Priority Ramblers and People's Songs. I was the baby of us four. When Jackie, Greta, and I had arrived back in New York after our 1940's wartime dispersal, we missed our friend Dottie. She was in France working for an international women's peace organization, living Parisian (that is, poor and hungry) and sending home long, analytical, incomprehensible political commentaries. New York meant Jackie, Greta, and I hanging out, listening over and over to Greta's Lady Day records, sighing and singing. God, were we ever really that young?

I was distracted from my reverie by some movement outside the window on the terrace of the apartment below. It was the sparrows splashing in puddles and pigeons pecking at the AstroTurf, as usual. The Squire was watering his impatiens, and then he would vacuum up whatever it was the wind had blown in and readjust the plastic geraniums at the base of his two potted trees, all while dressed immaculately in a silk business suit. The sparrows flew away, and then the pigeons. My nose warmed, warning me of tears. Donna, coming out of her own thoughts, took my hand. We stood up slowly and embraced for the last time in that place. Then we picked up our coats and overnight bags and walked toward the front door, leaving the stubborn begonia on the sill. The chairs remained as they were, slightly inclined toward each other but facing outward toward the silent view of the busy bridge.

WRITING MOTHER JONES

I looked in the mirror one morning and recognized that I was old. With my jaw relaxed, my mouth looked grim. There were tiny incipient crinkles in my cheeks, puffs and puckers around the eyes, and that throat! I stared at the well-traveled geography of my face with both regret and amusement and announced to myself aloud, "Look at that, Ronnie, that's sixty-five-year-old you." I couldn't seem to reconcile my reflection with my notion of myself. But hadn't I been crawling through household routines lately, and hadn't Donna been complaining more often about having to wait for me? Maybe my genes were from my slow father rather than my quick mother. What a drag, to be slow in such an impatient world.

The memory of a recent episode bloomed: I stood in line at an ATM, watching an old fellow turn his card the wrong way and then punch in the wrong code while the guy up next shook his head, shuffled his feet, and made *tsk* sounds with his tongue. When the old man finally finished, the exasperationist charged forward, nearly colliding with him. I wasn't sure, but I thought I might have seen just a hint of spite around the old fellow's mouth as he walked away. Was I looking at my future?

It was at this juncture in my life that I ran into the ghost of the old woman who was to change it—Mary Harris "Mother" Jones. I was in the Appalachians on the *Love Will Find a Way* tour. Donna, pianist Julie Homi, and I had a two-day layover before our next date, in West Virginia. I couldn't afford to fly us home and back, so I called Guy Carawan, an old acquaintance from my Weaver days, the former music director at the Highlander Research and Education Center in Tennessee. I asked if he could recommend a conveniently located bed and breakfast.

"Sure I could," said Guy. "But Ronnie, you'll want to visit the Pittston coal strike, won't you? Surely you've heard about Camp Solidarity?"

A strike in the coalfields? Memories from my well informed, red-diaper-baby youth surfaced of John L. Lewis, the iron-fisted, bushy-browed, fierce United Mine Workers' boss of a half a century ago, and Mother Jones, the legendary agitator. But this was 1989. President Ronald Reagan had smashed the big air traffic controllers' strike of nine years earlier by firing and replacing the entire work force. Corporations got his message: "Union solidarity? Labor law? Worry no more!" Corporate lawyers had been forcing long-standing, hard-won workers' rights out of union contracts ever since. In an occupation where accidents and black lung disease were facts of life, the Pittston miners were striking to retain lifetime health benefits for themselves and their families.

So, instead of tromping around the hills of the Great Smoky Mountains smelling the flowers, we dropped in on 1,700 Appalachian coal-mining families, who were engaged in the most remarkable American labor campaign of the twentieth century. Escorted by a friend of Guy's, who kindly put us up in her home, we walked a long hillside footpath to Camp Solidarity, which had been set up on an embankment by the Clinch River.

Why wasn't the West Virginia strike big news on TV? A contest in the historically violent Logan and Mingo Counties of West Virginia (which had been the site of John Sayles's powerful 1987 film, *Matewan*) should have produced some gory stories, but the union leaders had adopted one of the guiding principles of the Civil Rights Movement—nonviolent civil disobedience. "No blood? Not sexy," a press journalist explained.

As we entered the canvas-roofed hospitality area, so did a column of men in battle-green camouflage uniforms. They marched in and broke ranks with military precision. Confused by the macho militarism, all I could think of were CIA-backed contras out to destroy the Sandinista government, but I reminded myself to open my Berkeley mind. "This is West Virginia, not Nicaragua," I told myself. It turned out they were strikers coming off picket duty for lunch.

We were invited to join the lunch line, along with the six or seven other visitors that day, and we learned that thousands more had visited the encampment that summer. Wildcat coal strikers from other states, labor sympathizers, and people from all over the world had come to West Virginia to observe and lend support, including representatives of the United States Airline Pilots Association, who were considering a contest of their own. Hundreds of individuals had come with tents and sleeping bags, and they had taken turns picketing and blocking scab access. All were welcomed and fed. The strike became a resistance movement of a kind not seen since the sixties. This remote piece of Appalachia had even turned international as miners from Poland, England, Czechoslovakia, and Japan mingled with rural American workers at Camp Solidarity.

A woman serving us told us that the lunch line had handled over a thousand people one day. Another said the Pittston Company had gotten the health department to shut down the kitchen for a time. But that didn't stop them. "I cooked forty pounds of macaroni salad in my own kitchen," she grinned. These women, who had turned this outpost into a home base for international labor solidarity, were the backbone of the strike. Led by two women miners, they had connected with women from an earlier failed strike against another coal company and organized themselves into a bulwark of female support, ready for anything—from selling souvenir caps to picketing and organizing mass rallies.

If they were arrested, many of the women identified themselves in court only by the name printed across the bosom of their red T-shirts: "Daughters of Mother Jones!" A small blond woman described blocking the entrance to Moss 3, a major coal processing plant. The governor had sent armed state troopers to roust the strikers who occupied it. "It was raining. We just took hands and sat down in the road. I knew that trooper wouldn't step in the puddle to grab me," she laughed, "his boots were too shiny."

We spent the day listening to strike strategy and singing old labor songs with them, and we heard an address by strike leader

Cecil Roberts. I thought about *The Autobiography of Mother Jones*, which I'd read at age fourteen, curious about an old woman who organized coal miners. I recalled the story of when Mother Jones and striking miners encountered a guard with a Gatling gun. She told the man behind it, "Fire one bullet and five-hundred miners with rifles watching from the hills will see to it that not one of your gang is left alive." Later, she wrote that she knew nothing about miners in the hills. "I hate violence," she said. "I prefer drama."

Now, I wanted to know everything about the legend whose spirit had been invoked by these women. Surely this rich character called for a play. Who better to make one for her than the sixty-five-year-old woman in the mirror? Folk singer Si Kahn, a fine political lyricist, thought so too. We agreed he would provide the songs.

I wanted to play Mother Jones as a real woman, not an icon. Greedily, I opened to the first page of her autobiography, but I was disappointed. "I was born in Cork, Ireland, and raised in Toronto, Canada, but always as an American citizen," she says in the first paragraph, in which she briefly talks about her father; she never mentions a mother or siblings. By the second page, she has been married, widowed, and bereft of four unnamed and genderless children in a yellow fever epidemic. I plowed ahead.

Throughout the half-century memoir, the names of fellow organizers come up, but never those of a lover or close friend. Who was this woman who talked like a street fighter and apparently lived like a nun? There were no clues in the autobiography. I learned later that the woman some called "Jesus Christ in disguise" had also been called a "whorehouse madam" and "the most dangerous woman in America."

Another truly serious disappointment awaited me: Mother Jones versus the suffrage movement. I could hardly bear it!

Mother Jones, that tower of female individualism and strength, who had born witness to the women's suffrage movement from nearly its abolitionist beginnings through to the passage of the Nineteenth Amendment, appeared not to have had a good word to say for it. A contemporary article from the *New York Times* quoted her: "I am not a suffragist. I have learned that women are out of place in political work.... Home training of the child should be [a woman's] task, and it is the most beautiful of tasks."

Mother Jones, touting the Victorian *Woman's Sphere?* I couldn't believe it. No wonder the present day women's movement ignored her. But, at the time, I was in love with Mother Jones and reluctant to let her go, even if she wasn't a suffragist. In retrospect, I believe the *Times* article was deliberately distorted. Actually, her position on voting was consistent with her socialist and anarchist views. She believed that the lot of the working class would be improved only by organization and direct action, not by any movement for suffrage. "Politics is the servant of industry," she insisted. "The government isn't in Washington, it's in Wall Street. And that gang of pirates plunders the land and the people at will!"

Ultimately, this issue about suffrage inspired one of my favorite scenes in the play: to help Mother Jones raise money for the starving families of striking Colorado miners, well-meaning socialite Mrs. J. Borden Harriman arranges for her to speak at her exclusive New York Colony Club for Women. Jones makes her dramatic pitch, but the well-to-do women insist on knowing where she stands on women's rights and suffrage. "I am not for women's rights nor men's rights—I'm for human rights!" she declares. "You don't need a vote to raise hell; I have never had a vote, and I have raised hell all over this country." Calling her "an anti," the women troop out. Afterward, she ruefully admits, "I wasn't much help to the strikers that night."

Writing the theater production *Mother Jones* was a three-year journey over a mixed landscape. A visit with my friend Larry Lillo, artistic director of the Vancouver Playhouse, was a precious gift early in the process. For a week, we laughed over how to get Mother Jones on stage in the present: "Her spirit could arrive from heaven on a beam of light. No, no—from hell in a clap of thunder and a cloud of smoke! What's a good stage effect for purgatory?" Finally, we decided to place her at her hundredth birthday celebration bragging to her guests about her triumphs.

Larry and I arranged to meet next at my home in Berkeley following the opening of his latest production at the Playhouse. But he didn't make it to California; he died of AIDS on June 3, 1993. I didn't have much heart for writing *Mother Jones* after Larry's death. I was tempted to drop the subject, preferably on her head, but the mysteries surrounding Jones's personal life fueled my desire for more information. Scouring the library and bookstore shelves for biographies, I found a gem, *Mother Jones Speaks*— page upon page of verbatim quotes from speeches, letters, and interviews, collected by labor historian Philip Foner. I pored over the book, soaking up her style, her language, and her personality. Reading about the suffrage movement's long, checkered history clarified my understanding of how race and class tear at the fabric of female solidarity.

Meanwhile, I continued to make my living in the music world, performing at East and West Coast venues, managed by Donna, who was both my life companion and my traveling companion. I was a frustrating, often infuriating partner for Donna, who struggled to keep our personal and professional lives on track. At the best of times, I am a foot dragger around business needs. Now my mind was elsewhere. I was writing a play.

While I was still working on the script, I got an offer from Wisconsin. John Dillon, the artistic director of the Milwaukee Repertory Theater and a friend from my Open Theatre days, phoned and asked if I had a project I'd like to do at the theater. I told him about *Mother Jones,* and all of a sudden I had a fine theater's resources to develop the play and book it when it was done. But uncertainty warred with excitement. I was an actor, but what did I really know about playwriting? Where was the justification for Mother Jones talking about herself for an hour and a half? But the voice telling me to do it pushed past my fears that I didn't know how, and I turned again to Foner's *Mother Jones Speaks,* my copy bristling with markers, the contents highlighted in different colors, and let it flow.

When it looked like I had something resembling a play, Donna invited a group of women friends to a reading in our living room. Their insightful responses were encouraging. Two of the women were independent publishers, and they saw the possibility of a book contract if I wrote an essay about my interest in Mother Jones to preface the play. (I took them up on it. The Windcall Program, a retreat for activists on a ranch in Wyoming, gave me a generous month of solitude to relax and write. Conari Press published the book as *Ronnie Gilbert on Mother Jones: Face to Face with the Most Dangerous Woman in America*.) My access to music audiences was perfect for telling people about the play and trying out the songs. Pianist Libby McLaren traveled with Donna and I on tour, and her piano accompaniments gave Si's tunes, composed on guitar, a theatrical stature.

At last, I took the play to Milwaukee, only to discover that John Dillon and managing director Sarah O'Connor had booked the Rep's Stackner Cabaret rather than the Rep's full stage for

Mother Jones. So there I was, with a three-hour work-in-progress that I needed to cut down to an hour and ten minutes!

Jack Forbes Wilson, a fine pianist, arranged the songs for a small acoustic ensemble. Director Norma Salizar, whom John Dillon chose for the project, was *Mother Jones's* champion. She plunged into the material with an enthusiasm that matched mine, and she even fought for a bit more playing time and won it. I've always loved the rehearsal process in theater—the hunting, digging, exploring, thinking, and rethinking. I got my happy fill of it in Milwaukee.

Mother Jones was given a perfect production on the tiny Stackner stage. My costume was elegant and comfortable. The painted background was extraordinary, a sepia-colored enlargement of part of the Bill of Rights, overlaid with old photos of strikes, factory children, and the old American flag. My script was hidden onstage in a big, beautiful book that looked natural to the set.

I worried about battling the noise of cutlery and drink orders in a cabaret; but I needn't have. The skillful Stackner waitstaff were careful and quiet, and the audience was unfailingly attentive. Although I rarely forgot my lines, one night I did get confused. But in a one-person show, you don't have to worry about a mistake throwing off another actor; you just need to keep your cool and not let the audience worry for you. So, as I checked the script, I quipped, "After all, she's one hundred years old—what can you expect?" This got an appreciative round of applause.

Ann Shepherd, a bosom friend and my first theater mentor, came up from her home in North Carolina to check out my first venture as writer and actor. She left me with kudos and notes of brain-tingling brilliance, reminding me of what, thirty years earlier, had drawn me like a magnet both to her and to theater. I left Milwaukee happy—I had firmly been dubbed "playwright" by John and his theater colleagues, and I was beginning to believe it.

Following the Milwaukee run, I took *Mother Jones* to the Sheldon Concert Hall in St. Louis for a few days. The Sheldon wasn't a theater, but the directors convinced me that they could make the technically primitive auditorium work for the play. We decided to try, with the objective of using *Mother Jones* as a catalyst to bring together the communities of labor activists and women's rights activists in the audience. The Sheldon concentrated on outreach, and they all came. I spent one afternoon with a lively women's group and another with a labor group, and I visited Mother Jones's burial place in Mount Olive, Illinois. Afterwards, I took the play to the Folly Theater in Kansas City for a single performance. It seemed that *Mother Jones* was on her way.

However, at this point, songwriter Si Kahn and I parted ways, having made a critical mistake. Instead of negotiating a business relationship at the start, we sailed along with the creative work, counting on mutual admiration and political fraternity for consensus. We later learned that we had deep underlying differences in perspective, not only about money, but also about the point of the undertaking and how to proceed with it. We could not proceed. It cost us our friendship and cost my play its momentum.

After casting around for months for another songwriter, I settled down and rewrote the songs myself. During the Weaver years, I had contributed lines and verses to many songs in our repertoire. I had also had ideas for original songs, some several verses long, but had never pursued them to completion. But now I was both wimpy me and powerfully self-assured Mother Jones.

Mother Jones won. When the Berkeley Repertory Theatre gave my play its first full-scale production, it had a brand-new set of songs, with words by me and music by the brilliant composer Jeff Langley, who played piano for the run.

As much as I loved the cozy Stackner Cabaret, the production of *Mother Jones* at Berkeley's Zellerbach Playhouse, directed by Timothy Near, had a feeling of expansiveness I hadn't imagined. The set had a "railroad line" walkway out to the audience (for Mother Jones, the traveler) and a rise upstage for scenes like the end of the first act, in which Jones and a fellow organizer walk up the mountain on a moonless night. She wonders if anyone will show up for the meeting she has called. At the top, they see dozens of lanterns in the dark, like tiny stars moving up the trails. "Oh, John, there's the star of hope," Mother Jones says (a direct quote, taken from Foner's book). "There's the miners' future, a new civilization, the star that will shine when all others grow dim."

The press was fairly enthusiastic. The *San Francisco Chronicle* critic's "little man" applauded, although, disappointingly, he failed to jump out of his seat. However, the review I most appreciated came two years later. Donna and I braved a wildly excited teenage audience to watch an Ani DiFranco concert at the grand Zellerbach Auditorium. In the seat to my left, a young woman of fourteen or fifteen kept staring at us through the first set. I figured it was because we were the only "old people" in the row. But, at intermission, she turned to me and asked shyly, "Are you Mother Jones?" To my surprised yes, she shouted, "I loved that show, I LOVED that show, I LOVED THAT SHOW!"

My ongoing relationship with *Mother Jones* survived various venues during the nineties. I even played her for an Irish audience. An old friend of mine, Gordon Rogoff, and his partner

Mort Lichter, who were living in Ireland and directing *Exiles Theater* in Cork City, brought me over. I was a bit nervous to be presenting *Mother Jones* in her birthplace, but the audience responded favorably. Present was His Right Worshipful Lord Mayor of Cork, whose costume confused me. He wore a most impressive heavy gold chain of office draped over his shoulders, which suggested brocades, but he wore an ordinary sort of workingman's Sunday-going-to-church suit. Confused by the mixed clues, I may have shown too much deference or not enough. Hard to say.

Director Maureen Heffernan worked with me on a revision of the play for a run at the Hasty Pudding Theatre (now the Zero Arrow Theatre) in Cambridge, Massachusetts. The stage set for the production was minimal, designed for easy traveling. I kept the pieces in my workspace closet, but I used them only twice and eventually gave them up. I became occupied writing another play, *Legacy,* based on the work of the author, historian, and social commentator Studs Terkel.

In 1996, I celebrated my seventieth birthday on tour with Holly Near. At each performance, Donna and Holly organized birthday cake and guest appearances from fellow performers and friends. The fun and moving trip marked the conclusion of my professional partnership with Holly and my lifetime of touring. The album *This Train Still Runs* was recorded during those performances.

I wasn't prepared for another solo singing career, but I also didn't want to give up my connection with an audience all together. So I put together bits of song and personal history from the labor movement, the civil rights movement, the election fights, and the political upheavals that I'd lived through into a one-woman show and called it *A Radical Life with Song.* Over the next ten years, I sporadically performed the piece for benefits and an occasional club date. At each presentation, I drew parallels with the topical issues of the day, hoping to light a few sparks and show that, no matter how bleak the news, we've faced these kinds of hurdles before and survived.

TWELVE

Women in Black

In 1982, I stood in a half circle in a garden with forty or fifty people from the Berkeley folk community. We were gathered together in celebration of *nueva canción* ("new song"), a movement that joined the musical genius of indigenous Latin America with the social awareness of its contemporary youth. The entertainment for the event was Lichi Fuentes's terrific band, and it was impossible to stand still to their bouncing, dimpling rhythms. Just as I was about to start dancing, a woman standing next to me whispered something my way.

"I'm sorry," I said to the attractive, dark-haired, dark-eyed woman with the unfamiliar accent. "I didn't quite hear what you said."

"*Nueva canción,* yes," she repeated, "but it makes me wonder."

"Wonder about what?" I said, still trying to hold on to the feel of the music.

"Why don't the songs of my people have a place in the movement if it's about musicians calling up their culture from under the heel of the oppressor?"

That little speech stopped me cold. What could I do but smile—in a friendly manner, of course. "Your people? Who are your people?"

"I'm Lebanese," she said.

My first thought was, that's silly. What can Arabic music, based on an entirely different set of harmonic and rhythmic principles, have in common with the deliciously complex but familiar music of Latin America? I didn't know the first thing about Lebanon.

"Okay," I gave in, "so why do you think there's no Arabic music in *nueva canción?*"

"Racism. What else but racism?"

Ugh, racism, I thought. Everything is racism. I was annoyed. "But how can it be racism? Look at these people. Dark-skinned, light-skinned, different kinds of hair, female, male ... "

"Yes, but not an Arab among them."

"Now, wait a minute," I said. "How would Arabic music relate? I certainly don't know how to listen to it. I bought a tape of Umm Kulthum, and I simply couldn't fathom where a song starts and where it ends ..." I trailed off, embarrassed. I could hear the racism squeezing out of me like toothpaste.

She smiled, held out her hand, and introduced herself. "I'm Tina Naccache," she said. "And I know who you are, my dear. But Umm Kulthum? Hers is the most difficult music, even for Arabs. Okay, Ronnie, if I taught you an Arabic song, would you sing it in public?" It was a challenge.

"Uh, certainly, of course, absolutely, why not, uh ... I mean, yes, if I could learn it. I'm pretty slow these days. You'd have to teach me—from scratch." And so she did.

And that's how it began, the crack in my wall of ignorance about the Middle East—with a new friend. Tina told me the song she found was from a play written and performed for children in the Palestinian refugee camps. Camps? I wanted to know what kind of camps she was talking about. Were they like the interim displaced persons camps established at the end of World War II, where thousands of refugee Jews waited to be sent anywhere but back to Europe? The camps Tina spoke of had been meant to be temporary, too, but for decades they had been the inhospitable home for hundreds of thousands of Palestinian refugees waiting to go back home to their villages and towns. Driven from Palestine in 1948, and again in 1967, women and men grew old and died in the camps. Children were born and grew up there and bore another generation. Tens of thousands of children had been living in abject poverty under Lebanon's reluctant sufferance, and, like their parents, they dreamed of going home to Palestine.

Meanwhile, inside the camps, life went on. A mothers' group devised a play for children about a fox who refused to eat meat, and the group recorded a sweet little song. I learned it in a few weeks and sang it at a concert at Berkeley's Greek Theatre, with Pete Seeger accompanying on banjo:

> Sing with me, let's sing to her,
> Call to her, and she will come.
> Don't be afraid, don't talk in whispers.
> The light of the moon and of the sun,
> The countries of the five continents,
> Are but a drop, a small drop in her ocean—
> Oh freedom, oh freedom.

Two women's groups, Jerusalem Women in Black and Serbian Women in Black, were co-nominees for a Nobel Peace Prize in 2001. The Balkan women had banded together in brilliant opposition to their war-thirsty leaders and compatriots during the Yugoslavian Civil War. They were inspired by the Jerusalem organization, whose members had been going out into the streets for three years to protest the Israeli Defense Forces' occupation of Palestinian territory. Although irate Israeli patriots threatened and insulted the Jerusalem women, the movement had spread throughout the country. My awareness of these Israeli women's activism sent me to the Internet to educate myself about the occupation from the Palestinian point of view, which was rarely expressed in American TV and newspapers. My vague feeling of disloyalty to Israel faded as I read reports from European newspapers and Israeli peace groups about the hell that was the occupation: US helicopter gunships and F-16 war planes were being used in densely populated areas; homes were demolished in the middle of the night and farmers' olive and fruit orchards were uprooted by bulldozers designed and produced in the United States; children were shot for throwing stones at armored tanks; sudden arbitrary curfews were being implemented; sick people and women in labor were being refused transport to hospitals less than six miles away due to the cruelty of the checkpoints. I saw that the vicious Palestinian suicide bombings and the heartless Israeli occupation were equal crimes against both peoples, and they thwarted any hope for peace. "In the kingdom of death," wrote Israeli peace activist Nurit Peled-Elhanan, whose thirteen-year-old daughter was killed in a suicide attack by a Palestinian youth, "Israeli children lie beside Palestinian children, soldiers of the occupying army beside suicide bombers, and no one remembers who was David and who was Goliath."

I helped start Bay Area Women in Black in 2001. Coming out publicly for an end to the Israeli occupation of Palestine is complicated, especially for American Jewish progressives, much more so than, say, speaking out for gun control. Anti-Semitism, shamed into dormancy for a time by the horrors of the Holocaust, is again on the rise in the world. Indeed, sometimes it seems our whole species is sick with racism, anti-Semitism, and tribalism. One doesn't want to give aid, even inadvertently, to xenophobes who use the misdeeds of the State of Israel as an excuse to unleash Jew-hatred. I cringed, for instance, at the sight of a placard in a peace demo that showed the Nazi swastika superimposed on the Star of David of the Israeli flag, as if the evil were in the ancient Judaic symbol itself.

In that same year, Jerusalem Women in Black sent out a call: "Tomorrow is the anniversary of the Israeli Army's illegal crossing over the green line into Palestinian territory. Stand with us against the Occupation … Stand with us tomorrow." I felt compelled to protest the policies of the State of Israel, even after their withdrawal from Gaza. The occupation of the West Bank, which is actually expanding, continues to this day, as does the denial of real statehood for Palestinians. As I protested, my memory unsurprisingly threw me a couple of long ones.

I remembered my mother and ten-year-old me, marching hand in hand down a wide avenue in New York City in the long-awaited May Day parade, part of the American scene of my childhood and a great yearly celebration of union labor and leftist activism. People lined the sidewalks along the route. Often, there was applause. We were marching with a huge contingent of women, the dressmakers' union—my mother's group. Behind us, before us, and around us were ranks of cloak makers, furriers, and milliners—the needle trades workers of New York City celebrating international labor's big day. We were walking and singing: "We shall not, we shall not be moved!" "Solidarity forever, the union makes us strong!" People lined the sidewalks.

Most simply watched; some applauded. Suddenly, I became aware that the singing just ahead of us was dying out, and at the same time I heard shouting from the sidelines. Up ahead, a spectator from the sidelines, his face blotchy red, his mouth twisted and wide, leaned out as if to jump at us and screeched: "Jews, kikes! Go back to Russia, ya dirty Jews!" I slowed down and drew back a little. My mother tightened her hold on my hand. Some people around the man laughed. They had hold of his arm, but they were screaming, too: "Dirty Jews, Sheenys!" Shocked, I looked up at my mother. Her head was tilted upward, her gaze focused on the ranks of marchers ahead. "Pay no attention," she said firmly and calmly, and she lifted her chin even higher as we walked by. I stuck my chin up as high as possible as we passed them, imitating her air of disdain. "Of course we are Jews," I thought. "And proud of it! Look, we're in the best company: unionists, socialists, Jews!" They, the ignorant haters, were beneath contempt. The singing soon picked up again, even stronger than before. The message was clear: we will prevail.

Another memory came to me, from years after the parade. Hillel and Aviva Rabinodov, two singers from Israel, were playing a guest set at the Village Vanguard, where the Weavers worked. Aviva's dancing fingers struck thrilling rhythms on a drum shaped like an hourglass, which she held under her arm. Hillel coaxed tunes from a hollow length of bamboo between verses. Afterward, they introduced us to a friend of theirs, "Captain Ike." He was a little guy, with an open boyish grin, his jaunty yachtsman's cap shoved back on his head, and his shirt collar open over the lapels of his threadbare jacket.

"You read about him, right?" asked Hillel.

"I think so," I lied, blushing. But then a picture came to me from a news story of two or three years earlier, before Israel: a

258 / *Women in Black*

rusty hulk of a ship loaded with Jewish survivors from Europe, being forced back to Europe by the British after having daringly run the British blockade and docking in the port of Haifa.

"Captain Ike was the pilot of that boat," said Aviva, her eyes tearing with pride.

"Oh, yes," I recalled, "The *Exodus*. The boat was called the *Exodus*, wasn't it?"

And then this memory:

MOTHER (ANGRY): I don't understand you, Ronnie. How can you support Israel?

ME (ANGRIER): How can you not? How can a Jew not want Holocaust survivors to have a home? Where were they supposed to go? No one else took them—not us, not the Soviet Union.

MOTHER (SHAKING HER FINGER IN MY FACE): But it's not good what they're doing there, the Zionists. They're lining themselves up with America against the Soviet Union ...

ME: Right, you don't like Zionists. But must you spout the Party line on this, Mom? Can't you ever think for yourself?

MOTHER (GOING FOR CLOSURE): That's the trouble with you, Ronnie. You don't read enough!

Typically, for Mother, the crux of the issue was socialism versus capitalism; for me it was free thought versus my mother. Neither of us, I realized sadly, ever mentioned the Palestinians and what was happening to them while the Jews "built Israel." And now I was out here protesting. What would Mother say? "Told you so"?

At the silent vigils in the Bay Area held by Women in Black, I met defenders of Israeli policy. One accused us of "doing the work of Hamas." Another spat at us. A man in a three-piece suit used his briefcase to smash a sign I was carrying. Enraged, I turned to yell at him, but I managed instead to take a couple of deep breaths, clamp my teeth, and hold back the expletive. My God, nonviolence asks a lot from us!

Jewish members of Women in Black hold with the centuries-old Judaic tradition of, to quote an Israeli peace activist brought up by parents who survived the Holocaust, "bearing witness, railing against injustice, and foregoing silence." Our silent witness was a shout to ourselves and to the world to pay attention. More than once, I've been asked, "Why pick on Israel when there is so much other injustice in the world?" And my answer is always, why not? Are Jews supposed to self-criticize only at Yom Kippur and then forget about it? And where does it say that a crime is canceled by a crime elsewhere? I have never had any religious training at all. I am the daughter of an atheist and am an atheist myself, and my relationship to my Jewishness is entirely secular: pride in our age-old need to probe, search out meaning, and delight in the life of the mind; pride in the long history of spirited Jewish participation in struggles for economic and social justice, not just for ourselves, but for all people; pride in our strength and endurance as a people despite injury and even calamity; and pride in our humor.

THIRTEEN

Learning to Be Old

August, 2013

I roll my walker to the corner, heading for the Seniors for Peace demonstration. A dozen residents are already out there in their chairs and walkers, waving appreciation to motorists for honking approval at the weekly demonstration of gray-haired activists. I thought I'd skip this week, but the news is impossible to ignore: rows of dead Syrian children killed by poison gas, and President Obama threatening to bomb Syria! The military use of poison gas is beyond horrific, but it isn't clear which ferocious side of Syria's civil war launched the gas rockets. Regardless, the rationality of the United States bombing the country escapes me. How many more Syrian children will die as collateral damage?

I choose a peace sign from a few unclaimed extras but hang back from joining the action. Do we honestly think songs sung off-pitch in Mill Valley will stir up a tsunami for peace in Washington? And in Iraq, Afghanistan, and now Syria? But as historian Howard Zinn wrote, "pessimism becomes a self-ful-filling prophecy. It reproduces itself by crippling our willingness to act." There was never a truer word. So we keep optimistic and keep protesting. But the fervent out-of-tune singing gives me a toothache. I should have learned to play the banjo.

September, 2013

The bombing is "on hold." President Obama and Russia's President Putin have agreed that Russia will monitor the removal and destruction of the Syrian stock of sarin gas. Did our little demonstration play a part in delaying America's involvement in the Syrian civil war? I doubt it, but maybe that's all one can really expect from a small group action: the feeling of having done something—anything. I remember Zinn again: "We don't have to engage in grand, heroic actions to participate in the process of change. Small acts, when multiplied by millions of people, can transform the world." It's true; the Vietnam War was not stopped by any single protest, but by eight years of actions taken by students, workers, soldiers, and old people.

I'm at another of the weekly Seniors for Peace demonstrations. I watch my special friends among the dozen or two activists: Warren in his wheelchair, a conscientious objector since 1944; Al and Betty, both one-hundred-and-one years old; Frieda, ninety-five, and Nora, ninety-four, their wheelies plastered with peace and justice signs. All of them are long-time veterans of movements against war. Year after difficult year, they make a new nest for hope, which Emily Dickinson described as that "thing with feathers … that sings the tune without the words and never stops at all." I pick up my sign and join the passionate, if somewhat off-pitch, tune: " … AND STUDY WAR NO MORE!"

262 / Learning to Be Old

January, 2014

International folk music icon and American activist Pete Seeger died at ninety-four on January 27. For six decades, he had been my musical mentor, working friend, and moral comrade, uncompromising in his commitment to making the world a better place. It was hard to imagine life without his indomitable energy. It was so typical of him that, a few days before he died, he insisted on splitting wood instead of resting in the hospital. Sadness aside, I was grateful he didn't survive to disablement; Pete Seeger and a wheelchair would have had a terrible relationship.

For weeks, my email inbox overflowed with condolences from strangers who responded to Pete's passing as if it were the loss of a personal friend. I wish that more of them had also known the other Seeger hero, Toshi-Aline Otah Seeger, Pete's wife. A producer, filmmaker, activist, and mother, Toshi dedicated her life to supporting Pete and the causes he stood for. Her support made his commercial success possible. She was "the brains of the family," Pete had said. "I'd get an idea, and she'd figure out how to make it work." Toshi had died just a few months earlier, at ninety-one.

July, 2014

Outside my window, three little finches scrabble at each other over positions on the seed feeder. It's plenty long enough for them all, but maybe they prefer struggle to peace. The birds remind me of the Middle East and my anticipated problem at the Seniors for Peace demonstration the next day.

Ten years old and going strong, the demonstration has a barrel full of good handmade signs with nice universal messages such as

"Peace Now" and "No War." But I'm planning to carry a different sign tomorrow: "ISRAEL STOP BOMBING GAZA!" It may infuriate the never-criticize-Israel peace activists among us, but I'm sick of choking back my fury at the horror of Israel's murderous barrage, using US-financed missiles on the imprisoned, unarmed citizens of tiny Palestinian Gaza. No matter what Hamas is doing in retaliation, nothing can compare to Israel's unbelievable destruction of Gaza's infrastructure—which has left the population, young and old, without power or water—and the deliberate shelling of a Gaza school, whose staff begged for time to evacuate.

I only have the one sign, which someone made for me. A few other folks express interest, so I find some photos of simple Jewish Voice for Peace posters online and print them on letter-size paper. Some of my friends are willing to pin the sheets onto their shirts. It's encouraging that others agree—this isn't a time when silent anti-war pacifism is enough.

August, 2014

Nancy Feehan, the facilitator of a support workshop I attended, had an old tape she was holding for a couple of other participants. These days, I mostly use an iPod, but I've still got my old-fashioned audio equipment gathering dust on a shelf, so I invited them to my apartment to listen to the cassette. The worn label on it said "depression"—not very appealing. But when we finally got it playing what we heard was a tiny scrap of song.

"Is that Holly Near?" Betty wondered.

"No, she doesn't play guitar," I answered. "But it's familiar … "

We turned up the volume.

What joy! It was a recording of old, beloved songs—"Ode to a Gym Teacher," "Sweet Friend of Mine," "Waterfall," "You've

Got Me Flying"—by the stars of the lesbian song movement: Meg Christian, Margie Adam, Cris Williamson, and yes, Holly Near. The tape turned out to be a precious recording of the 1976 Women on Wheels tour of California.

"I was there, I was there!" Betty cried. "I saw them, I heard them, I was there!" We sat together in my room for however long, singing those songs again and again, laughing, weeping, and remembering those marvelous years. Betty is turning ninety this week, I'm eighty-eight next month, and Audrey's seventy something, just a kid. She's getting there. I think of a few lines from one of Holly's songs, "We're Still Here," from the album *Peace Becomes You:*

> We're still here
> Choosing love over fear
> With walkers and canes we are standing
> And we're still here.

POSTSCRIPT

Ronnie took ill in mid-May, 2015. With grace and conviction she declined surgery, accepting an imminent death over the uncertainty of medical intervention. She was not in pain, and she was very much at peace with her decision. "What about the book?" she asked. "It's OK. You've done what you needed to do, and the book will have a life of its own," I reassured her.

Out of the hospital, Ronnie was cheerful and relaxed. Donna and I camped out in her room, telling stories, laughing, watching movies, knitting—sad times full of sweet moments. A friend, treating Ronnie to a session of energetic bodywork, commented, "Hmm. Ronnie has the strongest aura of anyone I've ever worked on." "No shit, Sherlock," Donna responded.

Ronnie lived her life fully and passed peacefully on June 6, 2015. She was eighty-eight.

Lisa Weg
June, 2015

INDEX

Abbe Alice Music, 237
Abraham Lincoln High School, 36
Adam, Margie, 264
Adler, Stella, 133, 137
Almanac Singers, 43, 48
Alper, Jackie (née Gibson), 43–44, 45, 49, 50, 52, 53, *figs. 3, 19*
America Hurrah, 137–39, 141, 142, 197, *fig. 9*
American Civil Liberties Union (ACLU), 61
American Labor Party, 61–62
American Nazi Party, 59, 60
Anacostia High School, 46–47
Arena Stage, Washington, 44
Asbel, Bernie, 43, 45
Asbel, Millie, 43, 45
Ashbee, Felicity, 139, 148
Awake and Sing! (play), 35

Baez, Joan, 175
Barsky, Edward, 28
The Beatles, 126, 174
Belafonte, Harry, 101, 105

Bennett, Gwendolyn, 28
Berkeley (city), 165, 173, 177, 214–15, 229, 237–38, 249, 252, 254
Berkeley Repertory Theatre, 249
Black Comedy & *White Lies* (play), 142–43
Blackman, Sara, 40, 42
Blakeslee, Dick, 53
Blue Note, Chicago, 92, 98
Boro Hall Academy, 37–39, 153
Brand, Oscar, 56, 64
Brighton Beach, Brooklyn, New York, 22–26, 29, 30, 33, 38, 39, 114
Brighton Beach Drum and Bugle Corps, 25
British Columbia, Canada, 167–68, 175–77, 178–96, 223
Broadway Open House (television show), 75
Brodie, Greta, 49, 50, 52, 53, 60, 77, 238–39, *fig. 3*
Brook, Peter, 143–45, 146–47, 149–52

Brown, Jim, 210, 215, 224, *fig. 11*
Brown, Sam, 120–21, 123–25

Camp Wo-Chi-Ca (workers children's camp), 26–30, 32, 35, 39, 48
Carawan, Guy, 240
Carnegie Hall, 1, 101–2, 116, 224
Carter Family Singers, 43
Chaikin, Joseph, 136, 138, 141–42, 145, 153, 163, 192, 196–202, 235, *fig. 10*
Charter Records, 60
Christian, Meg, 264
Ciro's, 88–89
Civil Rights Movement, 115, 175, 223, 241, 250
Columbia Records, 73
Coney Island, Brooklyn, New York, 33–34
Connoisseur (magazine), 153, 156
Coon Creek Girls, 43
Counterattack (paper), 75–76, 79–80, 81–82, 93–95, 98, 113
Cowan, Alec, 110, 159–60
Cowan, Ruth, 110, 159–60
Critchlow, Ernest, 27

Darling, Erik, 108, 115, *fig. 8*
The Dave Garroway Show (television show), 93
Davey, Jill, 225, 226–27
Decca Records, 72–74, 82, 83, 94, 96–97
Dobkin, Alix, 126
Dorsey, Tommy, 31
Ducoff, John, 129
Durban, Deanna, 23, 44
Dyer-Bennet, Richard, 48, 63

Eddy, Nelson, 23
Empire Room, 92–94, 98

Fast, Howard, 28
Federal Housing Authority, 40, 41–42, 44
Flynn, John, 6–7
Flynn, Mary, 6–7
Forrest, Helen, 31
Foy, Hope, 80

Gabler, Milt, 72
Garland, Judy, 23, 175
Gaslight South, 126
Gibson, Jackie. *See* Alper, Jackie
Gilbert, Charles (father), 3, 5, 8–9, 13, 22–24, 127–32, 181
Gilbert, Irene (sister), 8, 10, 22, 28, 40, 48, 217–18, *fig. 2*
Gilbert, Sarah (mother), 3–6, 8, 9, 28–29, 36, 37, 48, 181–83, 203–7, 215–22, 258, *fig. 2;* Alzheimer's, 215–22; divorce, 17–18; and IWO/union activism, 24, 28, 31; at Mariposa Avenue, 168–73, 216; medical treatment, 39–40, 44–45
Gilbert, W. S. and Arthur Sullivan, 35, 43
Ginsberg, Allen, 199
Glaser, Ray, 52
Glazer, Joe, 98
Glazer, Tom, 43, 45, 46, 56
"Goodnight Irene," 73, 78, 83, 88, 90, 97
Gordon, Max, 63–64, 70, 74–75, 78
Gottlieb, Dottie, 238, *fig. 19*
Goyan, Pat, 158–59
The Grand Theater, *figs. 15, 16*
The Grapes of Wrath (play), 32
Greenpoint, Brooklyn, New York, 10
Greenwich Village, New York, 49, 63, 197
Group Theatre, 113–14, 133

Guthrie, Arlo, 233
Guthrie, Woody, 43, 46, 67, 81, 83

Hagen, Uta, 133, 137
Haines, Connie, 31
Hambro, Leonid, 57
Hamilton, Frank, 115, *fig. 8*
Harburg, Edgar ("Yip"), 51
H.A.R.P. Tour, 233–34
Hartley, Michael, 180, 183–85
Hauptmann, Gerhardt, 56
Hays, Lee, 1, 64, 72, 88, 210, 212; and
  People's Songs, 48, 49; and the
  Weavers, 56, 62, 66–67, 70,
  84–85, 105, 108, 111–12, 115, *figs. 4, 8*
Hellerman, Fred (later Fred
  Brooks), 2, 100, 105, 124, 127, 214;
  and People's Songs, 48, 49; and
  the Weavers, 56, 58, 62, 66, 70,
  72, 74, 85, 90, 108, 110, 115, *figs. 4, 8*
Herrmann, Bay, 180, 190–91
Herrmann, John, 180–81, 186,
  190
Highlander Research and
  Education Center, 240
Hinton, Sam, 55
Hitler, Adolf, 32
H.M.S. Pinafore (play), 35
Hood, Sam, 126
Hoover, J. Edgar, 61
Horowitz, Amy, 228
House Un-American Activities
  Committee (HUAC), 1, 61,
  98–99, 103
Hughes, Howard, 90

International Ladies' Garment
  Workers' Union, 4
International Workers Orders
  (IWO), 24–26, 40
Israel, 111–13
Ives, Burt, 48

Jackson, Mahalia, 92–93
James, Harry, 31
Janov, Dr. Arthur, 161, 165–66
Javna, Jonah, 29–30
Jenkins, Gordon, 72, 74, 97
Johnny Got His Gun (novel), 32
Jones, Mary Harris ("Mother
  Jones"), 239–49; play about,
  245–51
Joplin, Janis, 175
Judge Street, 8, 14

Kahn, Albert, 28
Kahn, Si, 248
Kameron, Pete, 71–73, 75, 78, 79,
  81–83, 93, 99
Kapp, Dave, 72–73
Katzman, Alicia, 235–37, *fig 20*
Katzman, Harlene, 235–36, *fig. 20*
Kent, Rockwell, 28
Knight, Gwendolyn, 27
Korones, Donna, 234–37, 245–46,
  250, *figs. 17, 20, 21, 25*
Krause, Bernie, 115, *fig. 8*

Laguna Beach, 159–60
La MaMa Exerimental Theatre
  Club, 196, 202
Lamarr, Hedy, 33
Langley, Jeff, 174–75, 249
Lawrence, Jacob, 27
Lead Belly, 97, 225
Lee, Bill, 121–22
Lee, Canada, 27
Lee, Harvey, 37–39
Legacy (play), 250
Leib, Chaver, 25
Lev, Rae, 57
Leventhal, Harold, 71–72, 101–2,
  105, 116, 121, 126, 137, 237
Levinsky, Beatrice ("Beattie"),
  30–35, 40

Lifeline Tour, 224
Lillo, Larry, 245, *figs. 15, 16*
Linda, Solomon, 69
Lomax, Alan, 43, 45, 68
London, 110–11, 139–43, 148–51
Los Angeles, 169–71, 204–9, 216
The Loves of Isadora (film), 140–41
Love Will Find a Way (record),
    237
LSD-25, 116–18

MacDonald, Jeanette, 23, 44
Maeda, Jun, 201–2
Main, Leah, 179, 188
Maltz, Gerry, 178
Maltz, Judith ("Judy"), 178
The Man in the Glass Booth (play),
    151–52
Mann, Ann Sheperd. *See* Ann
    Sheperd
Ma Rainey, 44
Martin, Dolph, 29, 30
MBUBE, 69
McCarthyism, 69, 76, 93, 98, 101–2,
    104, 108, 114
McFarland, Spanky, 127
Meserole Theater, 10, 11
Mexico, 100
Meyer, Ruth, 140
The Mikado (play), 35
Miller, Glen, 31
Mill Valley, 158–61, 260
Milwaukee, Wisconsin, 231–32,
    245–48
Misciagna, Lou, 121, 123
Mora, Carlos, 50
Mother Bloor, 28
Mother Blues, 92, 126, 137
Mother Jones (Mary Harris Jones),
    239–49
Mother Jones (play), 245–51
Muir, Florabel, 88

National Women's Music Festival,
    227
Neal, Fred, 127
Near, Holly, 173–76, 211, 214,
    224–28, 231, 233, 237, 250, 263–64,
    figs. 13, 14
Near, Laurel, 176
New Denver, 178–80, 188
New York Times (newspaper), 83, 138,
    201, 213, 223, 244
New York World-Telegram (news-
    paper), 95
No-Name Quartet, 56. *See also* The
    Weavers
Norris, John, 188

Odets, Clifford, 35
Oida, Yoshi, 145, 148
Opatija, Croatia, 140
Open Theatre, 133–37, 141–42, 162,
    197, *fig. 10*
Otah, Takashi, 57
Otah, Virginia, 57

Paris, 143–48
Partnoy, Alicia, 228
Patton, Will, *fig. 12*
Peekskill, New York, 57, 60,
    61
People's Artists, 70
People's Songs, 48–50, 51, 55, 57,
    61–62, 70, 238
People's Songs Bulletin (newsletter),
    49, 62, 70, 80
Petric, Faith, *fig. 23*
Pins and Needles (musical), 46
Pinter, Harold, 139–40, 151–52
Pleasence, Donald, 140, 152
Pocket Theatre, New York, 138, 141,
    fig. 9
Primal Institute, 162–68, 178
Primal therapy, 161, 162–64

Primus, Pearl, 27
The Priority Ramblers, 43–45, 238

Rabinodov, Aviva, 257–58
Rabinodov, Hillel, 257–58
A Radical Life with Song (play), 250
Rainbow House Children's Radio
   Choir, 29, 40, 74
Reagon, Bernice Johnson, 228
Re-Arrangements (play), 201–3
Redgrave, Vanessa, 140–41
Redwood Records, 175, 237, 238
Reisz, Karel, 140–41
Rivington Street (novel), 219
Roadwork (production company),
   228
Robeson, Paul, 4, 27, 47, 52, 57,
   58–59, 83, 175
Rogoff, Gordon, 134–35
Rome, Harold, 56
*Ronnie Gilbert on Mother Jones: Face
   to Face with the Most Dangerous
   Woman in America* (book), 246

Sandburg, Carl, 71, 96–97
Sanders, Betty, 215, 263–64
San Francisco Bay Area, 157–59, 177
Scharf, Stuart, 136
Schwartz, Lois, 167–68, 177, 178
Seeger, Pete, 2, 30, 43, 107, 124, 177,
   212, 214, 233, 254, 262, *figs. 3, 4, 8;*
   contempt trial of, 103, 104–5; and
   People's Songs, 48–49; and
   Wallace campaign, 51, 52; and
   the Weavers, 55, 56, 57–59, 62,
   63, 64, 65–68, 70, 73, 74, 79, 81, 85,
   87, 94, 96, 107–8
Seeger, Toshi, 57, 63, 66, 68, 71, 96,
   106, 124, 177, 214, 262
Seniors for Peace, 260–61
Seratoff, Naomi Engel, 218
Shaffer, Peter, 134, 142–43, 179

Shepard, Sam, 198, 235
Shepherd, Ann, 113–14, 133, 247
Shumaker, Joanie, 237
Silber, Irwin, 80
Sinatra, Frank, 31, 78
Sing Out!, 70, 80–81
Sisterfire music festival, 227, 235,
   figs. 13, 14
Smith, Bessie, 44
Solomon, Maynard, 104
Solomon, Seymour, 104
"So Long, It's Been Good to Know
   Yuh," 81, 83, 88, 94, 97
Sorry, Wrong Number (play), 32
Soviet Union, 32, 51, 61, 207–8, 258
Spencer, Kenneth, 27
Springfield, Missouri, 18–22
Stalin, Josef, 32
Strand Theatre, 78
Sussman family, 18, 19–21, 31
Sweet Honey in the Rock, 228,
   230

Taylor, Glen, 51
Theatre Energy, 196
This Train Still Runs (record), 250
Top Girls, fig. 15
Tourists and Refugees (play), 202–3,
   fig. 12
Train to the Zoo (record), 70
Truman, Harry, 54
"Tzena Tzena," 73–75, 78, 83, 89,
   97

Upper West Side, Manhattan, 48,
   113

Vancouver, 179, 214–16
Vancouver Playhouse, 179, 245
Vanguard Records, 104, 107
Village Vanguard, 63–72, 75
van Itallie, Jean-Claude, 137, 142

Waiting for Lefty (play), 35, 114, 138
Wallace, Henry Agard, 51–54, 55, 81
Washington, DC, 40, 41–42, 44–45, 227–28
Watt, Dr. James, 116–17
Weaver Brothers and Elvira, 90
The Weavers, 55–119, 153, 175, 210, 213, 224, 237, 240, 248, *figs. 4, 8, 11*. *See also* No-Name Quartet; *names of individual members*
The Weavers' Almanac (record), 107–9
The Weavers at Carnegie Hall (record), xiii, 104, 106
The Weavers at Home (record), 107
The Weavers: Wasn't That a Time! (film), 224, *fig. 11*
Weg, Lisa (daughter), 101, 106–7, 110, 111, 113, 118, 174, *figs. 7, 18, 20, 24;* education, 119, 143, 155–56, 173; in Berkeley, 229, 237

Weg, Marty, 50, 57, 58, 60, 77, 79, 87–88, 89, 99–100, 124, *fig. 6;* divorce from Gilbert, 109–10
Weg, Sara Zoë (granddaughter), *figs. 21, 22, 24*
Weiss, Sid, 74
We Wish You a Merry Christmas (record), 96
White, Charles, 27
White, Josh, 63
Willens, Doris, 67–68, 71, 108
Williams, Reverend Claude, 49
Williamson, Cris, 264
"Wimoweh," 69, 97
The Winter Project, 196–209, *fig. 12*
Wolff, Bill, 52
Women in Black, 252–59, *fig. 23*
Worley, Jo-Lynne, 237

Yiddish, 12, 22–23, 25, 27